D0199742

VILLAGE
AND
BUREAUCRACY
IN
SOUTHERN
SUNG CHINA

VILLAGE AND BUREAUCRACY IN SOUTHERN SUNG CHINA

Brian E. McKnight

The University of Chicago Press
Chicago
& London

THE UNIVERSITY OF CHICAGO PRESS, CHICAGO 60637
THE UNIVERSITY OF CHICAGO PRESS, LTD., LONDON

© *1971 by The University of Chicago*
All rights reserved. Published 1971
Printed in the United States of America

International Standard Book Number: 0–226–56059–7
Library of Congress Catalog Card Number: 72–159834

Contents

Preface

In premodern China local residents serving as subbureaucratic workers did much of the routine work of local administration. These men were both the agents of the state and the leaders of the people. Our understanding of state and society in premodern China will remain inadequate until we understand these functionaries and the institutions that they staffed. An interest in the problem of these mediators led to the initiation of this study.

Analogous institutions existed from the beginning of the empire in 221 B.C. until its fall in A.D. 1912, but the Sung period (960–1279) has a particular attraction for historians interested in studying the structure and evolution of political institutions in China. It was a time of innovation and rapid change, during which many elements characteristic of later dynasties first appeared. Historians divide the Sung into two periods, the Northern Sung (960–1127) and the Southern Sung (1127–1279). Japanese sinologists have studied, in a preliminary way, the village-level subbureaucratic institutions of the Northern Sung, but the Southern Sung situation has been less fully described. This is unfortunate. Although the roots of most Southern Sung institutions and policies can be traced back into the Northern Sung, these institutions and policies frequently reach their full flowering only during the later period. Thus, I have directed my attention to the Southern Sung.

The scope of this book has been determined in part by preexisting interests, and in part by the character of the materials available to me. The most important single repository of primary source materials is the *Sung Hui Yao Chi Kao,* the remaining part of the huge collections of selected documents compiled under imperial auspices during the Sung. The *Sung Hui Yao Chi Kao* consists largely of proclamations and approved memorials, with occasional insertions of commentary. Unfortunately the sections on the village service system end in the 1220s. For this reason the description of conditions during the last fifty years of the dynasty is necessarily rather tentative. Within the period covered it is clear that the documents preserved represent only a fraction of those originally contained in the collections ancestral to the work we have today. Moreover, most of the entries have been abbreviated. There are many cases of miscopying in this work, and some passages appear garbled. And yet, for all its limitations this is still the most important collection of information on the institutional history of the Sung. I have sought to make full use of those sections of this work bearing directly on the subject of this book, and selective use of peripherally relevant sections.

The collected papers of Sung officials (*wen-chi*) rank second in importance as sources of information on the Southern Sung service system. The materials contained are not so abbreviated as those found in the *Sung Hui Yao Chi Kao* but unfortunately are usually undated. The huge bulk of such collections still extant from Sung times prevented me from checking them exhaustively. I have examined the memorials in those *wen-chi* available to me and have used such tools as are available in trying to locate in them other information relevant to my topic.

Thirdly, local gazetteers, annalistic histories, and other miscellaneous works provided a plethora of information on some topics, without providing adequate materials on others.

Taken together, these sources afford a plenitude of information on questions of structure, personnel selection, and the ways in which the government sought to distribute the costs of village services among the people, but they do not adequately depict day-by-day procedures, the actual costs of the services to the people involved, or the relations of the servicemen to their superiors in the offices of the towns.

Both the character of the data and the depth of our present ignorance about Chinese traditional society encouraged me to adopt an institutional rather than a functional approach to my subject. A sociological focus on change, on interrelationships between social subsystems, and on the dynamic roles of institutions would be of great interest, but in the absence of thorough previous studies, and given the types of information available it seemed wisest to devote this study to a descriptive analysis of the institution of village services and to deny myself the pleasure of following my social theories too far beyond the edges of the evidence. I have also resisted the tempting assumption that T'ang or Yüan institutions closely resembled Sung institutions. In many cases the institutions were no doubt similar, but this similarity cannot be assumed. For this reason I have made only limited use of materials not directly concerned with the Sung period.

I am indebted to those Japanese scholars, particularly Sudō Yoshiyuki and Miyazaki Ichisada, who have in a preliminary way surveyed these institutions. Their articles have made my work far easier than it would otherwise have been.

In giving translations of titles I have followed the practices established by E. A. Kracke, Jr., in his works on the Northern Sung. In citing dates in the notes and body of the book, I have used Hsüeh Chung-san and Ou-yang I, *A Sino-Western Calendar for Two Thousand Years* (Peking: Hsin Chih San Lien Shu Tien, 1957). In cases where only the Western year is given I have used that Western year which roughly corresponds to the Chinese year in question.

In quoting Chinese materials I have faced the translator's perennial problem: How literally should a writer render the words of the original? I can only hope that my translations satisfy both the scholar and the general reader.

Finally I would like to express my gratitude to the many friends and teachers who have aided me in my studies, to Professor Charles Peterson, who read the manuscript and offered valuable suggestions, and most especially to Professor E. A. Kracke, Jr., for his constant encouragement and advice.

Abbreviations

CHTK	*Chou Hsien T'i Kang*
CPCSPM	Yang Chung-liang. *Tzu-chih T'ung-chien Ch'ang-pien Chi-shih Pen-mo.*
CTCCC	Ch'en Ch'i-ch'ing. *Chia-ting Ch'ih Ch'eng Chih.*
CWKCH	Chu Hsi. *Chu Wen-kung Cheng Hsün.*
CYTC	Li Hsin-ch'uan. *Chien-yen I-lai Chao Yeh Tsa Chi.*
HAHS	Chu Hsi. *Hui-an Hsien-sheng Chu Wen-kung Wen-chi.*
HCP	Li Tao. *Hsü Tzu-chih T'ung-chien Ch'ang-pien.*
HNYL	Li Hsin-ch'uan. *Chien-yen I-lai Hsi Nien Yao Lu.*
HSCH	Chen Te-hsiu. *Hsi Shan Cheng Hsün.*
HSWC	Chen Te-hsiu. *Hsi Shan Wen-chi.*
KCC	Ch'en Ch'i-ch'ing. *Kuei Ch'ang Chi.*
KCSMC	Mei Ying-fa. *K'ai-ch'ing Ssu Ming Chih.*
KCSMHC	Mei Ying-fa. *K'ai-ch'ing Ssu Ming Hsü Chih.*
"KRNB"	Miyazaki Ichisada. "Kyo-ri no baibi o chūshin to shite."
SHY	Hsü Sung. *Sung Hui Yao Chi Kao.*
"SIFS"	Nieh Ch'ung-ch'i. "Sung I-fa Shu."
SKSK	Sudō Yoshiyuki. *Sō-dai keizai-shi kenkyū.*
"SSKS"	Miyazaki Ichisada. "Sō-dai shu ken seido no yurai to sono tokushoku."
SZS	Sogabe Shizuo. *Sō-dai zaisei-shi.*
TITC	Li Yüan-pi. *Tso I Tzu Chen.*
TSKSK	Sudō Yoshiyuki. *Tōsō shakai keizai-shi kenkyū.*
YLTT	Yao Kuang-hsiao. *Yung-lo Ta-tien.*

]1[*Introduction*

The Chinese imperial state, like all states, faced a set of fundamental problems. The preservation of peace and order, the transmission of information between rulers and ruled, and the collection of taxes to finance operations formed an irreducible triad of political functions. Like all polities the Chinese state used a unique style of administration in performing these tasks. The style was a complex resultant of many factors. The myths, reasons, and traditions used to justify the existing political institutions, the relations between the formal state and other social groupings, and the distribution of power all conjoined to form a pattern of politics unique in time and place. Distinctive both in theory and practice, the government of imperial China still seems in many ways curiously modern and familiar. Bureaucratically organized, and dominated by a graded civil service led by men selected through competitive examinations, it was both a model for and a precursor of the complex administrations of our contemporary world. And yet this traditional Chinese government differed from its later counterparts in one most curious way: it was ruled by a handful of professional civil servants.

The members of this upper bureaucracy of civil servants, organized into nine grades (*chiu-p'in*), were said to hold their posts "within the stream" (*liu-nei*). They were distinguished from the rest of Chinese society by dress, by life style, by career expectations, and by a host of other traits.

But perhaps most centrally in Sung times, these graded civil servants were set apart by the presumption that they shared a community of values fitting them for service as the guides of the people and the limbs of the state. These values were enshrined in the Confucian Classics. To ascertain potential officials' mastery over this body of values and attitudes, the Chinese created an elaborate, brilliantly constructed, and wholly voluntary system of political indoctrination and testing—the examination system and its supporting educational institutions. This was not a system of technical training and certification designed to fit a man for the mundane triviality of bureaucratic routine, but rather the most profoundly effective mechanism the world has yet seen for assuring that fellow officials agreed on fundamentals. The system by no means ended partisan strife or personal animosities, but it did mean that in most instances those in positions of power argued their cases in the same language. The high standards of Confucian socialization that examination demanded of graduates largely precluded basic conflicts of value, but this underlying stratum of agreement was bought at a price. The number of those able to pass the examinations was limited. During the Sung, many low-level posts in the graded civil service were filled by men whose orthodoxy had not been formally certified.[1]

1. According to figures cited by Kracke, during the thirty years beginning in 1142, examination graduates would seem to have provided between 37 and 44 percent of the average number of needed civil service replacements. Edward A. Kracke, Jr., "Family versus Merit in the Chinese Civil Service Examinations during the Empire," *Harvard Journal of Asiatic Studies* 10 (1947): 120. Thus, a small majority of men in the graded civil service probably entered without having passed the regular examinations. However, it is clear that men with degrees almost monopolized the higher positions. See Brian E. McKnight, "Administrators of Hangchow under the Northern Sung," *Harvard Journal of Asiatic Studies*, 30 (1970): 205. Two other points are here worth noting. First, although very bitter political disputes did occur within the civil service itself, after the flowering of the examination system in Sung times the most abusive politics arose when power was given into the hands of those who could not be presumed

Furthermore, local control by these graded civil servants was made possible only through their continuing use of two sets of political functionaries not considered to be full members of the civil service—the clerical subbureaucracy and the village officers. The degree to which these two groups shared the values of their superiors could not easily be ascertained. The state, in administering local areas, was therefore faced with a fundamental political problem: How could it feel confident that its policies would be enforced when it could certify the orthodoxy of only a handful of its servitors and had to rely on the administrative activities of many men who did not stand within the circle of the elect?

Different dynasties dealt with this problem in different ways, but in all cases one element in the answer was attention to the balancing of authority and functions. The degree of control sought could in part be assured through the judicious distribution of functions and powers among the parties concerned—the central authorities, the local administrators, the clerks and runners, the village officers, and in the last dynasties the "gentry." In pre-Sung times, when Chinese society was more aristocratic, there was less emphasis on formal testing of beliefs; greater powers were granted to local officials; and the gulf between civil servants and their helpers was not heavily stressed.[2] Under the

---

to share in this community of values; this was particularly true of periods when eunuchs were influential. Secondly, although it is true that during the Sung there was no "orthodox" interpretation of Confucian philosophy (such as was inculcated in Ming and Ch'ing times), the wide areas of agreement on basic values in ethics are sufficient indication that fundamental Confucian assumptions themselves constituted an orthodoxy.

2. Aristocracy has been defined as a form of government in which supreme power is invested in the principal persons of a state or in a privileged order. In this sense it would seem reasonable to use the word to describe conditions in China from the Three Kingdoms to the late T'ang. The late T'ang and the Five Dynasties are part of a transitional period to the system that becomes mature only in the Sung.

dynasties that followed the Sung the central government
sought to obviate many problems by placing stricter limits
on the authority of local officials,[3] by bringing a greater
proportion of the population into the indoctrinated atmo-
sphere of the examination life,[4] and by permitting the use
of special agents to guard against clerical abuses.[5] The Sung
is therefore revealing as a period of transition between the
looser central control of the preceding more aristocratic
period, and the near autocracy of the last dynasties with
their gentry-dominated societies. And yet this period, although transitional, was no mere admixture of elements of
the earlier and later situations. The Sung rural social order
resembled the rural social orders of other eras in Chinese
imperial history but differed from them in certain critical
ways. Its unique character was reflected in a distinctive
system of local control in rural areas, marked by a constel-
lation of powers and functions peculiar to the Sung.

In one sense this period from the rebellion of An Lu-shan to A.D. 960
might be included with the Sung as part of the postaristocratic era,
since the decline in the power of the great families was already manifest by the middle of the eighth century, and yet this period was certainly marked, as was the earlier era, by loose central control, by a
lack of extensive use of examinations for the certification of officials,
and by a relatively weak emphasis on the division between the levels
of assistants of the principal local political figures. For these reasons
I have chosen to regard this period as one part of the pre-Sung era,
albeit a peculiar one.

3. For a brief comparison of the powers of local administrators in
the various dynasties see Yang Lien-sheng, "Ming Local Administration," in *Chinese Government in Ming Times: Seven Studies*, ed.
Charles O. Hucker (New York: Columbia University Press, 1969).

4. Chang Chung-li, *The Chinese Gentry: Studies on Their Role in
Nineteenth Century Chinese Society* (Seattle: University of Washington Press, 1955). See especially part 3. For a general description of
the role of the gentry in supporting control in rural areas under the
Ch'ing, see Hsiao Kung-ch'üan, *Rural China: Imperial Control in the
Nineteenth Century* (Seattle: University of Washington Press, 1960).
Dr. Hsiao's book is easily the fullest description available of those
institutions which, during the Ch'ing, performed the functions that
in the Sung were handled by the village officers.

5. Ch'ü T'ung-tsu, *Local Government in China under the Ch'ing*
(Cambridge: Harvard University Press, 1962).

The clerical workers, one key group in this system of powers, acted as secretaries, accountants, clerks, and miscellaneous functionaries in government offices. These operative personnel, although they were themselves organized in a manner reminiscent of the elite civil service, and although they were in some cases recruited through examinations not wholly unlike those used to select their superiors, were never considered to be full members of the upper bureaucracy. These clerks were not presumed to share fully in Confucian values. Indeed, during much of Chinese history they were presumed not to share them at all; they were stereotyped as dishonest and venal.

The village officers, the subjects of this book, collected taxes, transmitted documents, maintained local order, and provided a number of services to residents and officials within rural areas. Because these men were well-to-do, in the eyes of the government they were presumptively literate. Given the character of traditional Chinese education, where even the primers were expositions of Confucian philosophy, village officers had begun the process of Confucian socialization. They had already taken the first step from the tradition of the peasantry into the set of patterns exemplified by the mandarins. Because of the vital functions they performed, these officers were an irreplaceable link between the country people and the relatively small group of clerks and officials who in theory controlled the rural areas.

The village officers must not be confused with the gentry of the Ming and Ch'ing. The functional roles of the two groups are similar but by no means identical. The gentry supported the moral order and the examination system in ways not characteristic of the village officers, could not properly participate in tax collection, and led militia forces only under unusual conditions. Furthermore their juridical functions were extralegal, if widely accepted. The village officers by contrast collected taxes as a matter of course, frequently led militia units, and were key figures in the

legally established law-enforcement system. They bore burdens which in the Ming and Ch'ing were spread among the
gentry, the *li-chia*, the clerks and runners, and the *pao-chia*
leaders. Finally, the gentry of the last dynasties were men
whose ideological orthodoxy had at least in theory been
proved. Gentry status was a question of being an official, an
ex-official, a degree holder, or an imperial student, not of
merely being rich. But during the Sung the use of the
examination system as a means of indoctrinating the higher
levels of Chinese society was in its infancy. In the Sung there
were men with official status, there were various groups
possessed of miscellaneous privileges, and there were the
rich, but it seems fair to say that there were no gentry. The
more aristocratic society of earlier times in which local
political influence tended to remain in the hands of certain
families for generation after generation was dead, and the
gentry society of later times had not yet been born. As a
result the local elite consisted, not of the hereditarily influential or of the indoctrinated gentry, but simply of the rich.
During the Sung more than during any other period of premodern Chinese history economic position determined
membership in the nonofficial segment of the ruling class.
Perhaps the most that can be said of the functional equiva-
lence of the Sung village officers who were chosen from the
rural rich and the socially active gentry of later times is that
in both periods the paucity of officials and clerks necessi-
tated dependence on nonofficial agents in rural areas. A
brief examination of the size of the official-clerical group
makes the importance of such agents immediately obvious.[6]

6. The use of "gentry" here has no connection with the definition
of the term in the various works of Wolfram Eberhard. In the evidence examined there is simply no indication of the existence of the
gentry as he defines that term. Rather, I am using the definition accepted (with some important differences in detail) by Ch'ü T'ung-tsu,
chap. 10, and Chang Chung-li. This "gentry" group with its center in
the *shen-shih* group also corresponds in part to the elite dealt with
by Ho Ping-ti in *The Ladder of Success in Imperial China* (New
York: Columbia University Press, 1962). Ho is concerned with the

In the 1160s, when between 50 and 60 million people lived in the dominions of the Southern Sung, the civil service of regular graded civil officials "within the stream" (*liu-nei*) seems to have numbered only about 12,000 members.[7] Since our data on numbers of officials is fragmentary, general in character, and often difficult to interpret, this figure of 12,000 must be considered a tentative approximation. Nonetheless, the major sources of our information on such questions make it clear that the graded civil service was tiny when compared with the number of people over whom it was supposed to exercise control.[8]

Most members of this small group of graded civil

group with potential or previous access to office—a group that does not correspond exactly to the "gentry" as defined by the other two authors—and he raises cogent objections to the use of the term "gentry," but, given the wide currency of the word, I have chosen to use it here, though with some reservations.

7. The population figures are for the 1160s. Kato Shigeru, *Shina keizai-shi kosho* (Tokyo: Toyo Bunko, 1952–53), 2: 319, gives population figures for this decade ranging from 11,139,854 households (in 1162) to 12,335,450 households (in 1166). If, to obtain a rough approximation of the population, we estimate that a household averaged between four and five members, we arrive at the figures fifty to sixty million. The estimate of civil service personnel is for the period 1165–73. Kracke, "Family versus Merit," 120. This situation in the 1160s was not unique. In the period 1065–67, when the population of the empire was about sixty million, there were only about 25,000 officials, including military officials. E. A. Kracke, Jr., *Civil Service in Early Sung China* (Cambridge: Harvard University Press, 1953), p. 55 for the civil service estimates, and Kato, p. 318 for the population figures. Such population estimates are of course only approximate. Arriving at acceptable estimates for the population in Sung times is difficult. There is already a considerable literature on the problem of interpreting Sung population statistics. In addition to articles in Kato, see Koiwai Hiromitsu, "Sō-dai kokosu mondai ni kansuru shiken," *Bunka* 22: 641–57; Werner Eichhorn, "Gesamtbevölkerungsziffern des Sung-Reiches," *Oriens Extremus* 4: 52–69; Yüan Chen, "Sung-tai hu-k'ou," *Li-shih Yen-chiu* 3 (1957): 9–46.

8. Some general information on numbers of officials can be found in T'o T'o et al., *Sung shih* (Taipei: Yee Wen Publishing Co., 1956), *chüan* 169; Ma Tuan-lin, *Wen Hsien T'ung K'ao* (Kuo Hsüeh Chi Pen Ts'ung-shu ed.), *chüan* 47; and Wang Ying-lin, *Yü Hai* (Ch'eng-tu Wang Shih ed.), *chüan* 119.

servants seem to have worked in the capital. The empire had about 800 subprefectures. Most subprefectures had a subprefect, occasionally an assistant subprefect, frequently a sheriff, and often a registrar. Since there were few assistant subprefects, and since one man frequently filled several of the other offices concurrently, it seems safe to suggest that the average subprefecture had two or three civil service officials—for an empirewide total of 2,400 men. There were less than 170 prefectures, each apparently usually staffed by about eight civil servants—for a total of about 1,300 men. Circuit officials and other local officials cannot have added more than some hundreds more to this total, suggesting that about 8,000 civil officials worked in the central government offices of the capital and only about 4,000 were stationed in local posts. These calculations, admittedly very rough, nonetheless reveal how local administration spread like a thin film across the surface of rural life.[9] Direct per-

---

9. The tentative character of these calculations cannot wholly be eliminated. The extant sources seem to suggest that relatively few subprefectures had assistant subprefects, and in many areas one man served concurrently in more than one position. In some areas there was more than one sheriff in a single subprefecture. In addition to sheriffs some subprefectures also had police commissioners (*hsün-chien*) who, like the sheriffs had police duties (though these men should probably be considered members of the military hierarchy and not civil officials). There were also various (although apparently not numerous) miscellaneous officials in local areas, such as men to collect taxes at important taxgathering stations. Some men in this latter group were not regular officials "within the stream" and thus would not fall within the grouping being estimated here. Finally, changes were continually being made in the staffing of these posts. Assistant subprefects were added in some areas and eliminated in others. Registrars were newly appointed at some times, and at others their posts were eliminated. For these questions see *Sung Hui Yao Chi Kao*, ed. Hsü Sung (Taipei: Shih Chieh Shu Chü, 1965), *chih-kuan* 48.53a–91b. This work will be cited hereafter as *SHY*. These estimates are also very rough, since subprefectures were established and went out of existence, were lost to the Jurchen or Mongols, or were recovered. However, this estimate of two or three civil servants per subprefecture is also supported by evidence from the Northern Sung. In 1073 twenty-eight subprefectures in Hopei were abolished. Seventy-six civil

sonal central control reached down only to the subprefecture, where two or three civil servants might be responsible for tens of thousands of inhabitants spread over hundreds of square miles of countryside.[10] These few officials could perform their duties successfully only because they were aided by numerous non–civil service subordinates who acted as clerks, jailors, guards, accountants, secretaries, and miscellaneous laborers. An average Sung subprefecture probably had between 100 and 150 of these subbureaucratic clerical workers.[11]

This force of clerical personnel and officials, living and working in the subprefectural seat, did not actually direct the affairs of the multitude of people nominally under its control. Beyond the town gates, in the hamlets of rural China, there was another, still lower level of government. Actual management of the most basic functions of local administration—the collection of taxes, the

service posts were eliminated. See Li Tao, *Hsü Tzu-chih T'ung chien Ch'ang-pien* (Taipei: Shih Chieh Shu Chü, 1954), 246.9a–b. This work will be cited hereafter as *HCP*. The calculation for prefectures are also only approximate. Ch'in Hsiang-yeh, *Hsü Tzu-chih T'ung-chien Ch'ang-pien Shih Pu* (Chekiang: Shu Chü blockprint ed., 1883), 31.12a–15b, says that before 1112, prefectures averaged four to eight officials, but that in that year the complement was increased. The situation during the Southern Sung is not clear. Therefore, in seeking to obtain a rough estimate, I have assumed that there were eight officials per prefecture. In the T'ang, a *hsien* with between 5,000 and 10,000 households had, in theory, a staff of four civil servants with fifty-three assistants. Denis Twitchett, *Financial Administration Under the T'ang Dynasty* (Cambridge, Eng.: Cambridge University Press, 1963), p. 217.

10. In the 1160s the 50–60 million inhabitants of the empire lived in more than 800 subprefectures, an average of 70,000 persons per subprefecture. See Kato, p. 319.

11. In 1073, when twenty-eight subprefectures were abolished, 3,127 clerical personnel lost their jobs. See *HCP* 246.9a–b. Sudō Yoshiyuki, *Sō-dai keizai-shi kenkyū* (Tokyo: Tokyo Daigku Shuppan Kai, 1962), pp. 763–65, gives an estimate of 150 clerks in subprefectures in the middle of the Southern Sung. This work will be cited hereafter as *SKSK*.

transmission of documents to and from the rural areas, the making of fiscal and demographic registers, the preservation of local order, and the provision of a variety of services to residents and to officials—was delegated to organizations that in the early Sung were usually manned by unpaid personnel requisitioned for limited periods of service from certain household grades and types among the resident population. These village officers or village servicemen were essential to the day-by-day working of local government. Standing between state and society, and involved in the transfer of goods, services, and information in both directions, the village officers represented both the government and the people. Politically both subjects and participants, they embodied the will of the rulers and the aims of the ruled. The study of their functions, of their characteristics as personnel, of their responses to problems, and of the structure through which they worked illuminates not only one facet of the society of rural Southern Sung China, but also the ever-shifting balance between government sponsorship and popular initiative, between the domain of the sovereign and the power of the people.[12]

12. This type of subbureaucratic administrative service should be distinguished from corvée labor (*yao-i*). In theory, the corvée obligation had been commuted into a tax payment by the Twice-a-Year tax reform of Yang Yen in 780. In fact, in the Southern Sung, although corvée labor primarily involved physical labor by the soldiers of the provincial armies, the poorer members of the civilian population were also sometimes called. See Sogabe Shizuo, *Sō-dai zaisei-shi* (Tokyo: Dai Nippon Insatsu Kabushiki Kaisha, 1941), p. 90. This work will be cited hereafter as *SZS*. See also Sun Yü-t'ang, "Kuan-yü Pei Sung Fu-i Chih-tu Fan Ke Wen-t'i," *Li-shih Yen-chiu* no. 2 (1964). In the Southern Sung the lowest-grade (fifth-grade) rural households were called on to do corvée. *SHY, shih-huo* 14.44b–45a. However, the general policy was to use army personnel rather than civilians whenever possible. See the emperor's comments on this practice in Li Hsin-ch'uan, *Chien-yen I-lai Hsi Nien Yao Lu* (Peking: Chung Hua Shu Chü, 1956), 162.2649. This work will be cited hereafter as *HNYL*. Unfortunately Sung officials do not always specify clearly whether they are speaking of *yao-i* or of *chih-i*, i.e. of corvée labor or of labor services as the latter term is used in this book, so that frequently it is necessary to judge from context and content.

Highly organized village and clerical subbureaucratic systems had first appeared in Chinese history at a time when the political institutions inherited from the Western Chou (1122–771 B.C.) were being transformed into centralized bureaucratic governments.[13] Adequate studies of the growth of this new form of local political organization before the Ch'in have not yet been published, but the situation under the first empire is relatively clear. The Ch'in rulers divided their domain into thirty-six commanderies, which were subdivided into subprefectures. A central government appointee administered each subprefecture. Under the Ch'in, as under later dynasties, the yamen in the subprefectural town was the lowest-level center of national government control. Below this level the Ch'in selected influential and respected residents to serve as Canton Officers (*hsiang-kuan*) to manage the subunits into which the subprefecture was divided. The largest subunit, an aggregate that in theory numbered 10,000 households, was called the canton (*hsiang*), and boasted three types of officers—the Three Elders (*san-lao*), who oversaw educational and cultural affairs; Frugal Men (*se-fu*), who handled the general and fiscal administration of the area; and Traveling Justices (*yu-chiao*), who were responsible for maintaining local order. Each canton was divided into ten pavillions (*t'ing*) headed by Chiefs (*chang*). Each pavillion was divided into ten townships (*li*) which legally were supposed to number 100 families each, and were to be managed by Heads (*k'uei*). Townships were comprised of ten ranks (*shih*) of ten families each or of twenty files (*wu*) of five families each.[14]

Han rulers followed Ch'in precedents.[15] Han country

13. Heinz Friese, *Das Dienstleistungs-system der Ming-Zeit (1368–1644)*, (Hamburg: Gesellschaft für Natur- und Völkerkunde Ostasiens, 1959), pp. 12ff, suggests that the subbureaucratic labor services of premodern China were derived from the feudal obligations of service to the lord which existed in the Western Chou period.

14. Lao Kan, *Ch'in Han Shih* (Taipei: Chung Hua Wen Hua Ch'u Pan Shih Yeh She, 1964), p. 124.

15. Perhaps to avoid the stigma of legalism, later commentators

officers—members of powerful families, and the most important link between the populace and the upper levels of government—were key political figures in Han times. Moreover, the Han system of personnel selection permitted such men to enter the upper ranks of officialdom. Occasionally former country officers rose to national prominence. In the centuries that separate the Han from the Sui, administrative organizations patterned after Ch'in-Han practices remained nominally in force, but actual control in areas outside the imperial domains generally gravitated into the hands of great landowning families that maintained their positions for generation after generation. Country officers were neither as powerful nor as respected as they had been under the Han, although they continued to be appointed.

After the Sui had reunified the empire in A.D. 589 the domination of local politics by a handful of great families began to weaken. Well aware of the dangers inherent in the decentralization of political power, the Sui rulers set out to increase imperial control over local affairs. Although they continued to use the Ch'in-Han system of rural organization, they centralized control over appointments to low level local civil service posts.

The T'ang (A.D. 618–907) inherited their scheme of rural organization from the Sui. During the dynasty the structure and function of the village service system changed little, but transformations in other aspects of Chinese life

---

on these systems sometimes preferred to cite as precedent, not the practices of Ch'in, but the reports of the classical *Chou Li*. This idealized and rationalized description of the institutions of the "Sage Kings" of the Chou dynasty depicted an extremely elaborate administrative structure staffed by bureaucrats assisted by clerical personnel, and a system of organizing the people into a hierarchy of administrative subunits of 5, 25, 100, 500, 2,500, and 12,500 households. See *Chou Li*, Ssu Pu Pei Yao ed., 1.2a, 9.1b, 10.7a, 11.1b, 12.1a–7b, 15.7b–8a, 15.10a–14a. For an example of such a reference to the *Chou Li* system as a precedent for Sung institutions see Shih Yao-pi, *Lien Feng Chi* (Ssu K'u Ch'üan Shu Chen Pen ed.), 5.5a–9a.

combined to further lower the status of the village officers. The people were still registered in a hierarchy of subunits, from within which servicemen and yamen workers were drafted to serve as they had always served, but now these posts had lost their prestige. The decline in the influence and status of village and clerical personnel continued through the succeeding Five Dynasties period (A.D. 907–960). Appointment to this subbureaucratic and village stratum of government became in most cases a feared imposition, borne either by professional workers of low social standing or by those members of the general population who could not find any way to evade service.[16]

No major changes in this clerical and village service system were promulgated by the founders of the Northern Sung. T'ai-tsu and T'ai-tsung, who initiated many innovations in other aspects of Chinese political organization, accepted without cavil the subbureaucratic practices of their immediate predecessors. Their most influential reforms accelerated the trend toward centralization of power in the hands of the emperor that was to culminate in the near absolutism of later dynasties. They also worked to weaken the power of the military while increasing the prestige of civil office.[17] The division and circumscription of military au-

16. The preceding brief description of the post-Ch'in history of village officer systems is largely based on the opening pages of Nieh Ch'ung-ch'i "Sung I-fa Shu," *Yenching Hsüeh Pao*, no. 33 (Dec. 1947). This work will be cited hereafter as "SIFS." It should be pointed out, however, that even in the later part of the T'ang period there is evidence that the village officer post of *li-cheng* was being filled by men of some importance in their areas. Twitchett points out that of the eight *li-cheng* listed in the documents from Tunhuang P 3559 v°, P 3018 v°, P 2657, and P 2803, four were sons of officials. See Twitchett, p. 240. There is a considerable literature (in Japanese) on this level of local organization during the T'ang period. See Matsumoto Yoshiumi, "Rimpo-soshiki wo chushin toshitaru Tōdai no sonsei," *Shigaku Zasshi* 53 no. 3 (1942): 323–71; Naba Toshisada, "Tōdai rimpo-seido shakugi," in *Haneda Hakushi shoju-kinen tōyōshi ronso* (Kyoto: 1950), pp. 711–78.

17. The best work on the resumption of central control over the

thority contributed to both the strength and the weakness of the Sung dynasty. In no other dynasty were internal disturbances of so little historical consequence; but no other long-lived dynasty fared so badly in its wars against foreign enemies. To help compensate for the weakness that they had introduced into the military system the Sung emperors relied heavily on the production and deployment of ever more sophisticated weapons and an enormous standing army. Numbers and weapons were to overcome weaknesses born of poor training, poor leadership, and a confusing command structure. This legacy—internal security, external insecurity, and huge defense expenditures—must be kept in mind if the situation of the Northern and Southern Sung is to be understood.

These innovations and their aftermath coincided with major transformations in Chinese economy and society. By the thirteenth century Chinese life had reached substantially the form it would bear until the fall of the empire in 1912.[18] These changes, which began in the seventh and

military is still the article by Nieh Ch'ung-ch'i, "Lun Sung T'ai-tsu Shou Ping Ch'üan," *Yenching Hsüeh Pao* 34 (1948): 85–106.

18. For the best brief description of the general character of this social evolution see E. A. Kracke, Jr., "Sung Society: Change within Tradition," *Far Eastern Quarterly* 14 (1954–55); 478–88. A number of discussions of these changes have been gathered together in *Change in Sung China*, ed. James T. C. Liu and Peter Golas (Lexington: D. C. Heath and Co., 1969). There are a host of articles on various aspects of these changes, of which perhaps the most pertinent are, on industrial changes: Robert Hartwell, "A Cycle of Economic Change in Imperial China: Coal and Iron in Northeast China, 750–1350," *Journal of the Economic and Social History of the Orient* 10 (July 1967): 102–59; id., "Markets, Technology, and the Structure of Enterprise in the Development of the Eleventh-century Chinese Iron and Steel Industry," *Journal of Economic History* 26 (March 1966): 29–58; id., "A Revolution in the Chinese Iron and Coal Industries During the Northern Sung, 960–1126 A.D.," *Journal of Asian Studies* 21 (Feb. 1962), 153–62; id., "Classical Chinese Analysis and Economic Policy in T'ang and Sung China," *International Congress of Orientalists in Japan, Transactions* no. 13 (1968), pp. 70–81. On social and economic evolution: Denis Twitchett, "Chinese Social History from

eighth centuries, were well along toward completion by the opening of the Southern Sung. Rapid growth of population was accompanied by shifts in the concentration of people, wealth, and culture. In this period the Yangtse delta region of southeast China became the center of the empire. A group of cities grew up there which in the Southern Sung became the nucleus of a concentration of urban populations unmatched anywhere until late nineteenth-century Europe. During the eleventh century great regionwide markets grew up for the products of industries increasingly supplying goods for mass consumption. For many products the market was empirewide.

Industrial growth was accompanied by agricultural and technical advances, and supported by an increasingly sophisticated monetary economy. New crops were introduced. More farmers, especially wealthy ones, began to concentrate on the production of specialized crops for sale. Regional specialization increased. Areas of rice surplus traded their grain for the salt, tea, fish, metals, and handicraft products of less fertile regions. But these advances were accompanied by social changes which caused grave concern to the government. After the middle of the eleventh century the

---

the Seventh to the Tenth Centuries," *Past and Present* no. 35 (Dec. 1966), pp. 28–53; id., "Documents on Clan Administration: I. The Rules of Administration of the Charitable Estate of the Fan Clan. Annotated translation of the *I-chuang kuei-chü*," *Asia Major* 8 (1960): 1–35; id., "Lands under State Cultivation under the T'ang," *Journal of the Economic and Social History of the Orient* 2 (1959): 162–203; id., "The Monasteries and China's Economy in Medieval Times," *Bulletin of the School of Oriental and African Studies* 19, no. 3 (1957): 526–49; id., "Monastic Estates in T'ang China," *Asia Major* n.s. 5, pt. 2 (1956): 123–46; id., "Recent Work on Medieval Chinese Social History by Sudo Yoshiyuki," *Journal of the Economic and Social History of the Orient* 1, pt. 1 (Aug. 1957): 145–48; id., "The T'ang Market System," *Asia Major* 12 (1966): 202–48. On marketing and distribution: Ch'üan Han-sheng, "Nan-Sung Tao-mi te Sheng-ch'an yü Yün-hsiao," *Chung-yang Yen-chiu Yüan. Li-shih Yü-yen Yen-chiu So Chi-k'an* 10 (1942): 403–31; id., "Pei-Sung Pien-liang te Shu Ch'u-ju Huo-i," ibid., 8 (1939): 189–301.

median size of landholdings began to shrink, a phenomenon accompanied by an increasing concentration of land in the hands of estate owners, many of whom were officials. This trend continued to plague the dynasty until its conquest by the Mongols.

The Sung was also noteworthy for a flood of new technical advances, many of them contributing directly to industrial growth and commercial prosperity. New processes in metallurgy, new techniques in mining, and advances in shipbuilding and navigation—all contributed to promote economic expansion. This prosperity was made possible by an increasingly monetized economy. Paper money came into widespread use. Other instruments of credit were devised and employed, particularly in long-range commerce or trade in areas of difficult terrain. But despite this increase in paper instruments the basic unit of money remained the copper coin. The eleventh century saw an enormous expansion in the annual output of such coins. Finally, this period also witnessed a growth in the use of precious metals for fiscal transactions.

This unparalleled prosperity was reflected in a culture with few equals. Sung pottery, Sung paintings, Sung philosophical writing, Sung prose, and Sung historical expositions were rarely equaled by the works of other dynasties. The rise of printing and the growth of educational facilities no doubt contributed to this efflorescence. The rapid development of printing in the Five Dynasties and the early Northern Sung apparently lowered the cost of books, and made the products of a growing body of scholars and writers more widely available. At the same time the growth of formal facilities for education increased the size of the market for an increasingly commercialized printing industry.

But developments in foreign affairs continued to cast shadows across the glories of the Sung. Sung rulers never regained from the Khitan the occupied lands south of the Great Wall. The early fighting ended with the Peace of

Shan Yüan in 1004, but the continued presence of the Khitan was a source of concern to the wiser Sung officials and of temptation to the more stupid. On the western borders the Sung fought a succession of bitter campaigns against the Tanguts in the late 1030s and early 1040s. These military problems led in turn to increasing fiscal difficulties. From the middle of the eleventh century expenditures began to exceed revenues. Fiscal difficulties lent impetus to the reform movement led by Wang An-shih in the 1060s and 1070s. Wang sought to increase government income while hoping to reduce some categories of government outlays. But although some of his innovations were maintained, his most influential legacy to later times was a politics of bitterness and partisan strife.

Thus, when the twelfth century dawned, the Sung, for all its glories, was in a dangerous predicament. A faction-ridden bureaucracy, enemy forces in occupation of lands within the Great Wall, and a precarious fiscal situation faced the new emperor Hui-tsung. Hui-tsung and his ministers have suffered at the hands of later historians, who blame them for the fall of the Northern Sung. Whatever the virtues of their domestic policies, their foreign policy was disastrous. During the eleventh century a new power had appeared in the region north of China: a people called the Jurchen established a state to the east of the area of Khitan dominance and began a long series of forays and minor wars against their western neighbors. During the early 1120s the Sung, ever covetous of the Khitan-held lands south of the Great Wall, entered into alliance with the Jurchen and attacked the Khitan. During the ensuing conflict Sung armies did poorly, but the Jurchen forces overwhelmed the Khitan and then turned on their allies, the Sung. Sung armies suffered defeat after defeat. Hui-tsung abdicated, to be succeeded by Chin-tsung, but both were captured by the Jurchen invaders. The reins of government passed into the hands of Kao-tsung, the first emperor of the Southern Sung.

With Jurchen armies in control of north China, and Jurchen columns driving deep into the southeast, the fugitive court fled across the Yangtse river and moved from perfecture to prefecture to elude the enemy. The Southern Sung thus began its life as the harried remnant of a dynasty, its very existence in serious doubt, its armies routed, its territories invaded by foreigners.

The survival of the Southern Sung must be attributed in part to good fortune, in part to Jurchen deficiencies and the loyalty of the people and Sung officials, but perhaps most immediately to the appearance of a group of extremely able military leaders, who in a few years not only blunted the force of the Jurchen invasions but began to counterattack, driving deep into areas under Jurchen domination. Military successes posed political problems. The generals felt they could drive on to expel the Jurchen, but the Emperor Kao-tsung had doubts. Perhaps he questioned the accuracy of the general's forecasts; no doubt he was disturbed by the political implications of overly successful military leaders in command of large armies. In the event, he chose to negotiate a peace with the Jurchen which left them in control of much of north China. This peace lasted for several decades. In the 1160s there were more incidents with the Jurchen, but the life of the dynasty was not seriously threatened until the thirteenth century. Then in a series of events tragically reminiscent of the early twelfth century, the Sung helped further the fortunes of those who would become their destroyers. Within the area under Jurchen domination there lived a group of tribes called the Mongols. During the early thirteenth century these tribes were united under the leadership of Ghengis Khan. Grown strong, the Mongols turned on their masters and, aided by an alliance with the Sung, overthrew the Jurchen empire. Having conquered North China, they moved on to attack the South, which after decades of desultory but brutal warfare was finally overrun in 1279.

The broad outline of the foreign affairs of the Southern Sung is fairly clear; the internal development of the period remains almost completely unstudied. This domestic history is of great importance to our understanding of later Chinese history. The Northern Sung was a time of rapid development in many facets of Chinese life. The rapidity of this evolution was not matched under later dynasties. To what extent did this slackening in the pace of change occur in the Southern Sung? To what extent was it a result of the Mongol conquest and occupation? Adequate answers to these questions must wait on much further research, but even though our present knowledge is very limited it is clear that in some areas, such as shipbuilding, navigation, and overseas trade, the Southern Sung went far beyond the Northern Sung. And yet in almost all cases, whether the Southern Sung witnessed retreat or advance, it is possible to trace the origins of the changes back into the preceding period. In the Southern Sung there was new growth from old roots.

]2[The Northern Sung: Clerical Personnel and Village Officers

The Northern Sung subbureaucratic organization, modified by reforms during the eleventh century, was the foundation of the system in use during the Southern Sung. The Sung founders took over their predecessors' practices without altering them, but, since the context was different, the actual burdens and responsibilities of the subbureaucracy had changed. Sung China was a great empire, not a medium-sized country like the states of the Five Dynasties period. In time this alteration of circumstances forced the Sung rulers to make changes in all parts of the subbureaucracy. This subbureaucratic organization included three groups of workers: professional clerks, unpaid clerical personnel who served for limited terms in the subprefectural or prefectural offices, and village officers. At the beginning of the Sung the unpaid clerks were mostly village officers rotated to work in the yamen after having completed their terms as servicemen. This practice drew complaints in the Northern Sung because of the financial burdens it placed on those rotated. The statesmen of the time faced a dilema: they had to staff the clerical level of the local government, but they wished to avoid impoverishing those called first as village servicemen and afterward as unpaid clerks. The policy changes designed to deal with this problem culminated in the subbureaucratic reforms promulgated under Shen-tsung (1067–85). In most jobs salaried professionals replaced amateur clerical personnel, and for a few years even the vil-

lage officers were paid. When remuneration of village officers proved too great a strain on the treasury, the system of
unpaid officers was revived. These officers were now organized under rules that initially had been established by
Wang An-shih for the *pao-chia* militia. Despite the fluctua-
tions in policy that marked the reigns of Shen-tsung's successors Che-tsung (1085–1100) and Hui-tsung (1100–26),
pao-chia personnel continued to play a major role in village
services. The policy of using salaried professional clerks instituted under Wang An-shih also remained current practice under these last emperors of the Northern Sung. This
professionalization reduced the problem that had plagued
the first century of Sung rule but it also created a new problem which was to bedevil the officials of the Southern Sung.
In order to pay for the various reform measures, including
the system of hired clerks, the dynasty had to increase its
revenues. The Sung, particularly after the reign of Shen-
tsung, is noted as an era of both heavy taxation and inflation.
When, as a result of the invasions of 1127–37, military expenditures skyrocketed while the revenue base shrank, the
burdens placed on the tax-gathering village officers became
almost unendurable. During most of the Northern Sung
village servicemen suffered because they were rotated to fill
unpaid clerical positions; during the Southern Sung they
suffered because they were forced to submit quotas of taxes,
whether or not they had been able to squeeze these sums
from the men under their jurisdiction.

The professional clerks who served in the prefectural and
subprefectural offices were little touched by the spate of
reforms in the service system (*i-fa*) which occurred in the
Northern Sung. These professional clerks, who in the
Northern Sung already outnumbered requisitioned amateurs in the yamen, received either the income from certain
government-controlled enterprises or fees and bribes for the
work that they did. Even Wang An-shih's reforms merely
altered the source of their income, without fundamentally

changing the character of their positions. Occupying the highest subbureaucratic positions, thoroughly familiar with the Sung legal code and with local conditions, these men saw to it that their jobs remained secure, profitable, and in practice hereditary.[1] Since, as the decades passed more and more clerks were long-term salaried workers, by the end of the Northern Sung almost all such personnel were professionals.[2]

But as late as the early Southern Sung some yamen workers were requisitioned village officers. Under the requisition system a village serviceman who had completed his term might be rotated to the subprefectural or prefectural offices for unpaid clerical duty. Moreover, if the clerks in a prefecture were too few, the prefect might requisition supplementary personnel from subordinate subprefectures. The subprefect then had to draft additional personnel from among the village officers to restore his full clerical complement.[3]

1. Miyazaki Ichisada, "Sō-dai shu ken seido no yurai to sono toku-shoku," *Shirin* 36, no. 2 (July 1953): 117. This work will be cited hereafter as "SSKS." See also *SKSK* p. 658. Yeh Shih described the tendency of clerical personnel to pass their positions on within the family by pointing out that in his day (1150–1223) men said there were feudal clerks but not feudal officials. See Yeh Shih, *Shui Hsin Wen-chi* (Ssu Pu Ts'ung K'an ed.), 3.23b. See also *SZS* p. 104; *HCP* 5.8b, 389.18b. For a discussion in English of the Northern Sung system see Yu Ping-kuan, "The Reform of the Public Services of the Northern Sung Dynasty and Its Related Measures," unpublished Master's thesis, University of Washington, Seattle, 1959. See also James T. C. Liu, *Reform in Sung China* (Cambridge: Harvard University Press, 1959). For clerks see Liu, "The Sung Views on the Control of Government Clerks," *Journal of the Economic and Social History of the Orient* 10, nos. 2–3 (December 1967): 317–44.

2. Miyazaki Ichisada, "Kyo-ri no baibi o chūshin toshite," *Shirin* 30, no. 1, p. 35. Hereafter cited "KRNB."

3. For many positions, rules specified the length of the requisitioned service, the posts from which men might be selected, the value of the property they had to own to be eligible, and the household rank and type from which rotated men might be drawn. In addition for some positions a bond had to be posted. See Chao Yen-wei, *Yün Lu Man Ch'ao* (Ts'ung-shu Chi Ch'eng ed.), pp. 345ff.

The Northern Sung village officer system resembled the system used during the latter part of the T'ang dynasty, unpaid workers being conscripted from certain types and grades of households. For conscription purposes, the rural population was divided on the basis of wealth into nine grades before 1022 and into five grades thereafter. A requisitioned family had to provide a person to fill a particular village office for a limited period of time. When the term of duty was finished, the drafted person was generally allowed to return to his ordinary pursuits (unless he was rotated to the town yamen for clerical service), and another liable family was asked to provide his successor. This was called the "drafted service system" (*ch'ai-i fa*).

Village servicemen included Township Leaders (*li-cheng*), Household Chiefs (*hu-chang*), Elders (*ch'i chang*), Stalwart Men (*chuang-ting*), and Canton Scribes (*hsiang shu shou*) During the T'ang, one Township Leader was appointed in each grouping of one hundred households to act as a general administrator and to preserve local order; in the early Northern Sung, one Township Leader was chosen from a first-grade household in each canton, and as his major task he managed tax collection.[4] A number of Household Chiefs, selected from second-grade households[5] for three-year terms,[6] assisted Township Leaders in gathering taxes. If Township Leaders and Household Chiefs did not collect their assigned quota of taxes they had to contribute the difference from their own incomes, but, because tax rates were relatively low, these two positions were not considered burdensome until the last years of the Northern

4. Sudō Yoshiyuki, *Tōsō shakai kiezai-shi kenkyū* (Tokyo: Tokyo Daigaku Shuppan Kai, 1965), p. 566. This work will be cited hereafter as *TSKSK*. See also *HCP* 35.9b. For the T'ang see Twitchett, *Financial Administration*.

5. Ch'en Ch'i-ch'ing, *Chia-ting Ch'ih Ch'eng Chih* (T'ai Chou Ts'ung-shu ed.), 17.8a. This work will be cited hereafter as *CTCCC*. See also *HCP* 35.9b.

6. *TSKSK* p. 576.

Sung. After the reforms of Wang An-shih, taxes apparently became heavier, but the work demanded of the gatherers did not become onerous until the 1120s, when pressing military problems led to a sharp increase in the need for revenue.[7]

The Canton Scribes were also involved in the tax-collecting process, since they kept records used in assessing burdens. This office, first established during the Five Dynasties, was inherited by the Sung. During the first part of the dynasty one Canton Scribe was appointed in each canton from a fourth-grade household.[8]

Maintaining local tranquility was the responsibility of the Elders assisted by the Stalwart Men. The Elders were in charge of suppressing bandits, settling minor disputes, fire fighting, caring for roads and bridges, and encouraging agriculture and handicrafts. At the beginning of the Northern Sung the government commissioned three Elders from first- and second-grade households or from official households in each *kuan* (newly created administrative subdivision). Their assistants, the Stalwart Men, were drawn from fourth- or fifth-grade households.[9]

The system described above continued without any major alterations from the close of the tenth century until 1055. In that year the position of Township Leader was abolished. The job of collecting local levies passed entirely into the hands of the Household Chiefs. As a result the number of men called as Household Chiefs was greatly increased,[10] but, except for this change, the village officer system in most parts of the empire in the years immediately

7. *SZS* p. 133; "SIFS" p. 207.
8. *CTCCC* 17.8a. Even official households were sometimes called to provide Canton Scribes. See *TSKSK* p. 646.
9. *CTCCC* 17.8a; *HCP* 65.4b–5a. (The report suggests that *chuang-ting* were usually drawn from fifth-grade households.) On the origin of the *kuan* see Nakamura Jihee, "Sō-dai no chihō kukaku-*kan* ni tsuite," *Shien*, no. 89 (Dec. 1962), pp. 85ff.
10. *CTCCC* 17.8a; *SZS* p. 132.

prior to the reforms of Wang An-shih resembled that in operation in A.D. 1000.

Village officers during the first century of the Northern Sung did not fear the responsibilities of village service positions; they were afraid that they might be called upon to work as unpaid clerks in the prefectural or subprefectural offices. In particular, villagers dreaded the possibility that they might have to serve as Supply Masters (*ya-ch'ien*).[11]

The term *ya-ch'ien* first appears in the T'ang dynasty. Initially applied to the army guarding the emperor, after the creation of the Regional Defense Commandant (*chieh-tu-shih*) system in the mid-T'ang it referred to the troops under the direct command of the Regional Defense Commandant. When the civil and military hierarchies merged in the late T'ang and Five Dynasties, all members of the military advisory staff of the Regional Defense Commandants came to be called *ya-ch'ien*. At first the power of this staff increased, but during the Five Dynasties the *ya-ch'ien* gradually lost their connection with military affairs and were relegated to the job of controlling granaries. By extension they came to be charged with the management of other official property. This included the duty of overseeing the shipment of revenues to the treasury and accompanying civil service officials to and from office.[12]

Under the Five Dynasties the burden placed on these Supply Masters was not excessive. Since China was divided into a number of relatively small states, Supply Masters es-

11. Supply Masters is not a literal translation of *ya-ch'ien* but rather an attempt to indicate the major function of these men in Sung times. Liu, *Reform in Sung China*, p. 100, translates the term as "Office Servicemen," which is one step closer to the literal meaning of the words but does not adequately indicate the duties of the office. In fact, because of the evolution of the meaning of *ya-ch'ien*, no literal translation could be anything but misleading in a discussion of the situation during the Sung period.

12. For a description of the rise and fall of the position of *ya-ch'ien* see *SSKS* pp. 103ff. See also "KRNB" pp. 15ff; *SZS* pp. 103ff; Ma Tuanlin, *Wen Hsien T'ung K'ao*, 15.132.

corting officials and tax shipments did not have to traverse long distances. With the centralization under the Sung the duties of Supply Masters became extremely onerous. In convoying taxes and in accompanying civil servants, Supply Masters often traveled many hundreds of miles to K'ai-feng. They were responsible for goods lost or damaged in transit. Frequently they had to bribe the accountants at the capital before their goods would be judged acceptable.[13] As a result, a single term of service frequently impoverished village officers conscripted as Supply Masters.

The suffering caused by the Supply Master system was instrumental in stirring up much debate and some reform. During the first decades of the Northern Sung this problem was little discussed, but by the last years of the reign of Chen-tsung (997–1022) the need for improvements had become manifest. Before the accession of Shen-tsung (1067–85), changes in local government services were of two types: those designed to curtail total demand for servicemen, and those aimed at redistributing costs.

Aggregate demand could be lowered by reducing either the number of servicemen called[14] or the number of administrative units in the empire. Since each unit had a set mini-

13. "KRNB" p. 19; *SZS* pp. 108ff. Some of the Supply Masters were voluntary professionals who were able to squeeze some profit from their duties. These professional Supply Masters were called by various names—*ch'ang ming ya-ch'ien, li jen ya-ch'ien, t'ou ming ya-ch'ien, ch'ang ch'ung ya-ch'ien,* and *chiang li ya-ch'ien.* The last of these groups, the *chiang li ya-ch'ien,* might be called Military Service Supply Masters, since they were especially concerned with overseeing the transport of official goods and were subordinate to military officers. This position gradually disappeared during the latter half of the Northern Sung. The other terms given above were roughly synonymous. Although some *ya-ch'ien* were volunteers, there were circuits, particularly in North China, where there were not enough volunteers to fill all the needed Supply Master positions. Therefore village officers had to be requisitioned.

14. In the 1040s the number of men drafted is said to have been reduced by 23,622 men. See *HCP* 218.9a.

mum complement of clerical functionaries, the elimination of a unit automatically lowered the sum of legally required personnel. During the Northern Sung the statesman whose name was most closely linked with the policy of disestablishing administrative units was Fan Chung-yen,[15] but the policy had other supporters in both the Northern and the Southern Sung.[16]

Other reforms concentrated on reapportioning the burden of providing services. In some cases this meant reregistering the population and reassessing property,[17] but there were other, more radical attempts to reduce inequities inherent in the system. One famous measure limited the amount of obligation-free land that official households (*kuan-hu*) could own. These households often evaded regular land taxes on their holdings, nor could they be called on to fill most village officer posts.[18] It was felt that these privileges unjustly penalized the wealthy commoner families, which competed with official households for control of property while bearing the costs of local services. By restricting the amount of property that official households could hold free from fiscal obligations the government sought to promote a redistribution of administrative costs or of land ownership. Had this measure worked as envisioned by its sponsors, either official households would have helped to bear the cost of local services, thus relieving the local com-

15 A memorial of Fan Chung-yen on this topic is translated (into German) in Peter Buriks, "Fan Chung-yen's Versuch einer Reform des chinesischen Beamtenstaates in den Jahren 1043/44," *Oriens Extremus* 3 (July–Dec. 1956) : 78–79.

16. Ou-yang Hsiu, *Ou-yang Wen Chung Kung Chi* (Ssu Pu Ts'ung K'an ed.), 115.3a, and *HNYL* 176.2903 (1157).

17. "SIFS" p. 210.

18. There were a few exceptions to this rule. At the beginning of the Northern Sung, members of official households might be drafted to serve as Elders. See *TSKSK* p. 636. Also, the original exemption of official households covered only households where the official in question was of the seventh rank or higher. See "SIFS" p. 212.

moners, or they would hold down their investment in landed property, thus releasing land for purchase by others.[19]

In another type of reform, larger administrative units were used in assessing service burdens. This helped reduce inequities stemming from local disparities of wealth and population. In a fertile populous region, since a larger number of households would be accountable for service, any given household would be called on less often. Furthermore, a family considered rich in a poor area and ranked as a first-grade household might be only modestly well-to-do by the standards of a richer area and be classed as a second- or even a third-grade household. Therefore, when the responsibilities for a post were rotated among those eligible, families in affluent, densely populated regions did not have to serve as frequently as families in impoverished regions with sparse populations. And the richest families in fertile areas, being far richer than the most prosperous families in poorer localities, suffered less from the costs of office when they did have to serve.

This inequity could be mitigated by using larger units in drafting personnel. A subprefecture might have ten cantons and desire to call ten Township Leaders. If these Township Leaders were conscripted from the ten most opulent households in the entire subprefecture, this would probably be more equitable than if they were chosen from the individual cantons by taking the richest family in each of the cantons.

The most renowned reform of this type was inaugurated in 1055 when the position of Township Leader Supply Master (*li-cheng ya-ch'ien*) was abolished, and the post of Canton Household Supply Master (*hsiang hu ya-ch'ien*) was created to take its place. Under the Township Leader Supply Master system each canton had a register that listed

19. Ma Tuan-lin, 12.128–29.

households by grades in order of their wealth. First-grade households were selected from these registers, and required to provide someone as a Township Leader, after which this person might be rotated to serve as a Supply Master. Under the Canton Household Supply Master system each subprefecture had a similar register. Canton Household Supply Masters were drawn from the wealthiest households in the entire subprefecture. The effect of this innovation was to increase the share of service cost borne by the inhabitants of the more affluent cantons and to decrease the burden on poorer areas.

The memorial advocating this reform, submitted by Han Ch'i in 1055, said:

> Generally, in calling [people] for household service (*hu-i*, another name for subbureaucratic service), the assistants [to the subprefect] personally examine the registers. . . . With regard to the levies in each canton the broadness and material wealth [of these areas] is not the same. Supposing in one subprefecture there are two cantons—A and B. Canton A has fifteen households classed as number one grade, each worth three thousand strings of cash. Canton B has only five families classed as number one grade, and they are only worth five hundred strings. Then, in canton A each [liable] household serves [only] one term every fifteen years. In canton B [each household] has to serve a term every five years. Those who are rich are given excessive rest and those who are poorer work continuously. How is this in accord with the Court's intention of being the father and mother of the people? I ask that from now on you stop levying Township Leader Supply Masters and only levy Canton Household Supply Masters. [You should] order the Offices of the Fiscal Intendants to use the number of Township Leader Supply Masters presently being called in the various prefectures as the quota. [You should] order the assistants to the subprefect to take the Five Grade Registers [and] from among the various cantons of the whole subprefecture select one very wealthy household to

serve [by providing the Canton Household Supply
Master]. If, when you reform the drafting of men in
this fashion, subprefecture A has few qualified households and many positions to fill, then it should provisionally be permitted to requisition the needed men
from subprefecture B, which has an ample supply of
qualified households and few positions.[20]

The government accepted Han Ch'i's proposals, established Canton Household Supply Masters, eliminated
Township Leaders and Township Leader Supply Masters,
and in some parts of China inaugurated the five-grade system *(wu-tse fa)*. Under this system, Supply Master duties
were divided into five grades according to the hardship the
service entailed. The liable population was also divided
into five grades. First-grade Supply Master tasks were given
only to first-grade families, second-grade Supply Master duties only to second-grade families, and so on.[21]

The most noteworthy reforms of these decades were the
sporadic attempts to introduce the use of hired personnel
supported in part by special taxes. Since many clerical personnel were already professional (including many of the
Supply Masters), it was natural that attempts be made to
formalize and extend this usage in order to halt the requisitioning of unpaid Supply Masters. Supply Masters were
hired in some areas as early as 1034[22] and as late as 1052.[23]
In 1041 the Fiscal Intendant, Wang K'uei, introduced the
practice into Ching-hu Nan circuit. He added a new feature
when he began to collect "exemption money" *(mien-i
ch'ien)* from those who would ordinarily have been draft-
able for such service. This revenue was ostensibly to be expended hiring Supply Masters, but Wang K'uei set aside
300,000 strings for delivery to the central treasury. Thus,
the collection of funds to remunerate personnel and their

    20. *HCP* 179.7b–9a.
    21. Ibid.
    22. *HCP* 114.1b.
    23. *HCP* 172.20b.

misallocation to other uses both began at the same time.[24]

Tseng Kung, while prefectural vice-administrator of Yüeh prefecture in 1056–63, added a further refinement. Previously the clerks had been allowed to manage the state wine monopoly, a source of great profit. Tseng Kung decided to auction the right to the monopoly and use the proceeds to pay the clerks, including the newly engaged Supply Masters. If this income was insufficient, a special impost was to be levied on the rural rich.[25]

Finally, in 1062, Ssu-ma Kuang, who later became the most vigorous opponent of the policies of Wang An-shih, including the hired-service system, advocated utilizing wine monopoly income supplemented by a levy on wealthy urban residents as a fund for recompensing clerical personnel.[26]

Not until the rise of Wang An-shih were these piecemeal changes united into a system and used throughout the empire. Although the transformation of the services is closely linked with the name Wang An-shih, it should nevertheless be noted that the first initiative toward their thorough renovation came during the sixth month of 1067, while Wang An-shih was still serving at a local post in Chiang-nan. When the emperor Shen-tsung (1067–85) solicited advice on improving the services, his Finance Minister, Han Chiang, suggested that a committee of top-ranking officials be appointed to study the problem.[27]

Wang An-shih's rise to national prominence in the ensuing months was accompanied by a spate of reform decrees. In the eighth month of 1070 the Law of Granaries was

24. *HCP* 133.1b; Ma Tuan-lin, 12.129; T'o T'o et al., *Sung Shih*, 177.1b. It should be pointed out that it had been common practice from the early Northern Sung for city residents to pay money in lieu of service. See "SSKS" p. 116.

25. T'o T'o et al., 319.16a–b.

26. *HCP* 196.17a–b.

27. Ch'in Hsiang-yeh, *Hsü Tzu-chih T'ung-chien Ch'ang-pien Shih Pu*, 1.18b–19a; Shen-tsung's interest seems to have been aroused by an earlier report by Han Chiang. See *SHY, shih-huo* 65.1a–b.

promulgated, establishing legal fixed emoluments for the
clerks in the granaries of the capital. This enactment later
provided a pattern for the extension of salaries to other yamen workers.[28] Four months later the annals of the dynastic
history report that "for the first time the hired service system
(*mien-i fa*) was put into practice."[29] This hired system,
formally proclaimed in the tenth month of 1071, established
a graduated impost, the proceeds from which were to be
devoted to hiring professional clerical workers to fill posts
in the capital and in local yamen. This tax was to be collected twice a year, in grain or in cash. In rural areas the
top three of five household grades contributed; in urban
areas the top five of ten grades contributed. These households were to be regraded every three years in the cities and
every five years in the countryside. Groups that had
formerly been exempt now had to provide at least some
money to help defray service costs. The income was divided
into categories: exemption money (*mien-i ch'ien*) paid
by those groups that had been liable for conscription under
the old policies; aid money (*chu-i ch'ien*) given by those
groups that formerly had been excused from service; and
surplus money (*k'uan-sheng ch'ien*), a surcharge set aside
as a contingency fund. Salaries might be calculated on a
daily, monthly, or piecework basis. People were engaged
from the top three grades of taxpaying rural households.
Volunteers needed three guarantors. For some positions
there were other requirements. Supply Masters had to post
a bond, archers were tested, and scribes had to take examinations. Contracts, which ran for two or three years, were
subject to reconsideration when they expired.[30]

Initially the reformers had not intended to recompense

28. *HCP* 214.14b, 242.1b, 248.13b.
29. T'o T'o et al., 15.4a. This passage clearly refers to the beginning of a period of experimentation and not to the promulgation of
a finished system on a national scale.
30. *HCP* 227.2a ff; Ma Tuan-lin, 12.131.

village officers, but in the next few years the hiring of personnel was extended to the village level.[31] The cost of paying these workers proved too great, and in 1074 unremunerated service was reinstituted.[32]

Wang An-shih did not simply revive the old village officers. Instead he attempted to utilize a local organization created by another of his reforms—the *pao-chia* militia. The positions of Elders, Stalwart Men, and Household Chiefs were abolished, and their duties were assigned to *pao-chia* officers.[33]

Wang An-shih, desiring to reduce some categories of government expenditures, had sought to cut the military budget by decreasing the size of the professional armies. During the first century of Sung rule these forces had swelled until in the reign of Ying-tsung (1063–67) they numbered 1,162,000 men.[34] A great part of state income had to be committed to supporting this host. These soldiers were not engaged in productive occupations. They did not contribute to their own keep, nor did they pay taxes. Wang An-shih created a peasant militia, the *pao-chia,* to act as a supplementary military force to maintain local order. It was hoped that eventually this militia would replace the regular armies. Precedent for this reform was found in the *Chou Li,* in the peasant troops of earlier dynasties, and in the practices of the Sung. A local defense force called *pao-wu* already existed in some areas of China when Wang came to power.[35] Perhaps with these examples in mind, Wang designed a militia system, which was put into prac-

31. *HCP* 225.2a ff; 285.5b, 360.13b.

32. *HCP* 257.8a. The money saved by stopping the hiring of village officers was used to hire Bowmen, to pay the newly created Messengers, to pay militia expenses, or was sent to the central treasury. *HCP* 329.13b–14a; ibid., 2506.21b.

33. *HCP* 257.8a. See also ibid. 360.13a–b. For the pao-chia see also Lin Shui-han, "Sung Tai Pao-chia," *Ta Lu Tsa Chih* 20.7.4.

34. *SZS* p. 26.

35. *TSKSK* p. 579.

tice in the capital area in the first month of 1071. Under this system ten households were organized into a small guard (*hsiao pao*) from which one member of a well-to-do resident household (*chu-hu*) was chosen to act as a Small Guard Chief (*hsiao pao chang*). Five small guards formed a large guard (*ta pao*) from which one member of a wealthy resident household was selected to be the Large Guard Chief (*ta pao chang*). Ten large guards comprised a superior guard (*tu-pao*). Within each superior guard two men were appointed from very rich resident households. One served as the Superior Guard Leader (*tu pao cheng*) and the other as the Assistant Superior Guard Leader (*tu pao fu cheng*). Any household (whether resident or nonresident) with two or more adult male members had to donate the services of one of them to the militia. They were called Guard Men (*pao-ting*). Certain household types were released from this obligation.[36] In the autumn of 1073 this system was extended to the whole empire.[37] A few months later the number of households in each type of division was halved—five now forming a small guard; twenty-five a large guard; and 250 a superior guard—but the complement of officers remained unchanged.[38]

This *pao-chia*, initially an organization charged with suppressing local disorders, soon began to usurp village officer functions. In the years 1072–75 a series of orders abolished the position of Household Chief, Elder, and Stalwart Man.[39] In 1074 the taxgathering duties of House-

36. *SHY ping* 2.5a–b.
37. *HCP* 246.21b.
38. *HCP* 248.8a. In practice, different local militia systems were in use in different sections of the country. Several later decrees were concerned with unifying standards and practices. *SHY, ping* 2.9b, 2.19b–20a.

39. The sources do not always agree on the dates of these changes. *CTCCC* 17.8a and Ch'en Fu-liang, *Chih Chai Wen-chi* (Ssu Pu Ts'ung K'an ed.), 21.1a say that the position of Household Chief was abolished in 1072, but the *HCP* 257.8a records the abolition of this position (and its urban equivalent the *fang-cheng*) in 1074. The abolition

hold Chiefs were assumed by functionaries called Heads of Tithing (*chia-t'ou*). Households were to be organized into aggregates of from ten to thirty called tithings (*chia*). In each tithing one man, selected to be Head of Tithing, collected the taxes during a single tax period. Each household in the tithing had to provide a Head of Tithing when its turn came, the rotation of the position moving downward from the top in rank order of the wealth of the families.[40] In 1075 the position of Elder was eliminated and its police functions were turned over to the Superior Guard Leaders and their Assistants. The Large Guard Chiefs aided them in preserving local peace. At the same time the post of Stalwart Man was abolished. The newly established Messengers (*ch'eng-t'ieh jen*) assumed their document-carrying duties.[41]

Although the reformers found they could not continue to pay most village personnel, other aspects of the reformed service system of Wang An-shih seemed well on the way to acceptance and success. Many men who had originally questioned the feasibility or wisdom of his plans had begun to change their opinion. Then, in 1085, the emperor Shen-tsung died, and was succeeded by a minor, the emperor Che-tsung. During the minority of Che-tsung, the Hsüan-jen empress held actual power at court. She had long been critical of Shen-tsung's rennovation of the service system. One of her first acts was to place in power the archrival of Wang An-shih, the statesman and writer Ssu-ma Kuang.

Before the rise of Wang An-shih, Ssu-ma Kuang had written on the problems of improving local services. He had even advocated the hiring of clerks. However, by the time he became the leading minister in the reign of Che-tsung he had become a rigidly dogmatic opponent of Wang

of the Stalwart Men and Elders is dated 1074 by Ch'en Fu-liang, 21.3a, and 1075 by *CTCCC* 17.8b. See also *HCP* 2506.21b.

40. *HCP* 257.8a, 263.21b–22a.

41. *HCP* 263.21b–22a.

An-shih's policies. Within months of the death of Shen-tsung and the appointment to high posts of Ssu-ma Kuang and other enemies of Wang An-shih, the *pao-chia* was abolished and the older village service positions were re-established. At first this meant a return to the practice of using Elders, Household Chiefs, and Stalwart Men, but re-compensing them for their labors.[42] But a few months later Ssu-ma Kuang submitted a memorial attacking all aspects of the policy of hiring personnel with government funds.[43] Many officials who had previously disagreed with Wang An-shih did not accept Ssu-ma Kuang's opinionated criticism of the hiring policy. As a result, clerical personnel continued to be paid,[44] but after further criticisms of the compensating of village personnel[45] the government issued an order in early 1086 restoring the drafted service system (*ch'ai-i fa*).[46]

In the autumn of 1093 the Hsüan-jen empress died, and the emperor Che-tsung at last gained personal control of the government. He was an admirer of Shen-tsung and quickly recalled the partisans of the "New Laws." In the spring of 1094, Elders, Household Chiefs, and Stalwart Men were again given salaries. At first, personnel active in the newly resurrected *pao-chia* were not allowed to take the places of these village officers,[47] but in the autumn, at the request of the Finance Bureau, *pao-chia* officers were permitted to volunteer to serve concurrently as village servicemen. Superior Guard Leaders, their Assistants, and Large Guard Chiefs could act as Elders. Heads of Tithing could

42. *HCP* 358.4a–6b, 360.13a–14a; *CTCCC* 17.8a; Yang Chung-liang, *Tzu-chih T'ung-chien Ch'ang-pien Chi-shih Pen-mo* (Taipei: Wen Hai Publishing Co., 1967), 108.2b. This work will be cited hereafter as *CPCSPM*.

43. *SHY, shih-huo* 66.47a.

44. *HCP* 394.1a.

45. Ibid. 364.2b–6b.

46. *SHY, shih-huo* 13.3aff.

47. *SHY, shih-huo* 66.65b.

be Household Chiefs, and Messengers Stalwart Men.[48] In the second month of 1095 the final form of this system was established. Large Guard Chiefs replaced Heads of Tithing.

It seems that, while *pao-chia* leaders were in theory not paid (except when on active military training duty), when they volunteered for simultaneous service as village officers they were given the emoluments of such personnel. Thus, a Superior Guard Leader who acted concurrently as an Elder received an Elder's salary. A Large Guard Chief working as a Household Chief got the latter's salary. Messengers who took over some of the duties of Stalwart Men were also paid. If not enough *pao-chia* leaders volunteered to act as servicemen, then the authorities drafted Elders, Household Chiefs, and Stalwart Men from among the people.[49]

This system devised under Che-tsung permitted two different patterns of organization, which may be termed concurrent service and dual service. In the former, the *pao-chia* leaders acted concurrently as village officers. In the latter, two separate organizations existed in the rural areas—a *pao-chia* system and a village officer system. These rules, first set down during the 1090s, continued to be used during the succeeding reigns of the Northern Sung and were the basis of the service system under the Southern Sung.

48. Ibid., *shih-huo* 66.66b.

49. T'o T'o et al., 178.11b–12a; Ch'en Fu-liang, 21.3a; *CTCCC* 17.8a. The sources sometimes speak of hiring *pao-chia* officers, but it seems highly probable that the men in question were concurrently workers in service posts. There is no evidence that *pao-chia* leaders who did not provide village services were paid except when actively engaged in military training. For military pay see *CPCSPM* 71.6a. It is not clear whether the village officers drafted when there were not enough volunteers were paid.

The Southern Sung Village Service System: Functions and Procedures

The styles of organization of the Southern Sung service system varied, the concurrent variant being used in most regions and the dual variant existing in peripheral circuits, but the functions performed and the procedures followed were similar in all of the empire. Village service officers, in the Southern as in the Northern Sung, acted as soldiers, policemen, taxgatherers, record keepers, bureaucratic workers, welfare officers, road commissioners, and official hosts, and furnished men and materials for construction.

These tasks were usually carried out in accordance with defined procedures. Law or custom fixed time limits for the performance of duties and the transmission of documents, and warrants were used to guard against misuse of official power. Although extant sources only briefly detail daily routines, it would seem that procedures, like functions, changed little during the Southern Sung, and the distribution of tasks among the various officers altered little. Some servicemen had few functions, and most had a primary area of concern, but many were involved in a variety of sometimes overlapping minor tasks, and one—the Superior Guard Leader—was held at least partly accountable for almost all kinds of local problems that occurred in rural China. The burden of the office of Superior Guard Leader increased during the second half of the dynasty as the number of people under his jurisdiction began to exceed the limits set by law. He was clearly the pivotal figure in the administrative organization below the subprefectural level during this era of Chinese history.

Maintaining local tranquillity and capturing those who disturbed it had long been functions of the village service level of government. The paid constabulary headquartered in the prefectural and subprefectural seats were too few in numbers to deal adequately with the lawlessness endemic in pre–twentieth-century China. Assigning part of the responsibility for local order to village servicemen not only saved the state the cost of a large police force, it also created an organization that might aid in crime prevention and could even be used to supplement the regular armed forces in resisting invaders. During the Northern Sung the Elders, assisted by the Stalwart Men, were the chief agents for rural law enforcement.

During the Southern Sung officials repeatedly suggested that Northern Sung usages be revived,[1] and in some areas at some times Elders and Stalwart Men did exist as independent officers charged with maintaining local order.[2] However, at most times, in both dual and concurrent service regions Superior Guard Leaders were the key figures in rural law enforcement. Assisted in some cases by Guard Chiefs, and supplemented by the *pao-wu* militia, they upheld the law and presumably performed all the tasks of early Northern Sung Elders, while also acting as the chief agents in many other aspects of local administration. Yeh Shih (1150–1223) described the crime deterrence facet of village officer duties by saying that such men were to keep small quarrels from growing into great disorders and to teach the people in order to avoid having to punish them.[3]

1. *SHY, shih-huo* 14.25a (1135), 14.35a (1159), 14.46b–47a (1172); *HNYL* 167.2736 (1154).
2. *SHY, shih-huo* 14.22b–23a. In other regions they were usually concerned with tax collection, not police work.
3. Yeh Shih, *Shui Hsin Wen-chi,* 3.20b. There were contemporary observers, however, who questioned the ability of the village officers

On a more mundane level, the organization of the population into household groupings headed by village officers was the backbone of the system of crime prevention and detection through mutual surveillance and guarantee traditionally associated with the Ch'in reformer Shang Yang. During the Northern Sung, in addition to their participation in the ordinary system of mutual guarantee, village officers sometimes had to act as guarantors for such potentially troublesome people as itinerant brokers. In the Southern Sung, although village service organizations remained subject to rules covering mutual guarantee, the *pao-wu* militia units were the fundamental mutual responsibility groups.[4]

A memorial dated 1205 reveals both the positive and the negative sides of mutual surveillance. Describing the duties of *pao-wu* officers called *chia-shou,* an official asked that:

> If within the household grouping (*chia*) there are men who are well behaved and filial, this should be reported to the local authorities with a request that these men be rewarded. If there are men who are unfilial, unbrotherly, or contentious so that they injure the people, or if there are criminals or military deserters, then the household group leader (*chia-shou*) and the multitude should report them. The officials should punish them according to law. If there are those who momentarily cause dissension, the men from the household grouping (*chia*) should exhort [them to be peaceful]. The family of the household group leader (*chia-shou*) should be permitted to set up notices about defense against robbers. In times of dearth in rustic secluded places police posts should be established, and the household group leader should in a just and public way call on the men of household grouping to act as policemen (*hsün-ching*) in rotation.

---

to maintain order. See Huang Kan, *Mien Chai Chi* (Ssu K'u Ch'üan Shu ed.), 25.27a ff.

4. *SHY, ping* 2.48a–49a (1222); ibid., *shih-huo* 66.29a–b; *HNYL* 169.2766; Li Yüan-pi, *Tso I Tzu Chen* (Shanghai: Commercial Press, 1934), 2.11a. Hereafter cited *TITC.*

. . . The offices of the Judicial Intendants of the various circuits were ordered to devise measures for these purposes and to memorialize the Department of Ministeries about them.[5]

Hindering illegal activities involved not just mutual surveillance but also the elimination of conditions that might breed crime or attract criminals. The late Northern Sung handbook for local officials, the *Tso I Tzu Chen,* warns:

> Where there are empty kilns it is always imperative that they be filled up, and where there are gravesites that have become overgrown the roads leading to the graves should be cut clear. If these instructions are slighted then I fear that bandits will gather [at such places].[6]

The Elders were also advised to escort to the subprefectural borders young male beggars who were without crippling deformity or injury.[7]

Once disorders had occurred, whether because of attack from without or lawlessness from within, village service men took part in their suppression and in the subsequent processes of justice. During the Southern Sung, because of the existence of the *pao-wu* militia, the *pao-chia* organization played only a minor role in the defense against foreign invasions. In the early critical years of the resistance against the Chin there were scattered reports of *pao-chia* units taking part in the fighting—in Shensi in 1127,[8] in Ch'ing prefecture of Ching-tung East circuit in 1128,[9] in Yeh prefecture in Hopei West circuit in 1133,[10] and from several

5. *SHY, shih-huo* 66.29a–b. For another description of the role of the *pao-wu* in maintaining local order in the Southern Sung see Hsüeh Chi-hsüan, *Ken Chai Hsien-sheng Hsüeh Ch'ang Chou Lang Yü Chi* (Yung Chia Ts'ung-shu ed.), 15.4a–5a.

6. *TITC* 7.36a. The term translated kilns (*yao*) was also used in some parts of China for houses made of earth; so my translation may be misleading. Unfortunately the context does not indicate which idea is meant here.

7. Ibid.

8. *HNYL* 8.204

9. *HNYL* 12.273

10. *HNYL* 65.1101

prefectures in Ching-hsi South circuit in 1136.[11] After the frontiers with the Chin had stabilized in the late 1130s, *pao-chia* forces do not seem to have been used as soldiers, but *pao-chia* officers did sometimes serve as concurrent commanders of *pao-wu* units. In the late twelfth and the thirteenth centuries in Szechuan, Hunan, and Hupei, Superior Guard Leaders and their Assistants were concommitantly heads of the militia forces in their areas.[12]

Although *pao-wu* detachments were the more important local defense organizations and were the basic collective responsibility groups, the *pao-chia* system played a more influential role in the other facets of the rural police and judicial systems. In most dual service regions as well as in concurrent regions, Superior Guard Leaders and their Assistants were held accountable for the investigation of crime and the apprehension of brigands,[13] military deserters,[14]

11. *HNYL.* 99.1621. There are also reports of the use of *pao-chia* that do not mention the region involved. Ibid. 24.494 (1129).

12. Yao Kuang-hsiao, *Yung-lo Ta-tien* (Chung Hua Shu Chü facsimile edition), 2217.18b (describing Szechuan during the reign of Ning-tsung 1194–1224). Hereafter cited *YLTT*. See also *SHY, ping* 2.47a–48a (Hunan and Hupei in 1196). Sometimes it is not clear whether it is a question of *pao-chia* officers or other village service officers acting concurrently or of militia officers with the same title. For example, one *pao-wu* leader in Szechuan was called the *chia-t'ou*—the same title used for the tax collector in the Head of Tithing system. Since there is no evidence that the Head of Tithing system was ever used in Szechuan it seems likely that there were two distinct officers with the same title. See *YLTT* 2217.18b. There are also reports from the thirteenth century that *pao-chang* were militia leaders. Hu T'ai-ch'u, *Chou Lien Hsü Lun* (Ts'ung-shu Chi Ch'eng ed.), p. 17.

13. *CTCCC* 17.8b (1139); *SHY, shih-huo* 14.35a–b (1159); Ma Tuan-lin, *Wen Hsien T'ung K'ao*, 13.138 (1164); *SHY, shih-huo* 14.39b–40a (1164), 14.40b–41a (1167); Chu Hsi, *Hui-an Hsien-sheng Chu Wen-kung Wen-chi* (Ssu Pu Ts'ung K'an ed.), 99.1775–76 (1181), (hereafter cited *HAHS*); *SHY, shih-huo* 66.27b–28a (1197); Ma Tuan-lin, 13.138 (1199); *SHY, shih-huo* 66.28a–b (1199), 66.31a–b (1221). See also Ch'en Yüan-chin, *Yü Shu Lei Kao* (Ssu K'u Ch'üan Shu Chen Pen ed.), 1.1a. Ch'en calls these men *li-cheng* but this is a synonym for *pao-cheng* as is shown by Sudo in *TSKSK* p. 606–7. See also *HAHS* 19.296.

14. *SHY, shih-huo* 14.22b–23a (1134)

and illegal salt dealers.[15] They apparently had the assistance of the Large Guard Chiefs,[16] and presumably a posse drawn from among their neighbors.[17]

It is far from clear, however, how the law enforcement duties of Superior Guard Leaders and their Assistants were integrated with those of the Bowmen (*kung-shou*) stationed in the prefectural and subprefectural towns. These Bowmen guarded the offices of the local authorities under the command of the subprefectural sheriff (*wei*).[18] They were used throughout the Southern Sung. Each locality had a quota which in practice was not proportional to population, apparently being determined by the amount of disorder in the region.[19]

Every month the sheriff, accompanied by Bowmen, made a tour of the cantons in his subprefecture.[20] In addition to this regular circuit, Bowmen, with or without the sheriff,

15. *SHY, shih-huo* 25.22a (1124)

16. *CTCCC* 17.8b (1139); *YLTT* 2217.18b (1194–1224); *SHY, shih-huo* 14.22b–23a (1134)

17. The *pao-wu* leaders, when dealing with troublemakers, used the "multitude." Presumably the same was true in the case of the *pao-chia. SHY, shih-huo* 66.29a–b. See also *SHY, shih-huo* 65.91a.

18. *CTCCC* 12.5b–6a; *SHY, chih-kuan* 48.60a.

19. T'o T'o et al., *Sung Shih*, 24.9a (1127); ibid. 27.16a (1134); Liao Hsing-chih, *Sheng Chai Chi* (Ssu K'u Ch'üan Shu Chen Pen ed.), 5.23b; Ch'ien Shuo-yu, *Hsien-ch'un Lin-an Chih* (Ch'ien-t'ang Wang Shih Chen-ch'i T'ang blockprint ed.), 57.6a–b, 58.2b–6b; Shih Hsiu, *Chia-t'ai Kuei Chi Chih* (Chia-ch'ing recarved woodblock ed.), 4.5b, 5.2a (1201). According to the original statutes the quota was proportional to population. *SHY, chih-kuan* 48.60a. These statutes were ignored in practice.

20. Liao Hsing-chih, 5.17b–18b; *SHY, shih-huo* 14.42b–43a (1167): ibid., *chih-kuan* 48.68a. After 1133 the Superior Guard Leaders kept the registers that the touring sheriffs were supposed to sign each month to indicate that they were in fact complying with this duty to visit rural areas. *SHY, chih-kuan* 48.70a–b. It seems possible that at this time certain lawsuit warrants were given out by the visiting officials to the village officers. Compare *SHY, shih-huo* 12.23a with ibid., *shih-huo* 14.41a, where two different explanations are given for the term *ts'u-hsi ch'ien*—the one indicating that it was money paid out when officials visited rural areas, and the other indicating that it was paid out monthly when the servicemen acknowledged their "quota of indebtedness" (?) *ts'u-e*. See also *TSKSK* p. 611 on this puzzling point.

might visit the countryside at other times in their pursuit of bandits. Presumably in many cases the original complaints about such bandits were sent by the village officers to the sheriff's office. When trouble first arose, rural people were supposed to aid one another. Shirking this responsibility was a crime.[21] If mutual aid proved an inadequate defense, the Superior Guard Leader or Elder was to dispatch an urgent appeal to the subprefectural authorities informing them that there were criminals too powerful to be suppressed by the local people and asking the sheriff's help. Failure to do this was punishable.[22]

The Superior Guard Leaders then paid the costs of entertaining the sheriff and his assistants. Liao Hsing-chih reported that in Hupei,

> the sheriff or the police commissioner (*hsün-chien*) suddenly dispatch Bowmen to inspect Elder jurisdictions (*ch'i*) or guards (*pao*). [The leaders of the] Elder jurisdictions or guards then apportion [the responsibility for expenses (literally a certain sum of money, a certain amount of grain)] among the small guards. For the most part households pay one or two strings of money and ten or so pints (*sheng*) of rice, or at least not less than seven hundred or eight hundred [cash] and half that amount of grain. This happens repeatedly during the year.[23]

21. Tou I, *Chung Hsiang Ting Hsing T'ung* (Taipei: Wen Hai Publishing Co., 1954), 28.6a, describes the degrees of guilt and punishments for those not helping others being attacked by robbers. *TITC* 6.32a says, "Whenever bandits arise or fires start, it is to be presumed that the neighborhood group (*lin-pao*) immediately will mutually inform one another and go mutually to aid [those in need]. It is not necessary to wait until a group has gathered for this would result in loss through delay. If officials investigate and discover by themselves, or if they are told by neighborhood leaders, that some men did not help, then the head of the offending household together with the locally responsible leaders should be equally investigated and judged."

22. *SHY, chih-kuan* 48.71b (1140); Huang Kan remarks that Superior Guard Leaders in reality had an easy role to play for when major problems of lawlessness arose, they simply informed the sheriff and passed the responsibility on to him. Huang Kan, 25.27a.

23. Liao Hsing-chih, 5.17b–18b.

When the local authorities had been notified of a crime they would ordinarily issue a warrant for the arrest of the accused. In cases involving fights or injuries it was recommended that witnesses be named on the résumé of the charge that was included in the warrant.[24] Elders and Superior Guard Leaders were warned to accept only warrants that referred to actual fights and brawls, in order to cut down the excessive number of judicial cases.[25]

Warrants imposed a responsibility for seizing offenders within a set time limit. If the accused parties were not apprehended in five days, the Superior Guard Leaders might be beaten. However, the Southern Sung handbook for local officials, *Chou Hsien T'i Kang,* cautions against too casual use of whipping:

> [As for] the subprefectural officials [managing] pursuit and arrest, they frequently assign the responsibility to the Superior Guard Leaders. If the Superior Guard Leaders pass the first time limit, you must not be hasty in beating them. Moreover, as for pursuing men involved in important troubles, if the [Superior Guard Leaders] pass the first limit of five days and you hastily beat them, and at the time of the next limit they still have not succeeded, if you do not again beat them then, they will be dilatory, and the first beating will have been pointless. If you do again beat them, with their wounds from the first beating five days before yet unhealed, not only is this contrary to law but also I fear that they may suffer injury and you will thus be guilty of cruelty.[26]

24. *TITC* 7.35a. This report deals with the dual system in the late Northern Sung. As is true of many of the questions involved in the functioning of the system of local services, we do not have enough information readily available to trace historical changes during the dynasty. A thorough exploration of all extant Sung sources might make possible a more adequate description of local law enforcement, but until such a study is completed we can only surmise that at least in broad outline the procedures of the Northern and Southern Sung were similar.

25. *HNYL* 167.2736 (1154).

26. *Chou Hsien T'i Kang* (Ts'ung-chu Chi Ch'eng ed.) 2.19. This work will hereafter be cited as *CHTK.*

These five-day limits presumably refer to the apprehension of individuals involved in minor breaches of the peace or other misdemeanors. There were time limits set for the capture of major offenders, but these limits were much longer, and in any case the responsibility for seizing major criminals seems to have belonged to the sheriff or to the police commissioner.

Time limits were also set for the transmission of the relevant documents. Apparently the authorities treated cases of ordinary lawlessness according to the rules covering regular government business, for the official handbook quoted above says that only in very serious matters—such as cases involving brigands whose crimes called for the death penalty—should "urgent communications" (*hsin-p'ai*) be employed.²⁷

In the period following receipt of the warrant but before the expiration of the time limit, Superior Guard Leaders were expected to put up "reward money" (*sheng-ch'ien*) to be awarded to whoever captured the wanted men. If they were caught within the time allotted, the Superior Guard Leaders had to pay "surrender money" (*chiao-yin ch'ien*) to the clerks, but if they were not caught in time, the Superior Guard Leaders had to put up "punishment money" (*fa-t'su ch'ien*).²⁸

27. *CHTK* 2.17. The completion of any piece of official business in rural areas seems to have been followed by the transmission, within a time limit of ten days of the relevant documents to the subprefectural offices. *TITC* 3.12a.

28. Ts'ai K'an, *Ting Chai Chi* (Ch'ang Chou Hsien Che I Shu ed.), 5.1b. See also *HAHS* 99.1775, which seems to indicate that this money was connected with the turning over of the documents involved. See also Chen Te-hsiu, *Hsi Shan Cheng Hsün* (Ts'ung-shu Chi Ch'eng ed.) p. 11. Hereafter cited *HSCH*. According to the rules of the Northern Sung, the "reward money" should have been raised by levying an exaction on all the families in the superior guard (except the poor who were exempt), but the Southern Sung text seems to imply that in practice the money came from the Superior Guard Leaders and their fellow *pao-chia* officers. *HCP* 2506.22a for the Northern Sung. At that time the rewards were not to exceed two thousand cash for thieves,

Once a suspect was apprehended, the Superior Guard Leader oversaw his transfer to the offices of the local authorities. The late Northern Sung handbook for officials, the *Tso I Tzu Chen,* says that Elders and Stalwart Men should always escort prisoners in person.[29] Village servicemen also traveled to the district headquarters to assist in the legal actions that followed arrest, and they were responsible for escorting to court men involved in civil disputes. The *Tso I Tzu Chen,* says:

> [When the Elders] receive a placard from the sub prefecture [instructing them] to gather men (*kou jen*) in all cases where there are two or more men involved, the date [for their appearance before the court] should be fixed so that they can both come forward [to accept their responsibilities]. In this way they will not be arraigned at different times at the place of arrest, for that would hinder agricultural work.[30]

During the Southern Sung most lawsuits seem to have resulted from disputes over landownership and over the levying of state imposts, including the drafting of village servicemen. Village officers frequently had to bear witness in land control suits. During the 1130s, because of the military disorders, there were numerous disputes involving lands abandoned during the invasions. In unclear cases, where ownership could not be determined by consulting documents, the Superior Guard Leaders and the Guard Chiefs testified as to the true owners.[31] Unfortunately they were not always trustworthy witnesses. It is said that corrupt families that initiated litigation to gain control over properties with ambiguous titles or boundaries worked hand in hand with dishonest Superior Guard Leaders and

---

and five thousand for violent robbers. (Given the paucity of descriptions of these fees, my translations of them are only provisional.)

29. *TITC* 7.37a
30. *TITC* 7.36b
31. *SHY, shih-huo* 69.52a (1133), 69.57b (1139)

clerks.[32] Some land problems in this era were particularly
knotty because village officers were unfair in their treatment
of refugees who had fled their farms and wanted to return.[33]
These visits to the local yamen were usually a burden to the
village officers, since they frequently had to give the clerks
money when they went to the town offices.[34]

Village officers also had to bear some expenses when the
authorities came into the rural areas to investigate certain
types of crimes. In cases of homicide the civil service officials were supposed to attend an inquest held at the site
of the killing.[35] Superior Guard Leaders had to help investigate the murder[36] and defray the costs of the inquest.[37]

Government parties also visited the countryside to carry
out other types of inspections. The Superior Guard Leaders
in the superior guards through which such parties passed
and at the site of the inquiries had to bear the expenses of
the food, drink, lodging, and entertainment of the officials
and their whole retinue of clerical personnel.[38]

The sources frequently state that the Superior Guard
Leaders were merely charged with suppressing brigands
and fire fighting; in practice this meant that they had to
bear the costs of and participate in almost every facet of
the judicial process on the local level. There is little evidence that Elders as independent officers played any major
independent role in law enforcement after the end of the

---

32. *CHTK* 2.16
33. *SHY, shih-huo* 69.59a (1146)
34. *SHY, shih-huo* 14.28a–b (1139). See also *CHTK* 2.17
35. *HAHS* 99.1775–1776; *SHY, hsing-fa* 6.1a ff. For the Ch'ing situation see Ch'ü, *Local Government in China under the Ch'ing*, p. 120.
36. *TSKSK* p. 606. In the Northern Sung, Elders and Stalwart
Men helped on the investigations. *SHY, hsing-fa* 6.3b. See also *SHY,
hsing-fa* 6.5b.
37. *SHY, shih-huo* 66.31a–b; *HAHS* 99.1775–76.
38. *HAHS* 99.1775–1776; *SHY, shih-huo* 14.40b–41a, 66.31a–b;
Ts'ai K'an, 5.1b. The money used to pay the costs incurred by official
parties en route to or from a visit was called *kuo hsiang ch'ien, kuo
shui ch'ien,* or *kuo tu ch'ien.*

Northern Sung;[39] the other village officers under the concurrent system seem to have been involved only in subordinate roles in the police side of village services. In most
regions only the *pao-wu* militia officers shared with the
Superior Guard Leaders the task of overseeing the pro-
motion and preservation of local order in the countryside.

In the collecting of taxes, their second major task, village
officers were involved in all aspects of the levying process,
from the creation of the property registers on the basis of
which taxes were assessed to the delivery of the revenues to
the agents of the officials. They gave warrants to the households, took in the taxes, dunned those who refused to pay
voluntarily, went to court if disputes led to lawsuits, and
in the end if the amount collected was insufficient they
contributed the balance out of their own incomes. Although
the land tax was their biggest problem, they also had to
oversee the gathering of a variety of other levies. Frequently
they had to bribe the clerks, for if they did not they might
become involved in expensive litigation or might be
whipped for having committed some minor infraction.
Fearing financial ruin the people tried desperately to avoid
this tax-collecting responsibility. In seeking to alleviate the
suffering of the taxgatherers, the state faced a dilemma:
it had to distribute costs so that the burden of overseeing
tax collection did not destroy the officer households, but
it needed to define legal liability clearly so that in cases of
defaulting or fraud a certain serviceman could be held
responsible. The attempt to reconcile these sometimes conflicting aims contributed to major changes in the selection
of personnel and the distribution of the costs of village
services. But, despite alterations in these aspects of the
system, the actual job of tax collecting, including pro-

39. There are a few passages that seem to indicate that in some
places at some times Elders did participate in maintaining local order.
See *SHY, shih-huo* 14.45a–b, 14.46b–47a; *HNYL* 167.2736 (1154).

cedures followed and imposts gathered, seems not to have changed markedly during the Southern Sung.

Villiage servicemen collected a number of levies; under some circumstances they might have to oversee certain tax-collecting centers,[40] and they had to collect the labor service money[41] and the male head tax *(shen-ting ch'ien)*,[42] but the most important impost they gathered was the land tax. Collected twice a year, once at the summer harvest and once at the autumn harvest, it was called the Twice-a-Year tax. During the Sung the authorities usually collected the summer tax between the fifth month and the end of the seventh month.[43] It was assessed as a number of coins per Chinese acre *(mou)*—the rate varying with the quality of the land involved[44]—and was considered the more difficult part of the Twice-a-Year tax to manage.[45] The autumn tax, collected between the ninth month and the end of the year,[46] was assessed as a varying quantity of grain per Chinese acre.[47] It was thought to be the easier part of the Twice-a-Year levy to collect apparently because the rate at which it was figured was less subject to clerical and official manipulation.[48] The weight of this Twice-a-Year tax differed from region to region. In general, poorer and less populous circuits like Fukien were more lightly burdened, while the richer provinces paid at a higher rate. According to Chu

40. *TITC* 4.18b. The subject of the actual processes of tax collection in Sung times deserves far more extended study than it has so far received. For brief descriptions see *SZS* pp. 3ff, and Liu Tao-yüan, *Liang Sung T'ien-fu Chih-tu* (Shanghai: Hsin Sheng Ming Shu Chü, 1937).

41. *SHY, shih-huo* 66.31a–b (1221); *HCP* 2506.21b–22a.

42. *SHY, shih-huo* 12.18a (1170).

43. *SZS* p. 3

44. Ibid.; *SHY, shih-huo* 70.74a; Li Ching-te, comp. *Chu Tzu Yü Lei* (Ying Yüan Shu Yüan blockprint ed. 1872), 109.4379.

45. *SHY, shih-hou* 70.74a (1185).

46. *SZS* p. 3.

47. Li Ching-te, 109.4379; *SHY, shih-huo* 70.74a.

48. Li Ching-te, 109.4379–80.

Hsi, the closer a place was to the capital, the more oppressive its land tax.[49]

The just assessment of these imposts naturally depended on the keeping of precise records of land ownership. Property registers, said Ts'ao Yen-yüeh, were as vital in taxation as contracts in commerce.[50] Unfortunately these documents were frequently in error. This problem of inaccurate records, which existed at most times during the Sung,[51] led to disorder and confusion in the levying of taxes. In 1142, therefore, the Court accepted the suggestion of an official named Li Ch'un-nien that a major resurvey of property be undertaken. Local households were to draw up land registers showing the character of their properties.[52] Superior Guard Leaders and Guard Chiefs were to draw maps of their areas.[53] The maps of superior guards were to be assembled in groups of ten into larger maps.[54] (Chu Hsi suggested that the servicemen merely be asked to draw rough drafts and that the officials hire professional scribes to prepare the final maps.)[55] After the servicemen had drawn the maps, the area's landlords and tenants would be assembled. These maps would indicate the size, boundaries, ownership, and character of each parcel of land. After the landlords and tenants signed the maps to signify their legal responsibility, the Superior Guard Leaders, their Assistants, and the Large

49. Ibid.
50. Ts'ao Yen-yüeh, *Ch'ang Ku Chi* (Ssu K'u Ch'üan Shu Chen Pen ed.), 10.1b.
51. See, for instance, Wang Yüan, *I Feng Chi* (Yu Chang Ts'ung Shu ed.). 6a. Wang received his *chin shih* in 1163 and died in 1208. See also Ts'ao Yen-yüeh, 10.1a–b; Ch'en Ch'i-ch'ing, *K'uei Ch'uang Chi* (Ssu K'u Ch'üan Shu Chen Pen ed.), 4.19a (hereafter cited *KCC*); Liao Hsing-chih, 5.14a–15b; Ch'en Fu-liang, *Chih Chai Wen-chi*, 12.30a.
52. *SHY, shih-huo* 6.36a–40a.
53. *HAHS* 21.328.
54. *SHY, shih-huo* 6.36a–40a; *HYNL* 148.2390. This assembling of larger maps did not prove feasible.
55. *HAHS* 21.330.

and Small Guard Chiefs would countersign to signify their liability for the accuracy of the records. On the basis of these maps the subprefectural clerks would compile land tax registers (*chen-chi pu*) for each canton. Copies of these registers would be sent to the revelant subprefectural, prefectural, and circuit offices. The reliability of the records could be spot-checked by clerks dispatched into the rural areas for this purpose. If the ownership or control of a piece of property later changed hands, both of the parties involved were to inform the canton. The transfer would then be recorded on the old land register. Every three years a new register would be compiled and the old ones sent to the prefecture for storage.[56]

At times, variant systems were used in the resurveying;[57] at other times, different types of property records were compiled;[58] and there were periods when resurveying was only nominally carried out;[59] but throughout most of the rest of the dynasty in most parts of the empire, this scheme of Li Ch'un-nien was at least the legal basis for property registration and reregistration.

On the basis of these registers the clerks drew up tax warrants and records. They began work on the warrants for the summer tax at the beginning of the Chinese year, and for the autumn tax on the first day of the fourth month. These documents were to be completed within a forty-five-

56. *SHY, shih-huo* 6.36a–40a; Wang Yüan, 6a.
57. *HAHS* 21.330, 19.296; 100.1782.
58. For instance, in certain regions for some years after 1146 the guards drew up registers called *pao-wu chang*, which established a legal residence for each household. Every ten households would form a group called a *chia*. In accordance with the forms drawn up by the Ministry of Finance for recording the land survey, each *chia* would make a record which indicated the size and character of the property holdings of each family. These registers would be collected by the Large Guard Chiefs, who would forward them to the subprefecture and prefecture, where consolidated records were kept. See *SHY, shih-huo* 70.25a–b; *HNYL* 147.2365, 148.2390, 153.2462; Ou-yang Shou-tao, *Hsüan Chai Wen Chi* (Ssu K'u Ch'üan Shu) 15.36.
59. *SHY, shih-huo* 10.15a (1161); Wang Yüan, 6a.

day period.[60] The key records in the taxing process—called *p'ing-yu* or *yu-tzu*—not only indicated the amount of land tax to be paid by an individual household but also showed whether this was an increase or a decrease from previous collections, and whether the family had bought or sold land during the preceding year. Apparently the *p'ing-yu* specified the amount due from a given household, but in practice the subprefectural authorities merely demanded total amounts, the actual determination of quotas being fixed on the canton level and the taxes of individual families at least partly controlled at the superior guard level.[61] The *p'ing-yu* were distributed to the tax collectors one month before the beginning of the collection period along with a public notice from the subprefect advising the people to pay promptly and warning of the consequences of delay.[62] Under ordinary circumstances these warrants seem to have been given to the Household Chiefs, who gave them to the rural households,[63] but in poorer cantons with small tax quotas there were periods when only Superior Guard Leaders and their Assistants were appointed, and Household Chiefs were not called. In these areas the warrants were taken into the countryside by the clerks, and the taxes were brought in by the individual households.[64]

Under the dual service system the key officers in collecting the land tax were the Household Chiefs, who worked

---

60. *SHY, shih-huo* 70.4aff. The *Sung Hui Yao Chi Kao* here says four months and five days to complete the records, but the annotation of this passage in *Sō-shi shi tai shi yakuchū*, ed. Wada Sei (Tokyo: Toyo bunko, 1960), pp. 366 and 370, shows that this should be taken to mean forty-five days.

61. *SHY, shih-huo* 70.47b; *TITC* 4.19b; *SKSK* p. 482.

62. *SHY, shih-huo* 70.47b; *TITC* 8.41b.

63. *TITC* 4.19b; *SHY, shih-huo* 66.21a (1179). The same process of distributing warrants was also true for other taxes. For instance the Silk and Salt Money vouchers were distributed this way. See Hsieh Shen-fu, *Ch'ing-yüan T'iao-fa Shih-lei,* (Peiping: Yen-ching Ta-hsüeh T'u-shu Kuan, 1948), 48.29b.

64. *SHY, shih-huo* 70.74a–b (1185).

under the supervision of Elders. The routine under this system was described by Li Yüan-pi in the late Northern Sung:

> When you desire to collect taxes, you must first select in a single subprefecture a certain number of Household Chiefs. Each individual Household Chief should collect from a certain number of households a fixed aggregate of strings of cash, bushels, rolls of cloth, and ounces [of silver]. Also, each Household Chief should record the number of men he oversees and the total amount of his tax receipts. First he should write down the sum he receives from each Household [Group] Head (*hu-t'ou*). After this he must note what he gathered from the whole superior guard. These amounts should be written in one book. At each time limit he should merely be ordered to estimate the sum that has been paid in and the sum still owing. You should personally investigate this. If the quota due from the guard has been reached, since the proper total has been collected, the gathering of anything beyond this may be lenient. It does not matter if the amount from each individual household has been adequate.[65]

As this passage demonstrates, the Household Chiefs were in a position to manipulate tax burdens. The local authorities were advised to demand a set amount from the Household Chiefs but to be lenient about gathering taxes beyond that quota. The Household Chiefs therefore could undercollect from certain households or keep the taxes collected beyond their quota. They appear to have performed the same functions during the Southern Sung, both in dual service regions where they were Large Guard Chiefs acting concurrently.[66]

The Household Chiefs turned the warrants over to the

---

65. *TITC* 4.19b; the *hu-t'ou* mentioned in this document are said to be similar to *chia-t'ou*. Ibid.

66. For dual regions see *SHY, shih-huo* 14.22b–23a, and *YLTT* 2217.18b. For concurrent regions see below, page 82.

households in their area, with the adominition to pay before the first of the three tax time limits into which each collection period was divided. The process by which the taxes were actually paid into the local treasury varied greatly at different times and in different places. According to regulations in force at the beginning of the Northern Sung, people were supposed to take their grain to a designated granary and there surrender it to the clerks. Describing the late Northern Sung, the *Tso I Tzu Chen* says:

"[As for] the summer and autumn taxes . . . upon seeing [the notices] from the subprefectural offices indicating [the beginning] of the tax collection [the people] ought to abide by the time limits indicated on the face of the placards. They should take the opportunity of having goods [and personally] pay in [their taxes]. If they do not do this and subsequently give their money to the Household Chiefs, Heads of Tithing, [or other] tax collectors, [then] because of the undue delay the time limits may be passed, and [the taxpayers] may be called to court.[67]

Such payment in person also occurred in the Southern Sung,[68] but by that time it may have been the exception rather than the rule. During the Northern Sung a system of tax brokers grew up.[69] These men, who were closely allied with the local yamen clerks, received grain from the householders and for a fee turned it over to the yamen personnel. They also acted as agents in commuting grain into money to be used in paying certain levies. The brokers thus saved the rural people the time, trouble, and expense of going to the town offices to turn in their imposts. Because of their

67. *TITC* 6.31b. See also *SHY, shih-huo* 70.1b–2a
68. Such a system was requested in a memorial dated 1160 in *SHY, shih-huo* 14.36a–b (Kuang-nan in 1160). See also *SHY, shih-huo* 70.74a, 66.24a.
69. Su Shih, *Su Tung-p'o Liu Chi* (Ssu Pu Pei Yao, edition), 6.2a, reporting on taxes in Hangchow and noting the existence of these brokers there. Such brokerage was still practiced in the Ch'ing period. Hsiao Kung-ch'üan, *Rural China*, p. 96.

close connections with the local clerical personnel these brokers were also able to punish people who chose to pay in person. The clerks would cheat such individuals, thus discouraging future attempts to bring taxes in person.[70] (To reduce this problem local officials were advised to permit only the paying householders and the grainweigher to enter the granary. All unauthorized persons were to be excluded.)[71]

In other regions, householders surrendered their taxes to village officers or to agents of the village officers—to Heads of Tithing, Household Chiefs, or other tax collectors, who would forward the taxes to the Household Chiefs.[72] At times, the leaders of the local irregular militia forces (*t'u-hao* or *t'u-chün*) collected the taxes.[73] It is not clear whether or not these servicemen and militia men worked through brokers. Different systems were sometimes followed in collecting from different grades and types of people within the same area. In some periods "powerful households" (*hsing-shih hu*)—the households of village officers, clerks, and officials[74]—had their own registers controlled by the prefectural vice-administrators,[75] and at other times they were grouped separately for tax-collecting purposes.[76] One memorialist suggested that local officials personally oversee the gathering of taxes from official households and from

70. *CHTK* 4.38; Wang Ying-ch'en, *Wen Ting Chi* (Ts'ung-shu Chi Ch'eng ed.), 5.44. Chou Ying-ho, *Ching-ting Chien-k'ang Chih* (Ssu K'u Ch'üan Shu ed.), 40.20a ff.

71. *CHTK* 4.39.

72. *TITC* 4.19b; *CTCCC* 17.9a–b; Ch'en Yüan-chin, 1.1b–2a; *TITC* 3.10b, 3.11a, 6.31b; *SHY, shih-huo* 66.24a, 66.28a.

73. Liu Ts'ai-shao, *Fan Ch'i Chü Shih Chi* (Ssu K'u Ch'üan Shu Chen Pen ed.), 8.23a–b; *HNYL* 171.2812 (1156).

74. For a definition of "powerful households" see Hsieh Shen-fu, 47.23b. See also Yanagida Setsuko, "Sō-dai gyō-sei-ko no Kōsei," *Toyoshi Kenkyū* 27(3)[68.12] 100.

75. Wada Sei, pp. 365–68. See also *HCP* 12.1a–b.

76. *SHY, shih-huo* 14.14b–25a. See *HCP* 12.1a–b for the Northern Sung system.

the top three grades of commoner households.[77] On occasion, men were especially sent from the town offices into the countryside to oversee tax collection.[78]

In certain regions, taxes were not legally due at nearby granaries but at the frontiers. In effect, the people in these areas were called on to contribute, in addition to their land tax itself, a surcharge which would be used to pay the cost of moving the grain to border prefectures. In some periods this charge was assessed at so many coins per bushel of grain; at others it varied with household grade and was assessed in terms of distance.[79]

Village officers might or might not be involved in the actual shipment of grain to the local offices, but they were almost always used to dun those households that had failed to contribute their taxes on time. Although payment of the quota before the expiration of the time limits might lead to a lowering of future quotas and to advancement for the local officials,[80] procrastination in paying was very widespread. Under the dual system the Elders supervised the taxing and dunning of the tardy. They gathered at the subprefectural offices at the date of the middle time limit and were given printed sheets on which to verify tax collection. A few such sheets were handed out for each village. The Elders were also given warrants for the late gathering of the Twice-a-Year tax and another public proclamation from the subprefect to the tardy taxpayers.[81] In concurrent areas the Superior Guard Leaders managed the tax system and were usually charged with the task of dunning late paying

77. *SHY, shih-huo* 70.74a–b.
78. Hsieh Shen-fu, 47.1a.
79. In Shensi under Che-tsung, first-grade households were forced to pay a fee equivalent to a tax shipment of three hundred Chinese miles. Wada Sei, p. 423. For other information on surcharges for grain transport see *SZS* p. 59; *SHY, shih-huo* 70.17a, 70.44a.
80. *SHY, shih-huo* 70.4b.
81. *TITC* 8.42a. For the situation in the early Northern Sung see *SHY, shih-huo* 70.1b–2a (963).

families at the expiration of the second time limit,[82] but there were times when Large Guard Chiefs acting concurrently as Household Chiefs were forced to take on this duty.[83] Elaborate rules specified the punishments to be meted out for failure to have taxes in on time. Those involved were to be beaten a certain number of strokes, the number varying with the time limit in question and the percentage of taxes still not paid.[84]

If, as happened frequently, disputes over taxes led to legal actions, the village officers—Elders, Superior Guard Leaders, Guard Chiefs, and Household Chiefs—were called to the subprefectural offices at the time of the hearings. The Elders and Superior Guard Leaders were responsible for seeing that the principals were present at the hearings.[85] Village officers visited the yamen several times a month. Occasional suggestions were advanced for policies that would limit the number of such visits,[86] but officers continued to frequent the town offices, called there in many

82. For the general responsibility of these officers see *SHY, shih-huo* 14.18a, 14.18b, 14.22b, 14.32b, 14.39a–40a, 66.27b–28a, 66.28a–b; *HAHS* 99.1775. For the dunning procedure see *SHY, shih-huo* 70.44a (1153). See also Liu Ts'ai-shao, 8.23a.

83. *SHY, shih-huo* 25.20b–21a (1160); *CHTK* 4.38; *SHY, shih-huo* 66.24a. This practice was generally deplored. A document dated 1183 from the *Sung Hui Yao Chi Kao* says: "From now on the Large Guard Chiefs are not to be permitted to press for taxes. They are only to receive the tax warrants and turn these over to the households, ordering them to pay according to the time limits. If there are recalcitrant households with large debts, the Superior Guard Leaders should be commissioned to press these people." *SHY, shih-huo* 66.21a.

84. Hsieh Shen-fu, 47.17a.

85. *TITC* 7.36b; *CHTK* 2.17.

86. The author of the mid-twelfth-century handbook for local officials, the *Chou Hsien T'i Kang*, suggested a method by which the number of days on which village officers would be called to appear at court could be limited, and advised that the time limits for court appearances be adjusted to accord with local conditions. He felt that, if this were not done, witnesses and defendants would feel that they could not possibly reach the yamen on time and would bribe the Superior Guard Leaders to make false excuses for them. *CHTK* 2.17.

cases by the clerks, ostensibly so that tax matters could be checked but in reality so that the clerks could extort bribes from them. The authorities tried to stop this practice, and in 1139 it was decreed that men should be assembled only at the dates of the tax time limits,[87] but such rulings proved ineffective.[88]

In addition to their legally assigned quotas, these officers often had to pay extralegal fees established by the clerks and the officials.[89] In many cases they escaped punishment only by bribing the clerks who controlled the tax rolls.[90] (Village officers sometimes shared in the spoils, cooperating with corrupt clerks in failing to turn over to the officials all the tax revenues.)[91]

In the end, if the officers could not squeeze enough revenue from the people[92] and could not bribe the clerks to overlook their delinquency, they had to make up the deficiency from their own incomes.[93] This liability for taxes was a heavy burden, since old tax quotas remained in force even though they were based on outdated land registers that no longer reflected occupation and ownership.[94] The village officers had to pay in substitution when families had

87. *SHY, shih-huo* 14.28a–b (1139). Village officers had been called to the yamen once every ten days or once a month.

88. *CHTK* 2.17.

89. *CHTK* 2.23; *SHY, shih-huo* 70.43a (1152). There are also several passages in which prefectures or subprefectures were warned that they must not order Superior Guard Leaders and their Assistants to *"jih shu mao li"*—apparently in reference to a practice of calling these men in on spurious pretexts, just long enough to sign their names. This use of *mao* is still current in modern *pai-hua*. See *SHY, shih-huo* 14.29a–30a, 65.86a; *TITC* 4.196.

90. *CHTK* 4.38. See also *CHTK* 4.37.

91. *SHY, shih-huo* 12.13b (1161).

92. See Chao Shan-kua, *Ying Chai Tsa Chu* (Yü Chang Ts'ung-shu ed.), 1.6b.

93. Ts'ai K'an, 5.1b; Shu Lin, *Shu Wen Ching Kung Chi* (Ssu Ming Ts'ung-shu ed.), 3.11a; *SHY, shih-huo* 14.18b, 14.21b, 66.28a–b.

94. *SHY, shih-huo* 12.6b. For another general comment on this problem see Hsüeh Chi-hsüan, 16.4b–5a.

deserted their homes (*t'ao-hu*), when families had died out (*chüeh-hu*), when land was falsely registered,[95] and when families had lost their patrimonies without being removed from the tax rolls or had moved to other subprefectures or cantons and could not be dunned for defaulting.[96] If official fields (*kuan-t'ien*) were untenanted, the servicemen made good the lost revenue.[97] They paid when floods ruined crops, when the registers were lost, or even when influential families simply refused to pay. No matter what the problem, the village officers had to contribute the balance or suffer punishment.[98]

The financial responsibility seems to have fallen first on the Household Chiefs—in both concurrent and dual areas. As a result the people feared this post more than they feared that of the Superior Guard Leader or his Assistant.[99] The liability seems to have reached to the Superior Guard Leaders and presumably to the Elders only if the Household Chiefs were not able to make up the deficit.[100]

The transmission of documents between the subprefectural offices and the villages was another major concern of the village officers. Prior to the reforms of Shen-tsung (1067–85), Stalwart Men acting as assistants to the Elders had carried documents. When the positions of Elders and

95. Ts'ai K'an, 5.1b; Shu Lin, 3.11a; *HNYL* 174.2875; *SHY, shih-huo* 14.18b, 14.21b, 66.31a–b, 66.28a–b; 69.62b; Chang Shou, *P'i Ling Chi* (Ts'ung-shu Chi Ch'eng edition), 3.36. At times in the Northern Sung there were separate registers for families that had deserted their homes. See *Sung Ta Chao Ling Chi,* comp. Chung Hua Shu Chü (Peking: Chung Hua Shu Chü, 1962), 183.662.

96. Ts'ai K'an, 5.1b.

97. *SHY, shih-huo* 5.20b (1131).

98. *SHY, shih-huo* 14.21b, 66.21a–b, 63.225a (1203), 69.65b (1171); Shu Lin, 3.1a; Ts'ai K'an, 5.1b. There seem to have been some occasions when servicemen were excused from liability, but these appear to have been exceptional cases. See *SHY, shih-huo* 70.74a–b; T'o T'o et al., 25.3b.

99. Li Ching-te, 111.4385. See also Shu Lin, 3.11a.

100. This seems to be the implication of a passage in *HSCH* pp. 8–9. This version of the Sung tax system resembled that used in the Ch'ing. Hsiao Kung-ch'üan, pp. 95ff.

Stalwart Men were abolished in 1075, the message-transferring function passed to the newly created Messengers (*ch'eng-t'ieh jen*), who were subordinates of the Superior Guard Leaders. Under the late Northern Sung system devised under Che-tsung, both Messengers and Stalwart Men might work as message bearers—Messengers being used when enough men volunteered for that post, and Stalwart Men being drafted in regions where volunteers were too few. The document-transmission policies followed in dual service areas in the Southern Sung are not clearly described, but in concurrent areas the Messengers apparently continued to function as document carriers. An approved memorial dated 1170 suggested that in Liang-che the use of Messengers should be stopped and Stalwart Men should again be employed,[101] but there is no evidence that this policy was long in force, and there are indications that Messengers continued to exist after 1170. They are mentioned in a memorial dated 1190,[102] and the gazetteer of Hu prefecture in Liang-che, describing conditions around 1201, says that Ch'ang-hsing subprefecture had 105 Superior Guard Leaders and 105 Messengers.[103] It seems not unlikely that this gazetteer illuminates the generally approved practice—the appointment of one Messenger for each superior guard to act as the agent for carrying documents.

Although, legally, village officers were to take most documents into the countryside, subbureaucratic workers from the town yamen sometimes acted as carriers. These men used these trips as occasions for demanding bribes. Chen Te-hsiu says:

> The little people of the rural hamlets fear the clerks (*li*) like tigers. To allow the clerks to go down into the countryside is like permitting tigers to leave their

101. *SHY, shih-huo* 14.45a.
102. *SHY, shih-huo* 66.24a–b.
103. Li Ching-ho, *Chia-t'ai Wu Hsing Chih* (Wu Hsing Ts'ung-shu ed.), 7.6a. When they were first established in the Northern Sung there were two Messengers for each Superior Guard Leader. See *HCP* 2506.21b–22a.

cages. Bowmen (*kung-shou*) and the Territorial Soldiers (*t'u-ping*) certainly should be forbidden [to visit the countryside].[104]

Later in this same work Chen adds that *pao-chia* officers should carry messages from the subprefectural town to the villages. Clerical personnel were not to be permitted to visit the countryside without authorization, for when they entered rural areas they always caused great trouble. Apparently the use of clerical messengers was illegal but still widely practiced.[105]

The emperor himself was aware of the problem. In 1151 an official asked that the prefectures and subprefectures be forbidden to send lictors (*kung-tsao*) to the hamlets. He asked that the prefectures ship their communications to the subprefectures in wooden boxes (*mu-hsia*) and that the subprefectural officials give the documents to Messengers, who would carry them to the villages. The emperor remarked that he had seen the difficulties caused by lictors.[106]

Various devices were employed to insure the proper and careful dissemination of the information contained in communications and to guard against laxity and malfeasance. According to the late Northern Sung handbook for local officials, the *Tso I Tzu Chen,* the supervising village officer, in this case an Elder, was to draw up a register to record the receipt of documents. Each carrier (under this system they were Stalwart Men) was also advised to make his own list of messages he carried. Proper performance of local duties could be verified by comparing the lists. When Stalwart Men carried messages, the date and time were recorded on

104. *HSCH* p. 3.
105. *HSCH* p. 9.
106. *HNYL* 162.2646. Perhaps it was to this practice that Chu Hsi was referring when he said Superior Guard Leaders had to hire runners (*pen-tsou*) to carry messages. *HAHS* 21.326–27; 99.1771. There were also special cases with special carriers. In 1070 it was ordered that Guard Chiefs select in rotation Guard Men (*pao-ting*) to carry messages. *CPCSPM* 71.2a.

the notices. A corner was folded over the notation and a wooden chop was used as a seal to verify the contents. A résumé of its contents headed each communication. Notices intended for the public were written in large formal characters on signboards and placed in busy places in the villages or were copied on the whitewashed wall which served as a public notice board in rural hamlets. Such public notice boards seem to have been sacrosanct—messages on them to be erased or painted over only by the village officers, who were also charged with seeing that the walls remained in good condition. Elders, after receiving notification of their selection as village officers, were to assemble the neighborhood people as witnesses and the documents involved were to be read and signed in their presence.[107]

The problems facing the overseers of this communication system were increased because each of the four subprefectural offices—those of the subprefect (*ling*), the assistant subprefect (*ch'eng*), the registrar (*chu-pu*), and the sheriff (*wei*)—sent out their own distinctive types of documents (*wen-yin*) and placards (*mu-p'ai*).[108]

The Superior Guard Leaders also were burdened with a number of customary clerical fees connected with message transmission. The exact nature of some of these charges is difficult to determine, but they seem to have been connected with such steps as the surrender of documents, the meeting or extending of deadlines, the registration of messages, and the use of various official seals.[109]

---

107. *TITC* 7.35b–36b, 1.4a, 2.11a.
108. *HAHS* 99.1775–76.
109. Ibid. Chu Hsi mentions the following fees:
    (1) *ya-t'ou ch'ien*—a fee paid when the clerks notarized the face of the document?
    (2) *chiao-po ch'ien*—a fee paid when documents were surrendered?
    (3) *chan-hsien ch'ien*—a fee paid when the deadline was extended?
    (4) *ting-hsien ch'ang-hsien so yung chih ch'ien*—a fee paid at the time of the meeting of fixed and regular time limits?

The carrying of messages, like the other village officer duties, had to be performed within time limits set by the local officials. This was true under both the dual and the concurrent systems of the Northern Sung,[110] and was still part of the system during the Southern Sung. The author of the mid–twelfth-century handbook for local officials, the *Chou Hsien T'i Kang,* advises:

> In deciding whether a time limit should be lenient or not, it is necessary to consider whether the affair in question is urgent or not. If you do not measure urgency and always use the classification of "important," then the important and the unimportant will become confused. Many of those who receive the limits will be guilty. This cannot be done for long or in the end the confusion of important and unimportant will necessarily be calamitous! Therefore, "urgent communications" (*hsin-p'ai*) must not constantly be used, for if you overuse them, men will treat them as trinkets. They should only be used when sending "salary boxes" (*lu-hsia*) or "warrants for assembly" (*chui-hui*) to the superior offices (*shang-ssu* i.e. the prefectural and circuit offices), or when there is a bandit who has committed crimes warranting the death penalty (*ta pi chiang t'ao*). Those who err in delivery will then be few, men will not dare to be dilatory, and affairs can be managed.[111]

---

(5) *p'i-chu*—a fee paid when a red mark was made on a document?

(6) *feng-yin*—a fee connected with stamping the margin between two pages?

(7) *jih-ch'o*—a fee connected with stamping the date?

110. *TITC* 7.36b. Li Yüan-pi, describing the dual variant during the last decades of the Northern Sung said: "[If] the time limits on placards and documents that bear on their faces the words 'fiery urgency' (*huo-chi*) have been passed by one day (*wei-hsien i-jih*), [or] the time limits on documents marked 'urgent' (*chi*) have been passed by two days, [or if] the time limits on other documents have been exceeded by three days, and the affairs have not been completed, this should be investigated." *TITC* 7.36b.

111. *CHTK* 2.17.

The general nature of these time limits is explained further by the thirteenth-century official and writer Hu T'ai-ch'u:

> As for affairs in general, if there is disbelief, they will not be properly handled. How much more is this true of the business of a subprefecture. . . . Therefore, among important things nothing takes precedence over the firmness with which you establish time limits. But the fixing of deadlines has distinctions, and responding to time limits has steps. For the irregular and regular "warrants for assembly" (*fan ch'ang chui-hui*), only give a normal limit. Permit this to be extended three times. Before the third extension is over the people involved should be warned and thereafter given a fixed time limit which can be extended twice. Before the second extension is over the people should be warned and given a nonextendable warrant (*pu-chan yin*). This then really must not be again extended! If it is broken, this should be investigated, and those guilty should be beaten a certain number of strokes.[112]

When bureaucrats and their guests passed through a Superior Guard Leader's jurisdictional area, the officer had to hire the needed transport coolies;[113] supply miscellaneous provisions at each stopping place;[114] and entertain the officials, their guests and even the clerks in their entourage.[115] Providing for the clerical personnel in the touring party was especially expensive. If these men did not feel that they had been properly treated, they would demand money. If they were not paid, they would involve the Superior Guard Leader in costly and troublesome lawsuits.[116]

Superior Guard Leaders also had to provide many arti-

112. Hu T'ai-ch'u, *Chou Lien Hsü Lun*, pp. 19–20.
113. The money for hiring coolies was called *ti li ch'ien*. See *SHY, shih-huo* 14.40b–41a, 66.31a–b.
114. Liao Hsing-chih, 5.17b–18b.
115. *SHY, shih-huo* 14.42b–43a, 14.41a, 12.23a, 14.23a.
116. Liao Hsing-chih, 5.17b–18b.

cles for common use in the subprefectural offices,[117] including foodstuffs, wine, lamp oil, and local specialty products.[118] When the yamen buildings needed repairs, the Superior Guard Leaders had to supply both the materials and all sorts of construction workers.[119] In ordering these goods the authorities often used the precedent of the "equitable purchase" (*ho-mai*) system, according to which the Superior Guard Leaders should have been reimbursed at fixed rates, but sometimes nothing was returned for what had been delivered.[120] Officials also occasionally refused to pay after having forced the Superior Guard Leaders to contribute military supplies in times of emergency. Chen Te-hsiu reports that officials would order the Superior Guard Leaders to bring military goods and then not recompense them at market values or decline to pay at all. In some cases, not only did the Superior Guard Leaders have to provide these goods, but when the time came for delivery the clerks would even demand extra bribes.[121] Local government exactions were not confined to military provisions. There were cases of Superior Guard Leaders being dunned for extra levies of cloth,[122] bamboo, wood, earth, and granary salt.[123] Presumably these goods were treated as were military supplies; the authorities were expected to make restitution at fixed prices but in fact paid less or not at all.

The preceding description of services to local officials applies largely to the Superior Guard Leaders. Apparently the other concurrent service officers did not share most of these burdens, but there is one report that Large and Small

117. *SHY, shih-huo* 66.31a–b; *HAHS* 99.1775–76.
118. *SHY, shih-huo* 14.37a, 14.35a–b, 66.28a–b; *TSKSK* p. 613.
119. *SHY, shih-huo* 14.35a–b, 66.31a–b, 28a; *HAHS* 99.1776. In the Ch'ing such charges were added as a surcharge to the *ting* imposts. Hsiao Kung-ch'üan, p. 87.
120. *HAHS* 99.1776.
121. *HSCH* p. 10.
122. *HSCH* p. 9.
123. Ts'ai K'an, 5.1b. Ma Tuan-lin, 13.138.

Guard Chiefs did occasionally have to help with extraordinary levies.[124]

There is almost no information to indicate how these services were provided in Southern Sung dual service areas. Perhaps they were the responsibility of the Elders. During the late Northern Sung, Elders were said to have been liable for providing a guard for officials, certain examination candidates, and merchants who were staying at local hostels;[125] and it seems not improbable that these same Elders were charged with seeing to the other needs of their visitors.

Within their jurisdictions, village officers also had to supply a number of services to the residents, and had to oversee the maintenance of such utilities as roads and bridges. Managing local welfare services included both caring for afflicted transients and taking part in the state system of relief for the indigent or for those affected by natural disasters. During the late Northern Sung, if a traveler fell ill on the road and had no one to care for him, the Elder was to see that the patient was moved to a nearby hostel. The physician assigned to the hostel was to examine and prescribe for the illness. After the sick man had recovered and the proper reports had been filed with local authorities, the doctor would be reimbursed by the government.[126] Indigent and afflicted residents also received state aid. The mid-twelfth century handbook for officials, the *Chou Hsien T'i Kang*, reports that in midwinter the Superior Guard Leader and the Beggar Chief (*kai-shou*) had to decide on a quota for the relief granary (*ch'ang-p'ing i ts'ang*) in their area and inform the subprefecture of their decision. It is said that they often used this as an occasion for demanding kickbacks from those on relief.[127] When natural disasters

---

124. *HNYL* 166.2711 (1154). The indication comes in a memorial asking that the practice be forbidden.
125. *TITC* 7.37a.
126. *TITC* 7.36a.
127. *CHTK* 2.25.

struck, village servicemen helped in the relief process. They are said to have cheated their charges by diverting the relief goods into their own pockets.[128] Although they might be corrupt, however, they were virtually indispensable. Chu Hsi remarks that when he was trying to ascertain the number of the needy, he was told that his problem could be solved simply: he should gather the Large Guard Chiefs in a convenient temple and order them to state the number of the suffering, for they would naturally know this.[129] He had himself used Large Guard Chiefs as well as Superior Guard Leaders in recording information and checking on granaries set up under the community granary system,[130] and he speaks of Superior Guard Leaders, their Assistants, and Large and Small Guard Chiefs being used in investigations of assorted drought damages.[131] Even Heads of Tithing were sometimes involved in these relief processes.[132]

The village officers also had to oversee the upkeep of many public facilities. In dual service regions, these tasks were the responsibility of the Elders, and in concurrent areas, of the Superior Guard Leaders. Some of the Elders' duties are described in the Northern Sung handbook, *Tso I Tzu Chen*:

> [The Elders] should have charge over the repairing of roads and bridges and the removing of excess water [from the roads] so that the movement of men and horses will not be hindered.
>
> With regard to the ditches that run alongside the roads, [the Elders] should exhort the landowners to fill them up. If they are not taken care of then men and horses may be injured.

128. *SHY, shih-huo* 68.81a, 68.87b. The chain of command in the relief process ran from the subprefectural administrator through the canton clerks (*hsiang-kuan*) to the village officers. Huang Kan, 29.7b.

129. Chu Hsi, *Chu Wen-kung Cheng Hsün* (Ts'ung-shu Chi Ch'eng ed.), p. 12. Hereafter cited *CWKCH*.

130. *HAHS* 99.1771–73.

131. *HAHS* 99.1771–78.

132. *HNYL* 178.2939.

When there are wells close to the road, [the Elders] should be forcefully ordered to lay stone or brick [so that the well openings will be so] small and narrow that men cannot fall into them. On earthen wells where stonework or brick cannot be employed, they should use rough and large timbers to make a framework to cover the mouth of the well. Also, in each case a pavilion should be erected to shelter and protect [the well]....
[The Elders] should take care of the distance markers (*li-hou*), the whitewashed notice walls (*fen-pi*), and the placard displays (*pang-shih*) so that they do not deteriorate in the slightest degree.[133]

During the Southern Sung, Superior Guard Leaders in concurrent regions were not only responsible for fire fighting and the repair of roads and bridges,[134] but also for the repair of various sorts of public buildings and facilities such as "public offices" (*kung-chiao*), "police stations" (*hsün-pu*), "courier hostels" (*i-she*),[135] "postal mounds" (*p'u-hou*),[136] "courier posts" (*p'u-i*),[137] "shrines" (*tz'u-yü*), "lodgings" (*chiao-she*),[138] and "wayside inns" (*ch'uan-she*).[139] In caring for these facilities, as in building and repairing offices in subprefectural towns, the Superior Guard Leaders had to supply both materials and workmen but they frequently were not repaid.[140]

Village officers frequently gave money or gifts to the clerks. Sometimes these were given in return for services

133. *TITC* 7.35b–36a.
134. *SHY, shih-huo* 14.37a (1157), 14.40b–41a (1167), 66.28a–b (1194), 66.27b–28a (1197), 14.35a–b; *HAHS* 21.326; Liao Hsing-chih, 5.17b–18a; Ts'ai K'an, 5.1b.
135. Ts'ai K'an, 5.1b.
136. Liao Hsing-chih, 5.17b–18a.
137. *SHY, shih-huo* 14.39b–40a.
138. *HAHS* 99.1776.
139. *SHY, shih-huo* 14.37a. Some of these facilities were clearly located in rural areas. Others were probably in the subprefectural town. The translations are provisional. Some of the terms may even be synonymous.
140. *SHY, shih-huo* 66.28a–b; *HAHS* 99.1776.

rendered. When a clerk stamped a document or accepted tax vouchers he was performing a necessary task which might conceivably justify a demand for payment. These fees for work done have been described in the preceding pages. But there were other exactions not connected with services rendered which verged on extortion. When men were first called to serve, they had to feast the clerks.[141] When they were finished with the period of service, they gave money to the clerks as a token of their "gratitude."[142] They also contributed at the time of certain celebrations.[143]

Village officers were also involved in the making and keeping of maps of rural areas[144] and in the creation of the registers from which their successors would be chosen. The most detailed description of the making of registers is found in the Northern Sung handbook *Tso I Tzu Chen:*

> In making the five-grade registers, the Canton Scribes, the Elders, and the Household Chiefs should be in three separate places, so that they do not see one another. They should each be given stamped tax vouchers. For each household they should write out lists of family worth. Subsequently they should in one place compare [their results]. If there are major items that are not the same, this is evidence of fraud.[145]

Such registers were also drawn up in the Southern Sung, presumably in much the same way, but in concurrent areas by the Superior Guard Leaders and the Guard Chiefs rather than by the Elders and the Household Chiefs.[146] One report suggests that three copies of these registers were made. One

141. The fee was called *ts-an-i ch'ien.* See *SHY, shih-hou* 12.23a.
142. This money was called *tz'u-i ch'ien.* See *SHY, shih-huo* 12.23a.
143. *Huang Sung Chung-hsing Liang Ch'ao Sheng Cheng* (Taipei: Wen Hai Publishing Co., 1967), 51.14b; *SHY, shih-huo* 14.41a.
144. *TITC* 3.15b.
145. *TITC* 4.18a.
146. *HAHS* 21.328; ibid., 21.330; *HNYL* 148.2390.

remained in the superior guard, one in the subprefecture, and one was stored in the prefecture.[147]

During the late Northern Sung the Elders also were supposed to oversee agriculture and organize the peasants to combat calamities such as swarms of locusts.[148]

Finally, although by the Southern Sung most local government clerical posts were filled by long-term professional workers, at least during the early years of the period there were still a few jobs that were performed by unpaid amateurs drafted from the rural village officers. A report dated 1134 says that the Superior Guard Leaders, their assistants, and Guard Chiefs might be rotated to the subprefectural offices in Liang-che, Chiang-nan, and other circuits to serve as "orderlies" (*chih-hou*).[149]

The preceding discussion of the functions of village officers is necessarily tentative. Topics such as judicial process on the local level and the Sung land tax system need intensive study. On other topics the reports preserved in the sources are too fragmentary to permit adequate analysis of regional variations or changes over time. Some problems are discussed so sketchily and in so few places that it is impossible at present even to be certain of the nature of the tasks or procedures involved.[150] But, although there are

147. Mei Ying-fa, *K'ai-ch'ing Ssu-ming Chih* (Sung Yüan Ssu-ming Liu Chih, ed.), 7.3b. Cited hereafter as *KCSMC*.

148. *TITC* 7.36b; *TSKSK* p. 588.

149. *SHY, shih-huo* 14.23a. For a brief description of orderlies see Chao Yen-wei, *Yün Lu Man Ch'ao*, p. 348ff.

150. There are some cases in which we have only a single reference to a function, as in the statement describing the involvement of Superior Guard Leaders in revenue collection under the tea certificate system used in Hupei in 1158. See *HNYL* 180.2978. Or a reference to a recommended system of alternating calling of servicemen from the "two offices" (*liang ch'u*—the "two places"?). *HNYL* 163.2652. One particularly frustrating type of obscurity is a result of our lack of a complete record. During the Sung, one way in which legislation might be modified was by the emending of the rules involved by the adding or deleting of characters in the original text. We have several

many questions that must for the moment be left inadequately answered, it is nonetheless clear that the village officers were the vital link between the state and the people.

---

recommendations for adding or deleting characters, but in the absence of the original text it is often impossible to piece together the original ordinances. Here, as elsewhere, further research may throw more light on the problems posed. Since this study is not, and does not pretend to be, an exhaustive investigation into such important local functions as tax collection, police work, or postal services, it is to be presumed that when adequate studies of these topics are published they will modify some of the suggestions put forward in this chapter.

]4[

Structure
of the
Village Service System

In Imperial China the basic pattern of local administration evolved during the Eastern Chou period and was extended to the whole empire by the Ch'in. The empire was divided into a hierarchy of territorially defined units staffed by officials dispatched from the capital. Below these territorial units the populace was divided into household assemblages administered by men selected from the local people. That this general pattern continued in use until 1912 is sufficient commentary on the stability of at least some aspects of Chinese political organization, but this persistence of fundamental pattern was accompanied by countless differences in detail, which throw light on the distinctive characters of the dynasties and of regions within the empire.

During the Southern Sung, local government was administered through a two-level organizational hierarchy inherited from the Northern Sung. On the upper level—circuits, prefectures, and subprefectures—the divisions were territorial; on the lower level—cantons, townships, and superior guards—the units were groupings of households or territorial groupings that had evolved from groupings of households. The higher level was staffed by civil servants and clerical personnel, most of whom were professionals; on the lower level, administration was legally the responsibility of unpaid workers selected by higher authorities. Each subprefectural subdivision had a fixed quota of certain kinds of village officers, who were assigned definite duties for limited periods of time. The village service system used in most of the Sung dominions during most of the Southern Sung continued to be based on the *pao-chia* rulings of Che-tsung (1085–1100)—the concurrent pattern being most widely adopted but the dual pattern remaining in use in some peripheral areas. This relative uniformity of structure existed despite a host of local exceptions and some substantial changes as time passed. There were areas so difficult to control that the *pao-chia* system apparently was never established,[1] areas where there were no Superior Guard Leaders or Guard Chiefs because the clerks had been bribed not to draft anyone,[2] and areas where the clerks called either Superior Guard Leaders or their Assistants but not both.[3] There were regions that had never been asked to follow the usages of the rest of the empire,[4] regions that ignored the reform orders of the central government,[5] and regions where variations of the normal practices prevailed.[6] During the Southern Sung there were also occasional alterations in the numbers, tasks, and terms of service of these officers. These variations reflected the influence of economics and geography, local custom and the amount of discretion in the hands of local officials, external historical events and internal changes. Where deviation did occur, it

1. Fan Ch'eng-ta, *Wu Chün Chih* (Tse Shih Chü Ts'ung-shu ed.) 38.5a.

2. *HSCH* p. 11.

3. *SHY, shih-huo* 14.31b–32a (1149). This notice of 1149 is an order that this practice be stopped, but similar orders from 1152 and 1155 indicate that in fact it continued. Ibid., *shih-huo* 14.32a.

4. *HNYL* 159.2583, reporting on Ma-yang subprefecture in Ching-hu North circuit in 1149; *SHY, shih-huo* 66.22a, and Chou Ch'u-fei, *Ling Wai Tai Ta* (Chih Pu Tsu Chai Ts'ung-shu ed.), 4.10b–12a for Hainan; *SHY, shih-huo* 14.29a (1142) for Ch'iung prefecture in Kuang-nan.

5. *SHY, shih-huo* 14.38a–39a.

6. Shu Lin, *Shu Wen Ching Kung Chi,* 3.11a–11b, describing Hsi prefecture in Chiang-nan East in the 1130s.

sometimes demonstrated the willingness of the government to adopt policy to local conditions, while the modifications might indicate a continuing search for improvements in general policy. Yet the differences might also simply reflect the gap between law and practice, and some transformations occurred without apparent official consent or support. Despite deviations, the basic system remained uniform.

Administrative subunits based on household aggregates of various sizes had been employed under preceding dynasties for various purposes, including tax collection and local defense. In time, such units tended to become territorial rather than demographic. During the T'ang, subprefectures had been divided into cantons (*hsiang*)—groupings of five hundred households—and subdivided into townships (*li*)—groupings of one hundred households. By the late tenth century the canton was an areal subdivision of the subprefecture, and the township an areal subunit of the canton.[7] The Northern Sung inherited this canton-township pattern and passed it on to the Southern Sung.[8] At the beginning of the Southern Sung most subprefectures were

7. *SZS* p. 130–31.
8. The Northern Sung added to this system special-purpose units such as the *kuan*, first established by the Sung government in 974 as a subdivision of the canton, and the *ch'i*, a term designating the area under the jurisdiction of an Elder (*ch'i-chang*)—the officer responsible for the maintenance of local order in the early Northern Sung. See *SHY, shih-huo* 48.25a. For a study of the *kuan* see Nakamura Jihee, "Sō-dai no chihō kukaku-kan ni tsuite," *Shien*, no. 89 (1962): 85–115. Nakamura says that the cantons were abolished and replaced by the *kuan*, but although the decree involved may be construed in this way it appears that in practice the *kuan* were merely used as subunits of the cantons. The *kuan* remained in use throughout the Northern Sung. *TITC* 4.19a. For the *ch'i* see *TSKSK* p. 573. The early Southern Sung continued to use the *ch'i* but discarded the *kuan,* and used the canton-township system as its basic organizational pattern. On the abolition of the *kuan* see *TSKSK* p. 593–594, p. 624. On the continued use of the *ch'i* under the Southern Sung see *YLTT* 2217.18b. See also *SHY, shih-huo* 14.32b, 5.30a.

divided into cantons, which were subdivided into townships (*li*);[9] by the end of the dynasty the cantons in most of those sections of the empire about which we have information were composed of territorial units called superior guards—*tu* or *pao*—synonymous terms for the *tu-pao* unit originally established as a household aggregate division within the pao-chia system.[10] This transformation of units, originally defined in terms of numbers of households, into areal units may be an example of demographically determined institutional change. It seems probable that the major mechanism involved in this metamorphosis was gradual population growth. With a slow increase in population within an areal unit such as the subprefecture, the administrators of that unit were faced with a problem: they could

9. An example is Yen prefecture in 1139. See Ch'en Liang, *Yen Chou T'u Ching* (Ts'ung-shu Chi Ch'eng ed.), 2.132–35.

10. That *tu* and *pao* are synonyms becomes clear if we compare Fan Ch'eng-ta, 38.4b–5a, and Ling Wan-ch'ing, *Yü Feng Chih* (Peking National Library Rare Books microfilm), 1.1b–2a. In describing the same area at the same time one man calls *tu* what the other calls *pao*.

It should be noted that even in the early years of the Southern Sung there were some areas where cantons were divided into *pao* and *tu*. See *TSKSK* p. 438. And until the very last years of the dynasty there were areas which still used the township as the subdivision of the canton. See for example Ch'ien Shuo-yu, *Hsien-ch'un Lin-an Chih*, 20.2b describing Lin-an in the Hsien-ch'un period (1265–74). There were also cases of subprefectures where some cantons were divided into townships and others into superior guards. See Lo Yüan, *Hsin An Chih* (I Hsien Li Shih recut blockprint edition, 1888), 3.3a–4a; 4.2a–3a; 5.2b, 16a–b. The system used in Ming prefecture in Liang-che was a mixture of practices found elsewhere, with local peculiarities. Each subprefecture was divided into cantons. Each canton had associated with it a single township, which presumably was coterminous but subordinate. In some cantons there were no divisions below the township—in a sense the canton was the lowest unit. In other cantons the townships were divided into a few villages (*ts'un*). In still other cantons the townships were divided into superior guards. For instance, Hsiang-shan subprefecture was divided into three cantons (and three townships). Two of the cantons were divided into ten superior guards, and one into twelve. Whereas cantons were given names, the superior guards were merely numbered. See Lo Chün, *Pao-ch'ing Ssu-ming Chih*, 21.21b.

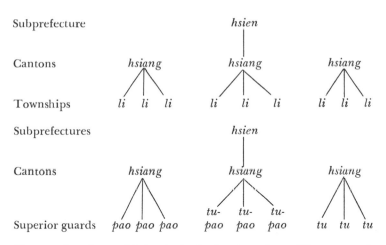

Fig. 1. Subprefectural Subunits in the Southern Sung. There were also cases, as noted in the text, in which there was a mixture of subunits, some cantons being divided into townships, and other cantons in the same subprefecture being divided into superior guards.

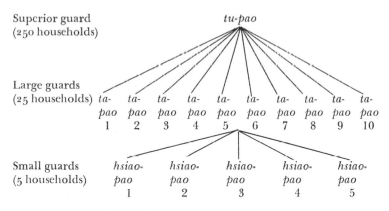

Fig. 2. *Pao-chia* (Village Service) Subunits in the Southern Sung

either add new population aggregate subunits (as legally they were supposed to do)[11] or they could merely append

11. *CPCSPM* 71.2a. For the increase in the size of these units see Lo Chün, 21.21bff. According to this work, in the Pao-ch'ing period (1225–27) there were thirty-two superior guards in a subprefecture with a total population of 13,380 households, an average of over 400

the added population to existing units, thus raising them beyond their legal limits. Accurate registration of the population occurred only rarely, but administrative decisions had to be made on a day-by-day, month-by-month basis. The only practical course over the long run was to define a unit legally composed of a limited number of households as being the households living within certain fixed boundaries.

This hypothesis may explain the transformation of the township and the superior guard into territorial units, but it cannot account for the replacement (within those areas about which we have sufficient information) of the township by the superior guard as the prevalent subunit under the canton during the late Southern Sung. Perhaps, as the superior guard approximated more and more, both in function and size, the preexisting township, the latter became administratively redundant. Then, for reasons unknown, decisions were made in many separate subprefectures to replace the township with the superior guard. There is no indication in the evidence examined that this change was the result of directives from higher authorities.

On the level below these areal divisions the Southern Sung population was organized into several kinds of house-

households per superior guard. The same situation existed in Lu-ch'uan subprefecture in Szechuan. Superior Guard Leaders there, during the reign of Ning-tsung (1185–1224), oversaw between 82 and 419 families. See *YLTT* 2217.18b. See also Ling Wan-ch'ing, 1.2b–3b, 1.18b, discussing the situation in K'un-shan subprefecture in 1251. There the total population of 54,368 households was divided into nine cantons and one garrison (*chen*); so an average canton probably had about 4,500 households. Six of those cantons were divided into two superior guards and three into three superior guards. The superior guards averaged almost 2,000 households apiece. This growth is also illustrated in the history of the canton, which in the Northern Sung varied from 200–300 at the smallest to 2,000–3,000 households at the largest. See *TSKSK* p. 627–28. During the Southern Sung, cantons in some areas ranged as high as 4,500 households in size. See Lo Chün, 21.21b.

hold groupings. The dominant system of household aggregates used in choosing village officers was derived from the *pao-chia* structure of the late Northern Sung. The regulations promulgated in the 1090s underwent little modification under Hui-tsung (1100–1126) and were taken over unaltered by the founders of the Southern Sung.[12] Under these rules the local authorities were permitted to organize service in two different patterns—the concurrent and the dual service systems. When the laws were first promulgated under Che-tsung, it was expected that under ordinary conditions officials would follow the concurrent variant. *Pao-chia* personnel—Superior Guard Leaders, their Assistants, and Guard Chiefs—would offer to act simultaneously as village servicemen—Elders, Stalwart Men, and Household Chiefs. Where not enough *pao-chia* leaders volunteered, the dual variant was to be used. Both *pao-chia* and village serv-

12. During the early years of the Southern Sung period there were cases of local variations in the sizes of the household groupings. Lin Hsiu-chung, writing in 1132, noted that ten small guards formed a large guard, and ten large guards formed a superior guard. See Lin Hsiu-chung, *Chu Hsüan Tsa Chu* (Ssu K'u Ch'üan Shu Chen Pen ed.), 3.7b. But it is clear that in general the legal rulings had not changed at this time. A directive of 1173 shows that the basic regulations had not changed by that year. It also indicates that the Southern Sung continued the Northern Sung procedures for dealing with groups of families and *pao-chia* units left over after the division of an area's population into small guards, large guards, and superior guards. As under the Northern Sung, if after assigning the people of an area to *pao-chia* units there were three or four small guards left over, these were formed into a large guard, and one Large Guard Chief was drafted. If there were less than three small guards, they were to be appended to other large guards. If there were five or more large guards, they were formed into a superior guard with a Superior Guard Leader. If there were less than five large guards, they were appended to other superior guards. See *SHY, shih-huo* 65.101b, 14.48a; *HNYL* 171.2902–03. A unit called the *pao-lin* also existed in the Southern Sung and was used in registering the population. See *SHY, shih-huo* 69.21b (1132). It also existed under the late Northern Sung. See *TITC* 7.36b. The term may be a colloquial synonym for a formal *pao-chia* unit (perhaps the superior guard) or an informal unit like our "neighborhood."

ice officers would be selected. *Pao-chia* personnel would perform *pao-chia* tasks, and village serviceworkers would perform village service duties, but membership in the two organizations would not overlap.

In fact, during the closing decades of the Northern Sung, the dual variant was widely used and seems to have been viewed as the normal arrangement. Then, during the disorders attendant on the Chin invasions of 1127–37, the concurrent variant was introduced and became common in Fuchou and the Chiang-che area. From Chiang-che it spread to other regions. It soon became standard in most of the empire, although in some peripheral circuits (including parts of Fukien and Szechuan) the dual system remained in use.

The existence of the dual variant during the closing decades of the Northern Sung is attested by the late Northern Sung handbook *Tso I Tzu Chen*;[13] the continuing use of this pattern in peripheral circuits at least until the 1190s is reported by various commentators. A document dated 1134 describes the dual variant in Fukien:

> In Fukien circuit the Superior Guard Leaders, their Assistants, and the Large and Small Guard Chiefs only have to catch military deserters and suppress smugglers and highwaymen. It is the Elders, Household Chiefs, and Stalwart Men who are the deputies of the subprefectural clerks in pressing for taxes and in gathering the Twice-a-Year tax. Nowadays the various subprefectures in Liang-che and Chiang-nan circuits all fail to hire Elders, Stalwart Men, and Household Chiefs, and merely draft Superior Guard Leaders, their Assistants, and Large and Small Guard Chiefs to manage [these tasks . . .] [i.e., the concurrent system had replaced the dual system in these circuits].[14]

And Chen Te-hsiu, writing in the middle of the twelfth century, indicated that this dual method of tax collection

13. *TITC* 3.10b, 3.11a, 4.19a, 6.31b, 8.42a.
14. *SHY, shih-huo* 14.22b–23a.

was still being employed in Fukien but did not exist in Hunan or Southeast China.[15] It remained current in parts of Fukien until at least the Ch'un-hsi period (1174–89).[16]

A similar dual service policy was enforced in parts of Szechuan in the middle of the twelfth century[17] and was still in use there during the reign of Ning-tsung (1195–1224).[18] In 1161, the administrator of Chung prefecture in K'uei-chou circuit in northwestern China complained that in Szechuan and Shensi village servicemen were being called according to the rules in force in the Huang yu pe riod (1049–53). In effect, a variation of dual service was in use.[19]

Variations in policy and practice are readily apparent; their causes are more difficult to discern. Why, despite the contrary intentions of the framers of the laws, was the dual system the normal practice in the late Northern Sung? Why did it give way to the concurrent system in the early Southern Sung? Why did dual service continue in some regions? The answers to the first and third questions can only be given by answering the second. But a distinction must be made between the immediate process involved in the introduction of concurrent service and the set of underlying conditions that transformed a temporary expedient into permanent policy. Two factors—military and economic—were involved in the initial introduction of the concurrent pattern in the decade 1127–37. Cheng Chü reports that, because of the military disorders, the state, unable to draft Elders, Household Chiefs, and Stalwart Men, had to force the *pao-chia* personnel to serve concurrently as village offi-

15. Chen Te-hsiu, *Hsi Shan Wen-chi* (Ssu Pu Ts'ung K'an edition), 29.4b–6b. Hereafter cited as *HSWC*.

16. Liang K'o-chia, *Ch'un-hsi San Shan Chih* (Ming woodblock ed.), 14.6b.

17. Wang Chih-wang, *Han P'in Chi* (Hu-pei, Hsien Cheng I Shu ed.), 9.16a.

18. *YLTT* 2217.18b–23a.

19. *SHY, shih-huo* 14.38a–39a.

cers.[20] But the military disorders were over by the late 1130s. Apparently the major reason for retaining the concurrent pattern was economic. The system proved particularly well suited (from the state's point of view) to the richer more densely populated regions, where taxes were heavy. A memorial dated 8 October 1169 says:

> It is decreed that all the men who collect taxes in the prefectures and subprefectures of Fukien should always follow the traditional [system]. If they have recently set up Heads of Tithing, Superior Guard Leaders, and Guard Chiefs to gather imposts, they should wholly abolish them. [This decree is issued because] some officials have said, "In the collection of the Twice-a-Year tax the use of Household Chiefs and Elders [i.e., the dual system] has been the rule. In Chiang-che, because of the number and complexity of the taxes, the Elders and Household Chiefs could not manage [tax collecting]. Therefore, provisionally, temporarily, and as a matter of convenience those responsibilities were turned over to Superior Guard Leaders and Guard Chiefs [i.e., the concurrent system was introduced]. After several years, various subprefectures and prefectures in Fukien followed the precedent of Chiang-che. But [to act in this way] is not to understand that the land of Fukien is less fertile, the people poorer, and the taxes lighter than in Chiang-che. We beg that you stop [Fukien from imitating the pattern of Chiang-che]."[21]

Although the authors suggest that concurrent service began in the rich lands of the Yangtse delta and later spread to the poorer circuit of Fukien, the first record we have of the use of the system during the Southern Sung is from Fukien.[22] However, this report describes Fuchou, which was economically highly developed. Despite its early introduction to this prefecture, the pattern seems to have remained un-

20. Ch'eng Hsün, *K'o-an Hsien-sheng Tsun Te Hsing Chai Hsiao Chi* (Chih Pu Tsu Chai Ts'ung-shu ed.), 2.15a–b.
21. *SHY, shih-huo* 14.44a–b. See also *SHY, shih-huo* 14.39b–40a.
22. Liang K'o-chia, 14.6a–b.

usual in the less-developed prefectures of Fukien, whereas it became universal in the rich Yangtse delta region.

But why should *pao-chia* personnel have proved more effective taxgatherers than the village officers they replaced? One possible explanation is that, since they combined both police powers and tax powers, they could more easily force men to pay their levies. This would have been particularly true in the Yangtse region, which was at the same time the key area of heavy taxes because of its inherent fertility and a difficult region from which to collect taxes at this time because it suffered during the military confrontation with the Chin. The very richness of this region made the system both possible and desirable (from the state's point of view). Under the concurrent system the financial burden placed on those called was considerably greater than that borne by men in dual service regions, but at the same time fewer men were called. Thus, the well-to-do who were liable for service were called on to invest less of their time but more of their money. Service was a dreaded burden, but at least it came less frequently than in dual regions. In poorer regions, the rich were, absolutely as well as relatively, poorer than the rich of the most favored circuits, and so might find it advantageous to offer the use of their time rather than of their all too limited financial resources.

Yet this does not explain why the concurrent system should have come into widespread use only after the advent of the Southern Sung. Fuchou cannot have been much richer in 1127 than it was in 1120, but it does not seem to have adopted concurrent service until 1127. It may be suggested that external events forced the government to withdraw from the people the option of choosing the preferred form of service (which seems to have been dual service). Under the rules of Che-tsung the *pao-chia* personnel were not paid, but the servicemen were. However, the rewards for acting as Elders, Household Chiefs, and Stalwart Men were not great enough to tempt men to volunteer for concurrent service. Therefore, so long as the choice was a free one, the dual services prevailed. With the advent of the Southern Sung, the government's fiscal position became desperate. The state had to have large revenues to shore up its military position at a time when collection of those revenues was exceptionally difficult. With the fate of the dynasty very much in doubt, the fate of those forced to collect taxes became for the moment irrelevant. The situation was most urgent in those rich regions which should have supplied the bulk of state income but which were also the chief sufferers during the Chin incursions. The authorities therefore inaugurated the practice of coercing *pao-chia* officers into "voluntary" concurrent service. There is abundant evidence of such coercion, and there is very little indication that at this period any substantial number of men actually volunteered for such work. The people probably would have preferred the dual system, but the authorities left them no choice. Instead, they placed heavy burdens on the *pao-chia* leaders and trusted that these *pao-chia* leaders would make use of their police (and at this time their semimilitary) powers to insure collection of sufficient revenues. Denied the right to choose the more convenient form, the people sought other means of easing the truly unbearable burdens of "voluntary" concurrent service. The outcome of this search was the professionalized service of the latter half of the twelfth century.

In outlying circuits, where collection of revenues was less important to the state's continued survival and where the people were less capable of bearing the strains of concurrent service, the dual pattern continued. Under this pattern the allocation of tasks between the village servicemen and *pao-chia* personnel was not the same in all sections of the empire; the defining characteristic of the dual pattern was not a specific division of labor but the coexistence of two separate organizations in the countryside. In Fukien the village officers were clearly concerned with taxgathering while the maintaining of law and order was in the hands of the *pao-chia*. But there seem to have been other areas where Elders traditionally managed problems of public peace and cared for roads and bridges.[23]

In concurrent system regions there seems to have been less variation in practice. The rules governing the concurrent pattern and the numbers of functionaries involved do not seem to have varied much from circuit to circuit nor to have changed radically during the course of the Southern Sung.

According to law, five families constituted a small guard, led by a Small Guard Chief. Five small guards formed a large guard, headed by a Large Guard Chief. Ten large guards composed a superior guard, headed by a Superior Guard Leader and an Assistant Superior Guard Leader.[24] Superior Guard Leaders and their Assistants were called for two-year terms. Large Guard Chiefs were also drafted for two-year stints before 1174,[25] but in that year their tours of duty were reduced to one year[26] and remained one year until at least the beginning of the thirteenth century.[27] Small Guard Chiefs seem to have worked for unlimited periods prior to 1172, when they were given terms of two years,[28] which remained standard until at least the opening years of the thirteenth century.[29]

23. *SHY, shih-huo* 14.46b–47a.
24. Ma Tuan-lin, *Wen Hsien T'ung K'ao*, 13.137. Ch'en Fu-liang, *Chih Chai Wen chi*, 21.3a; *SHY, shih huo* 66.21a.
25. *SHY, shih-huo* 66.21a (1174), 66.26b (1191); Ch'en Fu-liang, 21.3a.
26. *SHY, shih-huo* 66.21a. There is one piece of evidence inconsistent with this interpretation. Chu Hsi asked that the terms of Large Guard Chiefs be reduced to one year in a memorial apparently submitted in the 1180s. *HAHS* 21.327.
27. *SHY, shih-huo* 66.28b (1201–5).
28. *SHY, shih-huo* 14.46b–47a.
29. *SHY, shih-huo* 66.28b (1201–5). Ma Tuan-lin says that Small Guard Chiefs served two-year terms. This passage is so placed that it appears to be a general description of the Shao-hsing period (1127–63), but, given the *Sung Hui Yao Chi Kao* statement that up to 1172 Small

Before 1174, each man whose chief office was that of Large Guard Chief had to act concurrently as a taxgathering Household Chief for one tax period. During each of the two collection periods into which the year was divided a superior guard needed two Household Chiefs—a total of eight during the two-year tenure of a group of eight Large Guard Chiefs. Thus, during his biennial term a Large Guard Chief would have had to serve once as a tax collector.[30]

During the first, chaotic years of the Southern Sung, Superior Guard Leaders and their Assistants were sometimes asked to serve as taxgathering Household Chiefs.[31] After peace was restored in the 1130s the practice apparently declined, but reports from 1185 and 1191 assert that when there were not enough eligible Large Guard Chiefs, men who had served as Superior Guard Leaders were sometimes used as Household Chiefs.[32]

This flexibility was typically both a response to and an indicator of variations in local practices and conditions. But sometimes variations were due less to differences in regional character than to ambivalence in government policy. The state naturally was interested in the effective collec-

---

Guard Chiefs were called for unlimited service, we must assume that Ma Tuan-lin is really describing the system in use after 1172. See Ma Tuan-lin, 13.137.

30. Although this system is never described in detail its existence becomes obvious when comparing various reports on tax collection. See Ma Tuan-lin, 13.137; *SHY, shih-huo* 14.18a, 14.35a–b (1159), 66.21b (1179), 66.24a (1185); Shu Lin, 3.11a–b. After 1174, if the tenure of Large Guard Chiefs was in fact reduced to one year, the rotation policy would not have worked equitably without changes in other aspects of the system. Only half of the men called as Large Guard Chiefs would have had to act as taxgatherers during their time in office. Unfortunately the sources examined did not provide a solution to this puzzle.

31. *SHY, shih-huo* 14.18a (1131).

32. *SHY, shih-huo* 66.26b (1191); Yüan Hsieh, *Chieh Chai Chi* (Ssu K'u Ch'üan Shu ed.), 13.4b.

tion of revenues, yet it also had to design taxgathering systems that did not excessively burden the incumbent officers. The conflict between these not wholly compatible aims seems to have been at least one of the causes for the alternation between two different tax collecting systems—one using Household Chiefs and the other using Heads of Tithing. The Heads of Tithing system had three distinct advantages from the state's point of view: it was simple in organization, its units were small, and its officers had only one responsibility—to see that the tax quota was met. Yet it also had weaknesses, for it tended to become less and less effective as a taxgathering mechanism and more and more destructive of the fortunes of its officers as the years passed. Nonetheless, in times of trouble its good points seem to have outweighed its disadvantages in the eyes of the authorities. It was used in some regions in the first two decades of the Southern Sung, then between 1158 and 1172, for some years after 1189, and during the closing decades of the dynasty.[33] The system was first established in Fu prefecture in Fukien in 1127,[34] and its use on a national scale was advocated in 1130 by an intendant in Kuang-nan West circuit. It was tried in Kuang-nan West, found beneficial, and ordered extended to Liang-che, Chiang-nan East, Chiang-nan West, Ching-hu South, Kuang-nan East, and Fukien.[35] But in many places the orders were ignored and complaints were registered;[36] so in 1131 the Household Chief system was

33. *SHY, shih-huo* 14.17b (1128), 14.43b; Liang K'o-chia, 14.6b; *SHY, shih-huo* 14.17b–18a (1130), 14.19b (1131), 24b–25a (1135), 14.29a (1143), 14.36a–b (1160), 14.36b (1161), 14.45b–46a (1170); *CTCCC* 17.9a (1189); Ch'en Yüan-chin, 1.1b–2a (1189); Hu T'ai-ch'u, *Chou Lien Hsü Lun,* p. 12 (1230s?)

34. Liang K'o-chia, 14.6b.

35. *SHY, shih-huo* 14.17b–18a. *CTCCC* 17.8b gives the date of this change as 1127, but several other sources support the document in *SHY, shih-huo* 14.17b–18a. See *SHY, shih-huo* 14.18a; Ma Tuan-lin, 13.137; *HNYL* 36.696. Presumably the author of *CTCCC* was confused by the existence of the system in Fu prefecture from 1127.

36. *SHY, shih-huo* 14.18a (1131).

revived.[37] Although from 1131 until the late years of the dynasty these two systems alternated, the Household Chief pattern was the more common of the two, having been in use during a larger number of years than the Heads of Tithing system. Even when the latter was being practiced, it was not used throughout the empire, and at some times it seems to have been confined to a single circuit.[38]

There were many local variations on the basic Head of Tithing pattern, indicating both differences in local needs and the freedom of local officials to respond creatively to particular problems within their areas of jurisdiction. A comparison of two such patterns—one used in Kuang-tung in 1135 and the other in Che-tung about 1189—will give some idea of the amount of variation possible and of the common elements shared by the practices subsumed under the rubric Head of Tithing. It will also portray in brief the process of policy determination and the considerable scope given local administrators in altering general directives. The arrangement employed in Kuang-tung is described in a memorial dated 1135:

> The office of the Fiscal Intendant and the Intendant of the Ever Normal Granary in Kuang-tung says: "Recently the assistant subprefect of Ch'ang-chou subprefecture in P'ing-chiang prefecture, Lü Hsi-ch'ang, reported, asking: 'How can the Large Guard Chiefs [in charge of] tax collecting in a superior guard personally reach to the distant? If the [time] limits are passed [even] before men are pressed, [the Guard

37. *SHY, shih-huo* 14.20a (1131) *Chia-t'ou* continued to be used in Fu prefecture until 1137. Liang K'o-chia, 14.6b. See also T'o T'o, et al., *Sung Shih*, 28.7a.

38. *SHY, shih-huo* 14.24b–25a; *HNYL* 95.1579; T'o T'o, et al., 28.7a; *SHY, shih-huo* 14.29a; *CTCCC* 17.8b; *SHY, shih-huo* 65.91b, 14.29a; Liang K'o-chia, 14.6b; *SHY, shih-huo* 14.37b, 14.42b, 65.91b–92a, 14.45a–b (1170), 14.45b–46a (1170); *CTCCC* 17.8b. For some years after 1189, in T'ai prefecture in Liang-che the Heads of Tithing seem to have been used. *CTCCC* 17.9a; Ch'en Yüan-chin, 1.1b–2a; Hu T'ai-ch'u, p. 12.

Chiefs] are put in the cangue and beaten, and in the vexations of the investigation lose their patrimonies. I beg that this be changed and Heads of Tithing be used, with powerful households (*hsing-shih hu*—i.e., the households of village officers, clerks, and officials) collecting from powerful households, and ordinary households (*p'ing-hu*) collecting from ordinary households.' We have already received a directive [saying that] the benefits or injuries of using Household Chiefs and Heads of Tithing in collecting taxes differ in the various regions, and ordering the various circuits to evaluate such usages in order to report on them. Now we would like to see you follow the request [of Lü Hsi-ch'ang] to change and use the Heads of Tithing. The assistants to the subprefect should be given sole responsibility for taking the powerful households and the ordinary households and, in accord with the amounts that they pay in taxes, dividing them into three grades each. The names should be recorded, with every group of thirty names forming a tithing, the names being arranged in rank order to make a register. Afterward, when you have called men all the way through the tithing you should begin again at the top. Indeed this could be practiced for a long time and still be beneficial." The memorial was approved.[39]

The system employed later in Che-tung resembles that described above in some ways but contains interesting differences. Under the Che-tung policy—the designing of which is credited to the circuit intendant Yüan Shuo-yu—the unit of taxation was the canton. Within the canton, neighboring families were grouped together according to the amount of taxes that they paid, the upper households being divided into groups of twenty and the lower households into groups of thirty. Each tithing created its own register, from which one man was chosen to act as the taxgathering Head of Tithing. If during his term of duty he collected the proper quota, then his duties passed on to the next most well-to-do family in the tithing. If the quota was

39. *SHY, shih-huo* 14.24b–25a.

not met, the duties did not rotate. Under this policy, households are said to have been terrified of the consequences
of not collecting enough and so applied themselves dili-
gently to their tasks.[40]

These examples indicate how local exigencies frequently
led to attempts to create Head of Tithing structures. The
coincidence of the establishing of such systems with times of
invasion (1120s and 1130s, 1160s, mid–thirteenth century)
suggests that Heads of Tithing were particularly useful
when the regular *pao-chia* forces were busy keeping local
order.

The persistence with which local authorities advocate the
establishing of these organizations indicates their useful-
ness; their repeated abolition suggests that they posed as
many problems as they solved. The case against Heads of
Tithing was stated forcefully in the 1130s. These functionaries were not chosen on the basis of wealth; any household
with two adult males had to serve its turn, and in this way
many poor families were ruined. This policy also required
the services of a much larger number of local people than
did the Household Chiefs policy. The docket of disputes resulting from disagreements over the drafting of officers was
thus increased, creating an overloaded court schedule, and
taking many farmers away from their proper pursuits.
Furthermore the Heads of Tithing, often simple peasants,
were not powerful enough to make the rich pay, nor
wealthy enough to make good the debts of defaulters, nor
did they understand the ways of officials.[41]

Critics of the Heads of Tithing point to flaws inherent

40. *CTCCC* 17.9a–b; Ch'en Yüan-chin, 1.1b–2a.
41. *SHY, shih-huo* 14.18b (1131); *HNYL* 44.803 (1131). For the
large number of men called see the estimate of an official who said a
subprefecture had to call more than 600 *chia-t'ou*. See *SHY, shih-huo*
14.46a. This figure tallies well with a report by Wang Ying-ch'en,
Wen Ting Chi, 5.45 where he describes two subprefectures one of
which had 862 and the other 700 *chia-t'ou*.

in the system itself; critics of the Household Chiefs were usually concerned with abuses in procedures, such as corruption among clerks and the rich, rather than with weaknesses in the system.[42] Since Household Chiefs were selected at least in part because they were well-to-do, presumably they were better able to make the powerful pay, to deal effectively with clerks and officials, and to contribute missing imposts without being financially ruined. Because of their very wealth and sophistication, however, such households were more likely to be aware of the possibilities of making collusive agreements with the clerks. Furthermore, athough the officers' police powers might make it more difficult for defaulting households to evade payment, those powers also meant that the officers' time was divided. When invasion was imminent, they might have to abandon their tax collecting duties to concentrate on military preparations and actions.

When these *pao-chia* officers added military tasks to their other duties, they began to encroach upon the functions of the *pao-wu* militia. The Northern Sung *pao-wu* militia had in theory been displaced by Wang An-shih's *pao-chia*. But since the *pao-chia* soon became a local service (*i-fa*) organization, the *pao-wu* was in fact retained as a local self-defense force.[43]

Southern Sung officials frequently did not distinguish between the *pao-wu* and the *pao-chia;* they often speak of "*pao-chia* units" when describing organizations that in terms of structure and function are clearly *pao-wu* militia, and they sometimes say *pao-wu* when talking about *pao-*

42. Wang Ying-ch'en, 5.44.

43. Sudō Yoshiyuki has assembled a large body of evidence indicating that this *pao-wu* existed in most circuits of the empire during most of the Southern Sung. See *TSKSK* p. 683–735. The *pao-chia* had retained certain military overtones in the late Northern Sung. See Chai Ju-wen, *Chung Hui Chi* (Ssu K'u Ch'üan Shu Chen Pen ed.), 10.8b.

chia.[44] Their confusion is understandable. In some cases the terminology of the two systems is nearly identical,[45] and at times their functions overlapped. Early in the period, *pao-chia* members fought as soldiers.[46] In the middle of the period, *pao-chia* officers were sometimes concurrently commanders in the militia.[47] And, during the second half of the Southern Sung, the *pao-wu* militia began to take on welfare functions, apparently because officials felt that the *pao-wu* records were more accurate than those kept by the *pao-chia.* Thus, the militia was sometimes used in distributing famine relief and in registering the population.[48]

The militia rolls were more precise than the village serv-

44. *SHY, ping* 2.44b–45a; ibid., *shih-huo* 66.29a–b, 14.37a, 14.20a–b.

45. In one *pao-wu* system in use in Szechuan in 1222, 5 families formed a *chia*, 25 families a small guard (*hsiao-pao*), 125 families a large guard (*ta-pao*). See *SHY, ping* 2.48a–49a. *Pao-wu* leaders were also sometimes given titles identical with titles used in the village service system. A *chia-t'ou* could either be a Head of Tithing or a leader in the militia. For *chia-t'ou* as military leaders see *HNYL* 192.3222 (1161) and *YLTT* 2217.18b (1194–1224). It is probably to these men that Chu Hsi is referring when he speaks of *pao-t'ou* leading the *pao-wu*. See *CWKCH* p. 13–14. See also *SHY, ping* 2.47a. The title *pao-chang* was also used both in the service system and in the militia. For its militia use see Hu T'ai-ch'u, p. 11. The titles *tu-pao cheng* and *tu-pao fu-cheng* were also used in what Huang Kan called *pao-wu* units. Huang Kan, 32.1a, although in this case it seems possible that the organization described by Huang Kan was really the *pao-chia* organization, and his use of the term *pao-wu* was a mistake.

46. *HNYL* 8.204, 12.273, 24.494, 65.1101, 73.1209, 99.1621.

47. In the late twelfth and the thirteenth centuries *pao-chia* officers —Superior Guard Leaders and their Assistants—are described as leaders of *pao-wu* units in Szechuan, Hunan, and Hupei. *YLTT* 2217.18b; *SHY, ping* 2.47a–48a.

48. Huang Kan, 32.1a. See note 11. See also *TSKSK* p. 711. *Pao-wu* personnel might be used to perform other local functions. In 1155 they were ordered to report illegal wine production and sale. See *HNYL* 169.2766. In cities they might be used in fighting fires. See *CHTK* 2.23. Even in these cases we may make a functional distinction between the two organizations in that the *pao-wu* added duties can be seen in some sense as extensions of the duty to preserve order, through prevention as well as through suppression.

ice lists because the Southern Sung *pao-wu* units—unlike the *pao-chia* units, which grew in size beyond the limits set by law and became territorial divisions—remained closer in practice to the original rulings and smaller in size. Thus, their registers were thought to reflect more exactly the state of the rural people.[49]

A combination of factors was responsible for the transfer of vital functions from civil agencies to organizations originally devised for military or paramilitary ends—from the village service organization of the Northern Sung to the *pao-chia,* and from the *pao-chia* to the *pao-wu.* First, it may be suggested that because of their character, potentially dangerous to the state, military and paramilitary organizations were more closely controlled and more tightly organized than were civil agencies. In this regard the character of the Sung itself is relevant. It was a period of continuing external threat but also of great internal stability, ruled by a house particularly fearful of the dangers inherent in the wide diffusion of military power. The government was prompted to create militia units but to withhold from them major means of military force, particularly after some units were accused of participation in rebellious activities.[50] These well-organized groups were then available for alternative uses. They were effective in times of trouble because their leaders, like the leaders of the *pao-chia* organi-

49. In Lu ch'uan subprefecture the population was divided into two types of militia units which in theory were to number five households or twenty-five households. In fact, in this area the units were very close in size to these legal limits. See *YLTT* 2217.18b–23b. The use of five families as the basic units of the militia is also noted in 1127 (*HNYL* 6.168), in 1163 (*SHY, ping* 2.43a), in 1196 (ibid., *ping* 2.45a–b), and in 1222 (ibid., *ping* 2.48a–49a). Occasionally units of ten are reported. See Hu T'ai-ch'u, p. 12; *SHY, ping* 2.43b. Units of five were also used in organizing such special groups as the families of seamen along the coasts. *HNYL* 36.686, 89.1491. In practice it appears that fishermen and urban workers were not registered in the *pao-wu.* See Liao Hsing-chih, *Sheng Chai Chi,* 5.17a.

50. *HCP* 365.3a.

zations, seem mostly to have been drawn from relatively wealthy (and presumably relatively powerful) rural families. This frequent consonance between the formal and informal hierarchies of influence and power helped stabilize the rural social order while providing an effective structure through which to deal with sources of disorder such as natural disasters or lawlessness, though it did create increased opportunities for corrupt practices and oppression of the peasantry.[51]

In drawing rural leaders from this common source, the rural rich, the state provided a common thread which unified the otherwise complicated fabric of diverse rural agencies—militia and service organizations in dual and concurrent service regions, with local variations at different times and places.

51. Liu Ts'ai-shao, *Fan Ch'i Chü Shih Chi,* 8.23a–b, comments on this consonance of leadership, citing it as a root of rural problems.

5

Selection of Personnel: Privileged Households

The Confucian persuasion that molded the thoughts of most government leaders in premodern China contained certain unavoidable tensions. Confucians saw society as inevitably hierarchical. Men, if not born unequal, became obviously unequal as they matured. Households also occupied different ranks in the hierarchy, and the government granted privileges to certain favored types, particularly those of officials and nobles. This favoritism, expressed in pre-Sung times in differential burdens and freedom from some other impositions, was reinforced by the character of Chinese society during the period from the late Han to the mid-T'ang, when a relatively small group of families dominated the political and economic life of China.

At the same time Confucian philosophy contained elements that encouraged both the search for a broader social justice and attempts to distribute state burdens according to the people's ability to bear them. This led the state to grant privileges to handicapped groups. But the desire to provide a just system might also provoke a questioning of the right of these privileged groups to their privileges. Confucian admonitions could be cited to justify either the granting of benefits or their abolition. Actual state practice seems to have been based on practical political considerations, which reflected the continuing struggle of various groups to transmute their influence into concrete advantages, the desires of some influential factions within the government for social justice, and the bureaucratic demand for administrative practicality. Any basic shift in the distribution of privileges must therefore be considered proof of a more fundamental alteration in the balance of political power within the state.

During the Sung dynasty such a shift occurred. Sung authorities sought to create a progressive service system in which the heaviness of a household's burden was usually directly proportional to its ability to bear the expenses involved. The general trend was toward the elimination of vestigial practices that violated this principle. Southern Sung reformers succeeded in tying liabilities to actual wealth rather than to household grade alone, decreased the emphasis on the number of adult males in the family, reduced the benefits attached to many privileged statuses, and restricted access to other advantaged groups. The net effect of these changes seems to have been to reduce the relative number of the privileged and to place ever greater emphasis on money as the key factor used in assigning responsibilities and powers.

The Sung had inherited from previous dynasties the practice of freeing certain household types from some taxes and from liability for village services or services to local government.[1] These people seem to have been privileged because they were economically disadvantaged; because they had contributed in some important way to the proper functioning of state and society; or because collecting from them was impractical or impolitic.

During the Sung households were considered permanently disadvantaged if they were headed by a woman (*nü-hu*), if they had only a single adult male (*tan-ting hu*), or if they were headed by the elderly, the young, the sick, or the disabled. People in areas devastated by war or natural disasters also were frequently granted exemption from

1. Lü Tsu-ch'ien, *Li Tai Chih-tu Hsiang Shuo* (Hsü Chin Hua Ts'ung-shu ed.), 3.7b–8a.

some liabilities, by special dispensation and for limited periods.

Households were regularly honored for the contributions to society if they were headed by Buddhist or Taoist monks, by officials or the descendants of officials, or by some categories of students and examination graduates. Households might be given advantaged status if a member became known as a paragon of socially desirable virtues, if they fought bravely against the invader, if they were returned to allegiance after being under the control of the enemy, or if they were helping bring devastated farmlands back into cultivation.

Benefits were given to the preceding types of households in part to achieve social justice; some people, such as city residents, benefited not because of their disadvantages but simply because it was impractical to call on them to perform service or pay taxes in the regular fashion.[2]

During the Southern Sung the state gradually reduced the benefits accorded some of these groups, and made more elaborate the criteria for entrance into the advantaged statuses. Privileged groups came to bear a larger portion of the costs of government. In assessing obligations, the authorities placed increasing emphasis on wealth. By the end of the Southern Sung, the economic position of the household, which had always been one factor used in assigning burdens, in most cases far overshadowed all other considerations. The overall trend was toward a policy of treating the population as homogeneous in every respect but wealth. Not all privileges disappeared, but those left at the end of the Southern Sung were far less important than

2. It is difficult to decide where to place some kinds of families. For instance, salt producers generally seem to have been exempt from services, perhaps because of their economic importance. *HNYL* 56.986 (1132). However, it should be noted that at some times salt producers seem to have been liable for the costs of services. *SHY, shih-huo* 26.5a (1132); Ma Tuan-lin, *Wen Hsien T'ung K'ao*, 13.139. Families of miners may also have been exempted. Ibid.

those that had existed at the beginning of the period. As with many Southern Sung developments the roots of this transformation are found in the Northern Sung, but its fruition came during the twelfth and thirteenth centuries. During the Southern Sung, permanently disadvantaged households gradually lost many privileges. Southern Sung officials justified this change by pointing out that many people obtained disadvantaged status by fraud. By reducing the benefits of this status the state would diminish the temptation to cheat. Moreover, they argued, it was unfair to place all the burdens on ordinary households (*min-hu*), which might be poor, when there were rich households which fell into the "disadvantaged" categories. The most important benefit of permanent disadvantaged classification had been freedom from the village officer obligation or (in the cases of some groups with limited privileges) the right to hire substitutes. During the dynasty these households were forced to pay an increasing share of village service costs. Criteria defining membership also were made more detailed, apparently in order to restrict the number of families eligible.

One of the most important of these disadvantaged household types was families headed by a woman (*nü-hu*). At the beginning of the Northern Sung *nü-hu* had been freed from all *i-fa* obligations, but when the services were reformed under Wang An-shih their privileges were curtailed. They had to pay "aid money" (*chu-ch'ien*) to defray part of the cost of local services.[3] Under the Southern Sung, households headed by women continued to contribute aid money.[4]

In addition to this tax, the first decades of the Southern Sung, limited numbers of certain kinds of *nü-hu* were made liable for services. In 1135 it was ruled that households

---

3. "SIFS" p. 262. The amount of money they had to pay was reduced by half in the Yüan-yu period (1086–94). *SHY, shih-huo* 66.60a–b.

4. "SIFS" p. 262.

headed by women whose adult sons were Buddhist or Taoist clergy were to be liable for service obligations. Only one such household in a superior guard could be called in any single year, and the drafted household could hire a substitute to do the actual work.[5] This policy of counting Buddhist and Taoist monks as adult males if they were the sons of rich widows may have been in part an attempt to end one abuse of the exemption policy; there had been reports that sons had been forced against their own wishes to take religious vows.[6] The policy may also have been aimed at rich widows who purchased certificates of ordination so that their sons might evade services.

This new policy created a new set of difficulties. In 1149 a central government official named Wang Pao pointed out that, in some cases, overzealous local officials did not even bother to ascertain whether the sons in question were living or dead. He also complained that, in carrying out the directive, women who did not have any sons or grandsons, or whose sons or grandsons were minors, were being called on for service. He wanted to return to the old practice of exempting all *nü-hu*.[7] The Ministry of Finance replied to Wang's charges by denying that childless women household-heads were liable for services. Moreover, women who lived alone because their sons were certain types of students or examination graduates were also excused.[8] The emperor concurred with the ministry. He apparently felt that drafting some households headed by women was neces-

5. *SHY, shih-huo* 14.24b (1135); ibid., *shih-huo* 14.27a. See also ibid., *shih-huo* 14.31a (1149); ibid., *shih-huo* 65.101b–102a (1173).

6. Lin Hsiu-chung, *Chu Hsüan Tsa Chu*, 3.8a (1132); *HNYL* 88.1472 (1135).

7. *SHY, shih-huo* 14.30b; *HNYL* 160.2592. There is another, later request that all *nü-hu* be exempted, but this also was rejected. *SHY, shih-huo* 66.22a.

8. T'o T'o et al., *Sung Shih*, 30.14b; *HNYL* 160.2592. Women who lived alone because their sons were students in the Imperial Academy or were certified provincial graduates (*te chieh chü-jen*) were excused from service obligations.

sary because during the years when they had been wholly
freed from services, many families had falsely registered
as *nü-hu* to evade requisition.[9]

Pressure to tighten the rules for exemption existed
throughout the period. In 1137, two years after the first
ruling permitting the calling of some types of *nü-hu*, an official named Li Te-lin unsuccessfully advocated the drafting
of any households headed by a woman or having only one
adult male, so long as not more than five such households
were drafted in a superior guard in any one year.[10] In 1168
the rules governing liability were tightened. Rich widows
who remarried or rich women who were caring for aged
or infirm parents-in-law were to be treated like rich widows
whose adult sons were Buddhist or Taoist clergy.[11] In 1172,
because some families still fraudulently sought *nü-hu* status,
it was ordered that families that had illegally attained *nü-hu*
classification would be given a two-month grace period
within which they could confess without fear of penalty.
Thereafter, other men would be allowed to accuse them.
The accusers were to be rewarded according to the rules
covering informers.[12] In 1180 an official complained that,
despite their legal exemption, *nü-hu* were being treated in
accord with the Northern Sung rulings on the status of the
young, the old, the sick, and the disabled: they were being

9. *SHY, shih-huo* 14.31a.
10. *SHY, shih-huo* 14.26a–27a. The emperor, on the advice of the
Ministry of Finance, rejected the suggestion, but, feeling that Li Te-lin
had the welfare of the people at heart, promoted him five grades.
HNYL 109.1772.
11. *SHY, shih-huo* 14.43a. If these women owned property, it was
to be registered in their names. The document says that such women,
if they "personally have the official *yin* privilege, may be treated as
official households and are thus subject to the rules on the limitation of
liability-free landholding." It is not clear how such women could have
been given the *yin* privilege, unless we assume that official status was
a good that could be transferred by inheritance to women as well as
to men in this era.
12. *SHY, shih-huo* 14.47b.

called like ordinary commoners, and were merely permitted the minor privilege of not having to serve in person. He asked that the aged, the sick and the disabled remain liable for services with the option of hiring replacements, but that *nü-hu* and households headed by minors be exempt. The investigator appointed by the government reported that the problem had arisen because officials frequently, and mistakenly, added the characters for *nü-hu* and minor households to a ruling of 1179 which had reasserted the eligibility of households headed by the aged, the sick, and the disabled. The government accepted his recommendation that, in accord with the suggestions of the original memorialist, the full exemption of households headed by women and the young be reaffirmed.[13] Apparently these rules remained in force during the remaining decades of the dynasty. Most *nü-hu* remained free from the service obligations although they paid labor service money, but limited numbers of some types of widow households were liable for requisition.

Families with only one adult male (*tan-ting hu*) formed a second privileged group. Like *nü-hu*, these households gave "aid money" under the reformed system of Wang An-shih, paid at a reduced rate after the Yüan-yu period (1086–94), and continued to contribute during the Southern Sung.[14]

Although they had to give aid money, *tan-ting hu* benefits were still great enough to tempt men to act in antisocial or illegal ways to attain such registration. During the 1130s it was said that parents forced marriages on their adult sons, and brothers lived apart, so that their households could attain this status. It was even asserted that children were killed to lower the number of male family members.[15]

13. *SHY, shih-huo* 66.22a (1180).
14. "SIFS" p. 262. During the T'ang the authorities had also been forbidden to select service men who were the only adult males in households of low grade. See Twitchett, *Financial Administration*, p. 30.
15. Lin Hsiu-chung, 3.8a; *HNYL* 119.1927 (1138); *SHY, shih-huo* 14.21a (1133), 14.26a (1137).

Perhaps partly in response to these problems, the privileges of households with a single adult male were reduced in 1135. It was ordered that rich *tan-ting hu* might be asked to provide Superior Guard Leaders or Guard Chiefs, so long as not more than one such household was drafted in each superior guard in any one year. As with *nü-hu*, households with a single adult male were permitted to hire proxies to do the actual work.[16] Two years later an official complained that when only one *tan-ting* household could be called in each superior guard, the people still thought it advantageous to be classified as *tan-ting hu*. He asked that no limit be set on the number of solitary-support households that could be requisitioned. At the same time another official asked that the quota of liable *tan-ting hu* and *nü-hu* be raised to five for each superior guard. On the advice of the Ministry of Finance, both recommendations were rejected,[17] but later that year the ministry acted to restrict the certification of *tan-ting hu* by clarifying policy on some borderline cases. The ministry ruled that in situations where there were a number of adult males in a household, even though all but one of these men were of privileged status, the nonprivileged individual could not legally claim that he headed a *tan-ting hu*.[18]

Although another clarifying directive was issued in 1142,[19] and in 1145 the number of rich *tan-ting hu* that could be called in a superior guard each year was raised to two,[20] some critics felt that the system still enticed people

16. *SHY, shih-huo* 14.24b (1135). See also Lin Hsiu-chung, 3.8a.
17. *SHY, shih-huo* 14.26a-b.
18. *SHY, shih-huo* 14.27a. The ministry ruled that households in which there were two officials and one commoner were not *tan-ting hu*, and that households including one candidate qualified for the doctoral examinations at the capital (having been certified after local examination) (*chin-shih te chieh*), one *ying ch'ung chieh* (probably a prospective qualified candidate), one man who had been given official rank because he made contributions (for famine relief, etc.) (*chin-na te kuan*), and one commoner (*pai shen*) were not *tan-ting hu*.
19. *SHY, shih-huo* 14.29b.
20. *SHY, shih-huo* 14.46b.

into falsely claiming to be solitary-support households.
After 1172, as a result of suggestions by a reformer named
Yang T'an, *tan-ting hu* were apparently treated like ordinary households in the assignment of service obligations. From this year on, the "privilege" of *tan-ting
hu* appears to have been merely the right to hire substitutes.[21]

This hiring privilege was extended to some other disadvantaged household types, including families headed by
the elderly, the young, the ill, and the disabled. Such groups
seem to have been liable during at least part of the Northern
Sung, although they did not have to serve in person.[22] It
was reported in the early 1130s that men sometimes muti-
lated themselves to obtain the privilege of hiring accorded
the disabled.[23] The right of disadvantaged households to
hire substitutes was reaffirmed in 1137.[24] In the ensuing
decades the old and disabled seem at times to have been
treated as exempt, for in 1179 a ruling was handed down
specifically stating their eligibility. The purport of this
ruling was restated in 1180, when households headed by
minors were given complete exemption from liability for
services.[25]

In addition to these regularly privileged groups of disadvantaged households, other people were given limited exemptions following natural disasters or invasions.[26] Such
remissions of taxes and services occur from the earliest years
of the Southern Sung.[27] Usually they were extended for

21. *SHY, shih-huo* 14.46b.
22. *SHY, shih-huo* 66.22a, 14.27a.
23. Lin Hsiu-chung, 3.8a (1132).
24. *SHY, shih-huo* 14.27a.
25. *SHY, shih-huo* 66.22a. But from 1138, households headed by
aged individuals which included an adult son who remained at home
to care for his parents were treated according to the rules governing
widows with sons who were clergy. *SHY, shih-huo* 14.27b.
26. In 1162, some men in areas that had suffered invasions were
given temporary relief from services. *SHY, shih-huo* 14.39b.
27. In 1130 the court apparently acceded to the request of Chao
Ting that families in the general area of T'ai prefecture, Ming prefec-

fixed terms to delimited regions, but occasionally the whole empire received a reprieve.[28] At times remissions seem to have been put on a more regular basis. In 1209 it was suggested that relief from *i-fa* granted to drought-stricken areas be given according to a set scale, being reduced by varying amounts depending on local circumstances.[29]

People who lived in cities or in areas far from their native places, though not economically disadvantaged, received comparable benefits because it was too difficult to collect from them in the ordinary way. From the early Northern Sung, urban residents had been permitted to contribute a fee in lieu of personally performing service duties.[30] During the latter half of the Northern Sung and the early Southern Sung they continued to pay such a commutation tax.[31] Then, in 1142, they were made liable for conscription. Since they were permitted to hire substitutes, the effect of this ruling was to redistribute the fiscal burden and to clarify legal accountability. Instead of imposing a yearly impost on all city households of certain grades, money was demanded from individual families on a rotating basis. These households were allowed to serve in person, but apparently they frequently decided to engage others to do the work. They seem to have remained legally responsible for the proper performance of the duties in question.[32] This

---

ture, and Wen prefecture be forgiven one year's taxes and services. See Chao Ting. *Chung-cheng-te Wen-chi* (Ch'ien-k'un Cheng Ch'i Chi ed.), 50.16b.

28. In 1134 the dynastic annals report that, because of long-continued rains, all services that were not vital were to be stopped. See T'o T'o et al., 27.18a.

29. *SHY, shih-huo* 66.30a.

30. "SSKS" p. 116.

31. In 1086 the Executive of the Ministry of Personnel, Fu Yao-yü, said, "Humbly I say that in the villages on the basis of the number of adult males men put forth their labor, and in the cities on the basis of household grade men put forth their money. This is called drafting-paying (*ch'ai-k'o*)." *HCP* 388.7a.

32. *SHY, shih-huo* 66.26a–b.

apparently continued to be the policy for the rest of the dynasty except for a brief period from 1172 to 1179, when urban dwellers were not called for services.[33]

The sources do not make clear how this burden was assessed in the cities. Although in 1185 it was decreed that the property of urban dwellers was to be appraised and that such valuations were to be made in future every few years,[34] in the following year this order was amended. Assessment was to be carried out only where it was possible, convenient, and traditional. The memorial of 1186 does not indicate how the levying of services was to be determined in areas where the wealth of city residents was not evaluated in this way.[35]

During the Southern Sung many honored households, like most disadvantaged households, lost some of their privileges. The state issued increasingly detailed rules on admission to the most influential of the honored statuses—official households—and whittled away the benefits attached to membership in the two largest groups—official households and households headed by Buddhist and Taoist clergy. The minor categories of honored households apparently maintained their privileges intact, perhaps in part because very few families could claim classification in the minor groups and in part because the advantages awarded these groups had always been limited in character and were generally awarded for short terms.

These smaller and less important types of esteemed households included some categories that were rewarded according to established regulations, some groups that were granted advantages in special decrees, and some individual families that were honored by imperial grace. Certain cate-

33. *SHY, shih-huo* 66.21b (1172). The households of villagers who had moved to the cities and who were directly affected by the rulings on services or nonservice were called *chi-ch'an hu*. See *SHY, shih-huo* 14.46b; ibid., *shih-huo* 66.21b.
34. *SHY, shih-huo* 66.23b.
35. *SHY, shih-huo* 66.23b.

gories of students and examination graduates were routinely rewarded. According to one report an order was issued in 1133 that candidates for the metropolitan degree (*chin-shih*)—both those who were certified because they had passed the local examinations (*te chieh*) and those who, having already failed in the metropolitan examinations, were permitted to retake them without having to repeat the local tests (*ying mien chieh jen*)—were to be freed from service obligations.[36] In 1145 this privilege was extended to students in the Imperial Academy (*t'ai hsüeh sheng*).[37] But in 1149 an official complained that although, according to law, "provincial graduates" (*te chieh chü-jen*) who had already been examined and pupils in the Imperial Academy were exempt from service obligations, in fact such men were being requisitioned.[38] A few weeks later the court accepted the recommendation of the Ministry of Finance that Imperial Academy students and examined provincial graduates should be freed from the service liability if they had attempted the departmental examinations and were the only adult males in their families. If men had qualified as candidates because of special orders (*t'e chih*) or because of imperial grace without being tested (*ying en sheng mien chieh*), they were to be liable for the service requisition but could hire replacements.[39] None of the evidence examined

36. *HNYL* 64.1091. See also *SHY, shih-huo* 14.27a (1137).

37. *HNYL* 64.1091. There is some ambiguity in this report since it refers to *ting-i*—a term generally used as a synonym for *yao-i* (corvée labor). It would seem however that the report must be referring to *chih-i* (labor services). *Yao-i* was assessed only against the lowest grade of households in Sung times. It seems extremely unlikely that there were many fifth-grade household members among imperial academy students, and even more unlikely that these men would be privileged by being freed from corvée while their fellow students remained liable for labor services.

38. *SHY, shih-huo* 14.30a–31a (1149). He says that presented provincial graduates whose names were already entered in the T'ien Fu and Imperial Academy students who were already attached to the Shang Hsiang were being called for services.

39. *SHY, shih-huo* 14.31b.

indicates any changes in these rules during the rest of the dynasty. It seems probable that, from the mid–twelfth century on, men who had earned their place among imperial students and examination candidates in irregular ways were accorded the minor privilege of being allowed to employ others to act as servicemen. Men who came through the regular channels of the examination system—if they were the only adult males in their households—might gain full exemptions from services after having been tested in the capital.

The Southern Sung state, perpetually confronting war or the threat of war, rewarded its military and civilian supporters by reducing their fiscal and service obligations. The state sometimes released from service responsibilities individual military units and personnel. In some cases all personnel of the units were given temporary exemptions; in 1134 the militia that manned the water fortresses in T'ai, Ch'u, and Ch'eng prefectures were given ten years freedom from land taxes and local services.[40] In other cases members were given permanent relief; in 1166 it was ordered that the circuits of Ching-hsi and Li-chou should not tax or levy for services men who were "righteous defenders" (*pao sheng i shih*).[41] In 1127, militia officers were noted as being excused from having to serve in person as servicemen;[42] in 1177, immunity from certain tax and service burdens was granted to all militiamen except those from households in the top three grades, who remained liable for service as Superior Guard Leaders or Guard Chiefs.[43] Those who had fought bravely against the northern invaders were also frequently given temporary exemption because of their valor;[44] the most skillful village soldiers might even be made supple-

---

40. *HNYL* 82.1345.
41. T'o T'o et al., 33.20b.
42. *HNYL* 8.198–99.
43. *SHY, shih-huo* 14.44b–45a.
44. *SHY, shih-huo* 14.39a; T'o T'o et al., 27.12a, 16b, 21a.

mentary officials (*pu-kuan*). They thus became *kuan-hu* and might receive the privileges of that most desirable status.[45]

Men who, having been ruled by the Northerners, again became subjects of the Southern Sung were sometimes freed from the necessity of having to serve in person,[46] and farmers bringing war-devastated areas back into cultivation were forgiven taxes and services.[47]

Men who contributed grain in times of emergency sometimes were temporarily released from service obligations[48] or secured rank as officials through contribution, which in some cases they could use to obtain advantages through reclassification as *kuan-hu*.[49] At the beginning of the Southern Sung they might even bequeath these irregularly obtained privileges to their descendants, but in 1167 this practice was outlawed.[50]

During the Southern Sung men were sometimes honored as paragons of socially desirable virtues. After 1138, filial behavior under certain conditions was rewarded on a regular basis. When a son in a rich family remained home to care for aged or infirm parents, his family was classified with households of rich widows whose sons were priests. This classification greatly reduced the chances of his family's having to provide service. If called, it was permitted to employ substitutes to do the actual work.[51] The gazette of Yen prefecture in the Ching-ting period (1260–64) also records instances in which the authorities granted perpetual freedom from the service burden to sons famous for their filial behavior.[52]

45. *HNYL* 18.37a (1128).
46. *SHY, shih-huo* 14.27a (1137); T'o T'o et al., 34.6b.
47. *HNYL* 85.1399–1400 (1135); ibid. 161.2628 (1150).
48. *HNYL* 161.2611 (1150); *SHY, shih-huo* 66.30a.
49. *HNYL* 96.1585 (1133).
50. *SHY, shih-huo* 14.42b.
51. *SHY, shih-huo* 14.27b.
52. Cheng Yao and Fang Jen-yung, *Ching-ting Yen Cho Hsü Chih* (Ts'ung-shu Chi Ch'eng ed.), 5.65.

Another seemingly more numerous privileged group was households headed by Buddhist and Taoist priests. Originally the privileges had been accorded practicing clergy as a sign of the ruler's respect for religion and for the contributions the priests made to the proper functioning of society. By the Southern Sung, a "priest" was someone who held a certificate of ordination, and the government sold such certificates to raise revenue. The buyers were probably mostly affluent commoners who wanted the advantages attached to the classification of monk. Thus, this status, initially awarded in recognition of social and religious contributions, came to be one way in which the wealthy could avoid bearing their share of the costs of administration.[53]

Like some other privileged groups, Buddhist and Taoist clergy were first forced to contribute toward the provision of local services by the reforms of Wang An-shih. They continued to pay under the later Northern Sung and the Southern Sung, although at a reduced rate after the *Yüan-yu* period (1086–94).[54]

During the first decade of the Southern Sung the village service privileges of this classification were reduced very sharply. Households headed by rich Buddhist and Taoist priests could be conscripted like ordinary households. Their only remaining service privilege was the right to engage replacements.[55]

By far the most important honored families during the Southern Sung were official households (*kuan-hu*)—households headed by an official or in some cases by the descendants of officials. *Kuan-hu* had been privileged under the

53. For descriptions of the sale of monk certificates in Sung times see Yüan Chen, "Liang Sung Tu-tieh K'ao," *Chung-kuo She-hui Ching-chi Shih Chi K'an* 7, no. 1 (June 1944): 41ff. See also Kenneth Ch'en, "The Sale of Monk Certificates," *Harvard Theological Review* 49: 307–27.

54. *SHY, shih-huo* 66.60a–b.

55. *SHY, shih-huo* 14.24b (1135), 14.31a (1149); T'o T'o et al., 34.12a (1171); *SHY, shih-huo* 65.101b (1173); *HNYL* 88.1472.

T'ang dynasty[56] and under the Northern Sung.[57] They were free from the obligation to serve as village officers (and at times, apparently, from some taxes); in effect and in intent these rewards were part of their salaries.[58] At the beginning of the Northern Sung these privileges seem to have been confined to ranked civil servants of the seventh grade or higher,[59] but in 1036 they apparently were extended to all graded officials, their sons, and their grandsons.[60]

The advantages of *kuan-hu* increased the burden on ordinary households and decreased the revenues available to the state. In Sung times this problem was particularly serious. *Kuan-hu* were very numerous, largely because of the multitude of supernumerary officials. Their number was also swelled by the sale of rank and the use of "protection" (*yin*), which allowed some officials to pass their status on to their heirs.[61] During the Northern Sung these *kuan-hu* were major landholders, and the concentration of property in the hands of official families was apparently even greater under the Southern Sung.[62] This trend toward estate building by *kuan-hu* continued to plague state authorities to the end of the dynasty. In 1246 it was said that "the property holdings of *kuan-hu*, who are exempt from service obligations (*pao-i*), grow by the day."[63]

During the Southern Sung so much property was owned by *kuan-hu* and was therefore partly exempt from fiscal obligations that one author, Han Yüan-chi defined cantons where holdings of land by officials were particularly large as

56. "SIFS" p. 212.
57. For the situation under the early Northern Sung see *SHY, shih-huo* 1.19b–20a (1022).
58. Their exemption was not total. In the early Northern Sung they could be called on to provide someone to serve as an Elder. See *TSKSK* p. 636.
59. *HCP* 108.5a.
60. Ibid.
61. *SZS* p. 448.
62. *TSKSK* pp. 623–35.
63. T'o T'o et al., 173.26a–b.

"narrow cantons" (*hsia hsiang*) and cantons where the proportion of land held by *kuan-hu* was small as "broad cantons" (*k'uan hsiang*).[64] The term "narrow canton" had been used in previous times to describe an area where the population was dense in proportion to arable land. "Broad cantons" were areas where the population was sparse relative to the land available. It was assumed that in broad cantons more people were well-to-do and thereby eligible for service obligations.[65] Han Yüan-chi's redefinition of the terms "broad" and "narrow" reveals the seriousness of the problems caused by official estate building in the Southern Sung. He poses the quandary succinctly: "If a case should arise in which all the property in a canton were owned by official households without their having exceeded their quotas of obligation free land, who would be called to perform village services?"[66]

The government tried to solve the *kuan-hu* problem in three ways: by defining more precisely the qualifications necessary before a family could be listed as a *kuan-hu*; by reducing the advantages of that status; and by limiting the amount of land that an official household could own free

64. Han Yüan-chi, *Nan Chien Chia I Kao* (Wu Ying Tien Chü Chen Pan Chüan Shu ed.), 10.5a–b.
65. Huang Kan, *Mien Chai Chi* 25.7a ff. Yeh Shih portrays the same situation with more exactness. He notes that, in Ch'ui-i canton of Yung-chia subprefecture, thirteen households owned over four hundred and one *mou* of land; 59 households owned 151–400 *mou*, and 312 households owned 30–150 *mou*. But in Hsiao-i canton only 3 families owned more than 400 *mou*, 27 owned 151–400 *mou*, and 207 owned 30–150 *mou*. If all these households in both cantons were commoner households and thus liable for services, Ch'ui-i would obviously have been considered "broader" than Hsiao-i. But, since *kuan-hu* holdings were partly exempt from obligations, wherever *kuan-hu* owned a great deal of property the number of those liable was reduced. If, for example, in Ch'ui-i 11 of the 13 households in the richest group, and 50 of the 59 households in the second group were *kuan-hu*, while all the rich families in Hsiao-i were commoners, Ch'ui-i would in effect have been "narrower" than Hsiao-i. Yeh Shih, *Shui Hsin Wen-chi*, 16.12a.
66. Han Yüan-chi, 10.5a–b.

of obligations—an official household of a given rank could own a specified amount of property free from service obligations (and apparently at some times from some taxes), but any land owned above that quota was treated as if it belonged to a commoner family.

The policy of restricting the amount of obligation-free property that an official household could own was initially adopted in 1022 as one means of reducing the inequitability of a service system which overburdened ordinary households.[67] During the Southern Sung the policy of limiting landholdings was based on rules promulgated in the Cheng-ho period (1111–18). Restrictions applied to graded officials, and the aggregate that could be possessed free from obligations varied with rank. A first-grade official could hold one hundred *ch'ing* (about 1,513 acres) , a second-grade official ninety *ch'ing*, and so on down to a ninth-grade official who could own ten *ch'ing* (about 151 acres). Land beyond these quotas was treated as if it belonged to commoners and was thus subject to regular taxes and service obligations.[68]

During the Southern Sung the privileges of descendants of officials were sharply reduced. In 1159 it was ordered that the quantity of obligation-free land that could be held by a *kuan-hu* be reduced by half if the household's status was derived from an ancestor already deceased. A first-grade official could own one hundred *ch'ing*. Each of his heirs could possess fifty *ch'ing*.[69] In 1165 *kuan-hu* privileges were

67. *SHY, shih-huo* 1.19b–20b; Ma Tuan-lin, 12.128. This continued to be one justification of the system. *SHY, shih-huo* 61.80a (1170); *HNYL* 181.3009. Soon after its initial adoption in 1022 the policy was temporarily abrogated. See Maritami Katsumi, *Chung-kuo She-hui Ching-chi Shih* (Chung Hua Shu Chü), p. 206.

68. *SHY, shih-huo* 61.78a. This policy of land limitation must not be confused with the celebrated reforms introduced by Chia Ssu-tao in 1261–64. These reforms are only peripherally relevant to my main interest, and so I have not discussed them. For a description of them see H. Franke, "Die Agrarreformen des Chia Ssu-tao." *Saeculum* 9(1958).

69. *SHY, shih-huo* 6.2a–4a; *HNYL* 181.3009; Li Hsin-ch'uan,

further curtailed when it was ordered that all the heirs to official status could own together in total only half their ancestors' quota.[70] The rank to be used in determining the land quota varied according to the situation of the official in question. According to the rules in force at this time, when official households were headed by a living active civil servant, his current rank was to be used in determining the quota. When *kuan-hu* status was based on positions held by a father or grandfather who was no longer active, or on the rank of a man given posthumous office, the quota was half that allowed an active official of the rank in question. If there was a living grandfather of low official rank dwelling with a descendant who had a higher rank, the higher rank was to be used in setting quotas. Under the quota system all the land owned by a household in a prefecture was treated as a whole, even if located in several subprefectures. Special officials were to draw up the registers of official landholdings.[71]

Although *kuan-hu*, even within the quota allotment, could own enough property to be extremely wealthy by the standards of nonofficials,[72] they still tried in various ways to

---

Chien-yen I-lai Chao-yeh Tsa Chi (Ts'ung-shu Chi Ch'eng ed.), *chia-chi* 15.205. Hereafter cited *CYTC*. In the *HNYL* and the *CYTC* Li Hsin-ch'uan says that the memorial suggesting this limit was submitted by Chao Hsi-yang. *SHY, shih-huo* 61.78b, also says that it was submitted by Chao Hsi-yang. These limits applied both to land held in the name of the *kuan-hu* and land owned by them but held by tenants.

70. *SHY, shih-huo* 6.5a.

71. *SHY, shih-huo* 61.78b–79a. It was also noted that if an official was raised in rank (and therefore was given an increased quota of obligation-free land) after he had already been made responsible for services on the basis of his previous quota, he still had to finish paying for the requisition.

72. *Huang Sung Chung-hsing Liang Ch'ao Sheng Cheng*, 62.10b–11a.

evade the laws limiting exempt landholdings.[73] The state responded by tightening the rules against cheating.

An official said: "The court recently acceded to the request of the Intendants of Liang-che that the time limit for presenting registers (*chieh-pang*—that is to say, declarations of property owned) be two seasons. It was ordered that, if the families of officials and of ordinary people who have used fictitious names to conceal ownership of property have not come forward to confess by the end of this period of grace, they can be accused by canton scribes and others. [Now as for the problem of] those who have not themselves come forward to confess that they fraudulantly concealed ownership of property, even though the time limit for confessing is about to expire, I humbly say that, if you want to remedy this problem, the best thing would be to order the prefects to select one capable and honest subordinate official from each subprefecture, again extend the time limit, and have these appointed men devise ways and means to solve the problem. . . ." A decree ordered P'an Ching-kuei to design measures, investigate, and memorialize. Thereupon P'an Ching-kuei said, "In each subprefecture I desire that you set up wooden boxes (*mu kuei*) with two openings. These boxes will be locked and sealed [and put] on the subprefecture gate. Those who have falsified their names in order to conceal ownership of property will be permitted to insert in one of the openings true depositions (*shih feng*), personally confessing [their misdemeanor] within an extended time limit of ten days. [At the end of the ten day period] the subprefectural administrator should personally open up the box. Then [those men who had inserted depositions] should be listed with households that avoided guilt by confessing fraudulent land registration when pressed by the clerks(?). [As for] the other opening, when the time limit has passed various sorts of men including the incumbent servicemen in the yamen, yamen clerks, Canton Scribes, and even Superior Guard Leaders and their Assistants, Guard Chiefs, Household Chiefs, Messengers, and tax

73. *SHY, shih-huo* 6.2a (1159).

collecting householders should be permitted to write true depositions accusing people of falsifying names to conceal ownership of land.[74]

The problem posed by falsification of land ownership titles was also attacked in other more radical ways. In 1170, at the suggestion of the Secretariat-Chancellory, a system was tried in Liang-che under which landholding by *kuan-hu* was not limited but *kuan-hu* were not given exemptions from service burdens. Official households whose holdings ranked them in the first or second grade were to be drafted for two-year service terms. They were privileged only in that they were allowed to hire substitutes.[75] In 1185 an imperial order concluded that this policy was advantageous and instructed the Ministry of Finance to investigate it in detail.[76] Despite imperial interest and encouragement, the system does not seem to have been widely used.[77]

Other reforms were proposed but apparently not enacted. In 1180 it was suggested that the quota of obligation free property be cut by 30 percent.[78] Between 1142 and 1178, Han Yüan-chi suggested a "three-part reform." The territory of a canton was to be divided into three equal parts. *Kuan-hu* would only be allowed to own one-third of this total area free from obligations. If any individual *kuan-hu* owned more than its allotment under the Cheng-ho rules, it could be called for services. If all the *kuan-hu* holdings together exceeded one-third of the area of the canton, then—even if no individual *kuan-hu* exceeded its quota—

74. *SHY, shih-huo* 66.24a–25a (1190).

75. *SHY, shih-huo* 14.45b. This memorial was in response to a request of the emperor Hsiao-tsung that the high officials consider the problem of services. *SHY, shih-huo* 61.80a.

76. *SHY, shih-huo* 66.23b.

77. We know that systems of limiting landholding continued to be used. *SHY, shih-huo* 6.9a (1199). See T'o T'o et al., 173.26a–b. For the drive toward an equal treatment of *kuan-hu* and commoners see Hsieh Shen-fu, *Ch'ing-yüan T'iao-fa Shih-lei*, 48.24a–b.

78. *SHY, shih-huo* 6.7a–b.

the excess land owned by *kuan-hu* would be treated as if it belonged to commoners.[79]

The system of 1022 for restricting obligation-free landholdings was only the first step in reducing *kuan-hu* privileges. Under the reforms of Wang An-shih, official households also had to contribute "aid money" to help defray the costs of *i-fa*. The rate of payment was halved during the Yüan-yu period (1086–94).[80] *Kuan-hu* continued to pay at this reduced rate until the early Southern Sung. Then, in 1128, the amount paid by *kuan-hu* was raised to the same as that paid by ordinary families.[81]

The tariff was again cut in 1132, but in 1166 the Court agreed to a request that *kuan-hu* pay at the same rate as ordinary families.[82]

The advantages of official households were even more sharply curtailed in 1147, when the Court agreed to a request that, except for the privilege of avoiding being called for village services on a fixed quota of land, *kuan-hu* should provisionally be treated like ordinary households.

By the middle of the twelfth century, official households had thus been stripped of many privileges. Their fields now apparently bore the full land tax.[83] They were subject to

79. Han Yüan-chi, 10.5a–b. Han does not explain how he would decide which *kuan-hu* would be called on to bear the resulting burdens.
80. "SIFS" p. 262.
81. *SHY, shih-huo* 14.17a; Ma Tuan-lin, 13.137; Chao Ting, 50.9b; Ch'en Fu-liang, *Chih Chai Wen-chi*, 21.1b.
82. *SHY, shih-huo* 14.20a (1132); *SHY, shih-huo* 65.96b; *CYTC chia* 15.205. See also Chang Hsiao-hsiang, *Yü-hu Chu-shih Wen-chi* (Ssu Pu Ts'ung K'an ed.), 17.9b.
83. *SHY, shih-huo* 6.1b–2a. For many tax collection purposes *kuan-hu* and ordinary households had been provisionally treated alike since the 1130's. *HNYL* 78.1277. In law, taxes had been imposed on them from the early years of the dynasty (Ma Tuan-lin, 4.55) although *SHY, shih-huo* 6.1b–2a, makes it clear that in the early Southern Sung they were not expected to pay regular taxes. These orders call for provisional extension of taxes, but I have found no evidence that they were rescinded.

most other Sung imposts. Their major remaining advantage was that they could own a set amount of property without its being included in the assessment of village service burdens, and, when called for service duty, they generally could hire substitutes. Under certain exceptional circumstances they might even have to serve in person. Chu Hsi cites the example of Chiang Fei, who in the mid–twelfth century had to act as a Superior Guard Leader.[84] Chu Hsi complains that *kuan-hu* in his day (circa 1180) no longer were called for personal service because this policy of personal service embarrassed and inconvenienced local authorities.[85] However, there is evidence that, during the last decades of the Southern Sung, *kuan-hu* were sometimes put in charge of tax collection.[86]

Despite proposed and enacted restrictions there were still substantial benefits attached to official-household status. Men therefore tried in various ways to get their households classified as *kuan-hu*.[87] Sometimes men falsely claimed descent from local officials,[88] even making false gravestones to prove their case.[89] Very rich men contributed during emergencies or natural disasters and then used their honorary titles to avoid service.[90] Rich men might also purchase registration in the army or, through favoritism, secure titles

84. Chiang Fei graduated number one in the examinations during the middle of the Shao-hsing period (1131–63). He was active in official life during the last half of the twelfth century.

85. Li Ching te, *Chu Tzu Yü Lei*, 98.24b–25a.

86. Hu T'ai-ch'u, *Chou Lien Hsü Lun*, p. 12.

87. *SHY, shih-huo* 61.79b.

88. Yüan Ts'ai, *Yüan Shih Shih Fan* (Chih Pu Tsu Chai Ts'ung-shu ed.), 3.21a.

89. Liu Pan, *P'en Ch'eng Chi* (SSu K'u Ch'üan Shu ed.), 35.24a–b.

90. Li Chao-ch'i, *Yüeh Ching Chi* (Ssu K'u Ch'üan Shu Chen Pen ed.), 29.5b–9a; Feng Shih-hsing, *Chin Yün Wen-chi* (Ssu K'u Ch'üan Shu Chen Pen ed.), 4.2b–3b. For instance, in 1135 it was ordered that because of the need for famine relief grain anyone contributing 1,000 bushels would be awarded titles as *ti kung lang* or *ch'eng hsin lang* and classified as *kuan-hu*. HNYL 96.1584.

as supplementary officials (*pu-kuan*), which gave them *kuan-hu* status.⁹¹ T'ung Kuan is blamed for initiating a rule that men with purchased rank could be treated as *kuan-hu*. In the early Southern Sung these men with the titles of *ti kung lang* or *ch'eng hsin lang* would use the protection (*yin*) privilege to pass their privileges on for two generations,⁹² but in 1167 this was forbidden.⁹³ Men could also attain *kuan-hu* status by marrying members of the imperial clan.⁹⁴

Partly to counteract the increasing number of *kuan-hu* whose status was based on "protection" or on originally honorary offices, the Southern Sung government defined qualifications for official household classification ever more exactly as the decades passed. Since the privileges were justified as part of a bureaucrat's salary, it was obviously unfair to extend them to men not in fact acting as officials. Between 1134 and 1186, a succession of edicts dealt with the benefits of a variety of groups that had gained their official status in irregular ways: men who had been granted titles because they had contributed grain in times of emergency (1134);⁹⁵ men who were merely relatives of the imperial clan (1138);⁹⁶ *pao-chia* personnel classified as officials be-

91. *SHY, shih-huo* 6.1b–2b (1147).
92. *HNYL,* 77.1270.
93. *SHY, shih-huo* 14.41b.
94. Chu Yü, *P'ing Chou K'o T'an* (Ts'ung-shu Chi Ch'eng ed.), 1.3–4; Chang Pang-chi, *Mo Chuang Man Lu* (Ts'ung-shu Chi Ch'eng ed.), 10.107; Chao Pu-chih, *Chi Chu Chi* (Ssu Pu Ts'ung K'an ed.), 62.6a–14b; *SHY, shih-huo* 14.27b (1138); Hsieh Shen-fu, 48.25a–b.
95. In 1134 it was ordered that the men who gained office as irregular military officials of the sixth rank or lower through having contributed grain were to be given exemption for liability for services on five *ch'ing* of land. If they owned more than five *ch'ing*, they were liable for requisition on this excess amount. See *SHY, shih-huo* 14.22a; *HNYL* 78.1275. In 1149 it was noted that men who gained office through contribution but were not of titular court rank were liable for services but could hire replacements. *SHY, shih-huo* 14.31a.
96. In 1138 it was ordered that men who had married members of the imperial clan but who did not hold titular court rank were liable

cause they had gained honor in battle or in bandit suppression (1138);[97] *pao-chia* personnel who had official status without either military merit or merit from bandit suppression (1138);[98] descendants of supplementary officials of certain ranks (1150 and 1167);[99] or descendants of men given titles posthumously (1183);[100] supplementary officials who were of titular court rank (1156);[101] and various other supplementary officials (1186).[102] Rules were also drawn up to cover mixed cases in which some family members were regular officials and some were not.[103]

Two factors seem to have entered into decisions regarding the extension of privileges—rank, and whether the of-

---

for requisition but could hire substitutes. *SHY, shih-huo* 14.27b–28a.

97. In 1138 it was ordered that such men, if they were not of titular court rank, were eligible for services but could use substitutes. Ibid. See also *SHY, shih-huo* 14.32a.

98. Such men were liable unless they had reached the rank of *tai-fu* or above, but they could hire replacements. *SHY, shih-huo* 14.27b–28a; ibid., *shih-huo* 14.32a.

99. In 1150, rules were laid down covering several types of inheritance, and in 1167 these rules were further refined. *SHY, shih-huo* 14.32a (1150); *SHY, shih-huo* 65.96b (1167).

100. *SHY, shih-huo* 6.7b.

101. Most such men were to be considered as *kuan-hu* according to an order of this date. *SHY, shih-huo* 14.33a.

102. In 1186 it was decreed that non-irregular supplementary officials (*fei fan pu kuan*) and the seven sorts of supplementary officials (*ch'i se pu kuan*) who did not hold substantive posts in the Court, even if they held high rank, were not covered by the rules on limiting obligation-free landholding and were not free from being called for services. *SHY, shih-huo* 66.24a; T'o T'o et al., 35.18a. Rules also covered "specially selected names" (*t'e tsou ming*) and "irregular students" who wanted *kuan-hu* status. *SHY, shih-huo* 14.42a.

103. In 1138 it was ordered that a household containing three adult males—one a graded official, one not an official but entitled to the protection privilege (and therefore freed from service obligations so long as he lived in the household of the graded official), and one a commoner without the protection privilege, who had made contributions (without being raised to titular court rank)—had to provide village services although substitutes could be hired to do the work. *SHY, shih-huo* 14.27b–28a.

fice held was nominal or substantive. If the rank was high enough, even purely honorary titles usually carried with them the benefits of exemption;[104] if the office was substantive, in most cases it meant freedom from the service obligation.

The individual decrees dealing with the definition of *kuan-hu* status are elaborate and technical to the point of obscurity, but the general trend of which they form a part is quite clear. The Sung dynasty was a period marked by continuing attempts to reduce the number of people qualified in irregular ways for privileged status, and by the progressive reduction of the benefits attached to most such statuses. The tendency was to treat families as equal except for the criterion of wealth, but to extend to larger and larger groups the right to hire substitutes to do the actual work of village services.

The underlying causes of this trend are somewhat less obvious. However, it may be suggested that the reduction of privileges and the expanded use of commutation was merely a partial expression of the general transformation through which Chinese society was passing.

In the case of official households this transformation seems to have involved a lessening of the gap that separated them from commoner households. Perhaps this was a delayed reaction to the changes that had already occurred in the processes of selecting officials and in the social groups from which they were drawn. Officialdom itself had been transformed from a relatively closed group of men, many of whom secured their status through family connections or favoritism, to a more open body of examined scholar-bureaucrats drawn in large part from moderately well-to-do families very like those that provided village officers. The

104. This was true despite a feeling that substantive benefits such as fiscal exemptions should not be given to those holding purely honorary offices. *SHY, shih-huo* 6.7b (1183).

mandarinate had become less a privileged class and more a professional status group.

The decline in the privileges of Buddhist and Taoist clergy is probably best seen as a particular expression of the manifest decline in the influence of these religions on the life of the Chinese elite during this era. The lessened prestige of the religious life is also reflected in the growth and abuse of the system of selling monk certificates. Originally designed as a measure for controlling the religious community, this certificate system became through abuse a part of the government's regular fiscal system and a loophole through which the rich could reduce their financial obligations. It is hardly surprising that the state should belatedly move to restrict the privileges of such "clergy."

The reduction of the privileges accorded to some disadvantaged household types cannot be understood except when viewed against the general economic conditions of the era. It was the rise and spread of a money economy that made feasible the drafting of rich disadvantaged households. To call them and demand personal service would have been most unfair; to call them while extending to them the right to hire substitutes was both reasonable and just.

While it would be unwise to overemphasize the degree of these changes or their impact on Chinese society, it is important to understand their direction. Sung society seems to have been moving toward a more open social system, within which distinctions of status and personal condition were diminished in importance if not in numbers, while wealth per se became a key determinant of position in the rural social hierarchy.

6

Registration and Grading of Households

Information is power. The breakdown of the mechanisms that supply information to a government, or the interruption of its orderly flow upward, places the future of the rulers in jeopardy. As the size of the unit governed increases, the continuous working of these mechanisms seems necessarily to involve the collection and preservation of records—in the past, largely written documents.

The Sung, like previous Chinese dynasties, created many types of registers. Compiled by the village officers and local clerks, the various registers were supposed to be revised periodically; in practice, revision was not carried out as it should have been. Registers were usually presumed to be uniform in format throughout the empire; in fact there was considerable regional variation in their content and method of compilation.

Although no copies of these Sung documents now exist, enough partial examples can be drawn from printed materials to permit description of their general contents and uses, if not to answer adequately questions of regional character or temporal evolution. These examples reveal a government that dealt with its subjects as household units, and grouped these units into types based on wealth, role, and condition. "Condition" was mainly concerned with normal status, or disadvantaged status such as that of a household headed by a woman, having a single adult male, living in an area other than that of the root family, or led by young, sick, aged, or disabled individuals. Households were divided by social role into official households, households headed by Buddhist or Taoist clergy, several other small but honored groups, and commoners. Wealth had always been one of the chief criteria used in determining the assignment of fiscal burdens to the people. With the reduction of the benefits of privileged statuses during the Southern Sung, wealth became even more important as a determinant of liabilities. On the basis of registers of wealth, families were given a household grade which was often utilized in levying imposts. Finally, other sorts of documents were compiled on the basis of these registers of wealth, which thus were the key records in the local fiscal structure of the time.

Since land ownership was the major source of economic power in rural Sung China, property records were the most significant indicators of affluence. Village officers drew up these land registers. Copies were stored in the local offices. Changes in control of land were entered on the current records—a procedure called *t'ui-ko*.[1] Every three years new copies were to be created and the old ones sent to the prefecture for storage.[2] This triennial adjustment and the changing of the grades of households that accompanied it was called *t'ui-p'ai*.[3] According to law, adjustment should have happened every third year,[4] but in practice it did not occur for decades in many regions.[5]

1. "SIFS" p. 260.

2. *SHY, shih-huo* 6.36a–40a.

3. "SIFS" p. 260. There were areas of the empire where *t'ui-p'ai* was not practiced, for instance Hunan, Chiang-nan East, and Chiang-nan West circuits. *SHY, shih-huo* 66.23a–b, 28a.

4. *SHY, shih-huo* 69.23b (1142). It seems to have been felt that, given the rapidity with which the economic standing of a household might change in Sung China, a longer period would lead to inequities. Some men even felt that three years was too long. *HAHS* 18.16a.

5. Cheng Yao and Fang Jen-yung, *Ching-ting Yen Chou Hsü Chih*, 2.22 for Yen prefecture; Chao Shan-kua, *Ying-chai Tsa-chu*, 1.6a for the capital region; Liao Hsing-chih, *Sheng Chai Chi*, 5.14a–15b for

The inaccuracies resulting from infrequent rectification of records were compounded by deliberate fraud. Concealing of property ownership, although naturally illegal under Sung law and heavily punished, appears to have been common.[6] The guilty could reduce their sentences by confessing within a limited period after the reranking of households.[7] Sometimes such cheating was done by a family, but at other times the registers were falsified by the village officers. A document dated 1163 says: "If the Superior Guard Leaders or their Assistants have taken bribes to falsify the registers, then the people are allowed to use irregular channels to appeal their rankings."[8] But most frequently the doctoring of records required the cooperation of, or was encouraged by, dishonest clerks in the local yamen. Chen Te-hsiu in 1215 impeached a subprefect for blindly following the advice of his clerks. They had been demanding bribes from the people. If a household paid, the clerks would lower its rank. If it refused, they would raise its rank.[9]

Further problems arose when a household's fields were scattered in several cantons or even in different subprefectures. Moreover, some individuals did not live in the rural areas where they owned land. They might dwell in a nearby city, or in another canton or subprefecture. According to a decree of 1142 such men were to be considered as having a legal residence in one canton.[10]

The legal residence system for city people continued to be used until 1172, when it was abolished on the request of

---

Chiang-tung. See also Yüan Shuo-yu, *Tung T'ang Chi* (Ssu K'u Ch'üan Shu Chen Pen ed.), 10.5b; *KCC* 4.18a–19a; *HSWC* 12.30a; Ts'ao Yen-yüeh, *Ch'ang Ku Chi*, 10.1a; *SHY, shih-huo* 66.28a (1197), 35.15b–16a.

6. *SHY, shih-huo* 14.26a–b (1137); 35.15b–16a.

7. *SHY, shih-huo* 15.28b (1142).

8. *SHY, ping* 2.43a; ibid., *shih-huo* 66.28b for the procedure of irregular appeal.

9. *HSWC* 12.29b. See also *SHY, shih-huo* 66.21b.

10. *SHY, shih-huo* 14.46b, 66.21b, 14.28b.

officials who pointed out that men who had left their villages to dwell in distant cities were not listed on the rural rolls, so that it was extremely difficult to force them to contribute to village services. But the system of fixing a legal residence in one canton was reinstituted in 1179, after it was argued that to allow city dwellers to evade their local responsibilities merely increased the burden on the less well-to-do rural people.[11]

The problem of registering the landholdings of urban residents continued to plague the administration, and some attempts were made to rectify the situation. In 1185 the circuit intendants were ordered to instruct their subordinate prefectures and subprefectures to conduct a reassessment of the holdings of city dwellers during the upcoming slack agricultural season, and in accord with the new information to alter the old registers. It was further stipulated that the records should henceforward be kept up to date. Places that had already made new registers were to inform the Chancellory.[12]

In an empire as large and diverse as Sung China, such an attempt to impose a uniform policy naturally aroused discontent in areas that for legitimate reasons found it difficult to comply. One official who looked into the problem of wealth assessment reported in 1187 that in many areas it would be very difficult to carry out the directive of 1185. He noted that, since promulgation of the order, six prefectures had suffered drought, four had reported delayed tax time limits, one military prefecture had been the scene of warfare, one prefecture had reported that because of internal disorders it had not been able to reassess property, a border prefecture had indicated that it had never practiced property assessment, and many areas had asked for extended limits. Furthermore some regions had traditionally assigned taxes in unusual ways, not depending on

11. *SHY, shih-huo* 66.21b.
12. *SHY, shih-huo* 66.23b.

assessment of total wealth. Chiang-nan East and Chiang-nan West circuits followed a system which depended upon the "land quota" (*mou-t'ou*) rather than on registers of wealth. The official in question requested that the policy of 1185 be used only in areas where it had a local precedent and where prevailing conditions did not hinder its accomplishment.[13]

On the basis of information entered in the property registers, households were divided into resident and nonresident (or "guest") households, and then into grades according to wealth.[14] The term resident household (*chu-hu*) initially referred to families who were living in their registered native places. In Northern Sung times the significance of the terms was primarily fiscal—a resident household was subject to the Twice-a-Year tax and a guest household was not.[15] In the early Southern Sung, cases were reported of families' selling their properties and fleeing, so that they could be enrolled elsewhere as guest households and thus evade their fiscal obligations,[16] but by the late Southern Sung nonresident households came to pay certain taxes and were listed on the *pao-wu* militia rolls.[17]

13. *SHY, shih-huo* 66.23a–b. The document is dated Ch'un-hsi 11.7.12, but this is an error for Ch'un-hsi 13.7.12.

14. During the Northern Sung and the early Southern Sung most taxes and service burdens were levied only against resident households and varied with grade. Southern Sung authors claim classical precedent for such a system. Ch'en Ch'i-ch'ing cites Mencius to prove that making tax and service burdens proportional to land ownership was a "constant principle." *KCC* 4.18a–19a.

15. Yanagida Setsuko, "Sō-dai no kakko ni tsuite," *Shigaku Zasshi* 68, no. 4 (April 1959): 356–96.

16. *HNYL* 88.1471 (1135).

17. A document dated 1205 which includes an example of the format of these *pao-wu* registers first describes the information recorded about resident households and then says: "Such and such men head guest households. They originally are from such and such a place. They have been in this village for so many years. They pay the following taxes. They own so much land. They have so many adult males." *SHY, shih-huo* 66.29a–b.

Grades determined by economic standing were used in determining liability for some obligations, including, in some instances, the village service duties. The measures used were not absolute. A family worth a certain number of strings of cash might be rated a first-grade family in a poor area but only a second- or third-grade family in a richer area. During the first decades of the Northern Sung, resident rural households were divided into nine grades. Grades one through four were accountable for village services; grades five through nine were exempt.[18] The government apparently continued to use these nine grade registers for certain purposes during the rest of the Northern and the whole of the Southern Sung period,[19] but most evidence indicates that in rural areas, at least after 1022, the Sung generally used five grade registers in assessing *i-fa* and the Twice-a-Year tax.[20] It seems possible that this five-grade sys-

18. *SZS* p. 97; *HCP* 21.2b. This nine-grade system originated under the Northern Ch'i emperor Wen-hsüan (550–59). See Etienne Balazs, *Le traité économique du "Souei-chou"* (Leiden: E. J. Brill, 1953), p. 142. See also Ma Tuan-lin, *Wen Hsien T'ung K'ao*, 12.127. It continued to be used under succeeding dynasties, and in the T'ang village officers were selected from these nine-grade registers. This type of nine-grade register apparently continued to be the legal norm under the Five Dynasties, but in practice the household registers were frequently lost or destroyed. For this reason, in 963 Sung T'ai-tsu ordered a recompilation of household lists. Apparently women were not included in these early Sung lists. *HCP* 4.22a. It is possible that they also did not include the old, the young, and the disabled—that is to say, they included only adult healthy males. For legal purposes an adult male was a male between twenty and sixty years old (Chinese style). *HCP* 4.22a.

19. See *SHY, shih-huo* 66.25a–b (1190), which indicates the existence of nine-grade registers which were used in assessing *ho-mai*. The lower five grades were exempt. Mei Ying-fa, *K'ai-ch'ing Ssu-ming Hsü Chih* (Sung Yüan Ssu-ming Liu Chih ed.), 7.3b. This work will be cited hereafter as *KCSMHC*.

20. These grade registers were called *ting-ch'an pu, ting-k'ou pu,* and *wu-teng pu. HCP* 179.7b–9a; Chang Fang-p'ing, *Lo Ch'üan Chi* (National Library of Peking microfilms). 26.4a; *SHY, shih-huo* 11.13a, 1.19b–20a; Ch'en Fu-liang, *Chih Chai Wen-chi*, 21.2b. This division of the population into five grades had a precedent in Sung use of five

tem was not employed continuously in the decades following 1022,²¹ but it was the system used in the Hired Service System of Wang An-shih. In 1071, in order to exact money to pay for services, the rural population was divided into five main grades. These five grades were then subdivided: the top grade into five ranks, the second grade and third grades into three ranks, and the fourth and fifth grades into two ranks. In each subprefecture five registers were drawn up— one for each grade. On these records the households were listed in order according to their wealth.²²

During the Southern Sung the top four grades of wealthy households bore far heavier service responsibilities than

---

grades in assessing certain special exactions. For instance, in the spring of 962 T'ai-tsu ordered the revival of a latter Chou system, which divided the people into five grades for purposes of assessing contributions of lumber. *HCP* 2.5b.

21. *SZS* p. 98.

22. Ch'en Fu-liang, 21.2b. See also *SHY, shih-huo* 11.14b (1124). These registers were based on the tax vouchers (*yu-tzu*). *TITC* 3.18a. See also Wang Yang, *Tung Mou Chi* (Ssu K'u Ch'üan Shu Chen Pen ed.), 9.22b–24b; *HNYL* 140.2245; *SHY, shih-huo* 14.38a, 11.16b. This five-grade system was used only in rural areas. Cities had their own classification policy from the early part of the Northern Sung. We are told by Ou-yang Hsiu that in the cities the population was divided into ten grades. *SZS* pp. 98–99. This ten-grade system was used under the hired service system of Wang An-shih, and continued to be used under the Southern Sung. *SZS* p. 99; *SHY, shih-huo* 14.38a (1161), 1.13a, 69.23b. The top three grades were sometimes called "upper households" (*shang-hu*), and the lower two grades "lower households" (*hsia-hu*). Sun Yü-t'ang "Kuan-yü Pei Sung Fu-i Chih-tu Te Fan Ke Wen-t'i," *Li-shih Yen-chiu*, no 2 (1964), p. 148; *HNYL* 158.2573. Unfortunately for those reading Sung documents, the writers of Sung times also sometimes divided the five grades into three categories— "upper households" (*shang-hu*), which comprised first grade households, "middle households" (*chung-hu*), including second- and third-grade households, and "lower households" (*hsia-hu*), which comprised fourth and fifth grade households. *SHY, shih-huo* 10.19b; Ch'en Fu-liang, 21.2b. Thus, when a document simply refers to upper households or lower households, it is often impossible to tell whether the author is thinking of the two-category division or the three-category division of households.

the more numerous fifth-grade households. Lü Tsu-ch'ien, writing in the second half of the twelfth century, reported that in Yen prefecture in Chiang-che circuit there were only 10,718 adult males in grades one through four, but 71,479 adult males in fifth-grade resident households.[23] Village officers were generally drawn from grades one through four, but fifth-grade households, although legally exempt, were sometimes used as Household Chiefs[24] and Small Guard Chiefs.[25] In addition these poor households were liable for conscription for corvée labor (*yao-i*).[26]

Fifth-grade households were called for village services only irregularly and apparently illegally, but fourth-grade families were regularly used. Under the early Northern Sung, Stalwart Men were drawn from fourth-grade households,[27] and under the service system of 1071, Household Chiefs were from this grade.[28] During the Southern Sung, fourth-grade households were sometimes called on to supply Small Guard Chiefs.[29] Before 1156 they might also be called for Large Guard Chiefs,[30] and two separate memorials indicate that they were even being used as Superior Guard Leaders and their Assistants.[31]

A memorial of 1161 indicates the irregularity of levying Superior Guard Leaders or Assistants from fourth-grade households, the writer expressing his dismay that men as far down as the third grade were being called for these posts.[32] In fact these posts seem regularly to have been filled

23. Lü Tsu-ch'ien *Tung Lai Chi* (Hsü Chin Hua Ts'ung-shu ed.), 3.1a–2b.
24. *SHY, shih-huo* 66.28a–b.
25. *SHY, shih-huo* 65.89b (1158), 66.31a (1212).
26. *SHY, shih-huo* 14.45a (1170).
27. Liang K'o-chia, *Ch'un-hsi San Shan Chih*, 14.5b.
28. Ch'en Fu-liang, 21.2a.
29. *SHY, shih-huo* 65.89b (1157), 66.31a (1212).
30. *SHY, shih-huo* 65.89b (1156); Shu Lin, *Shu Wen Ching Kung Chi*, 3.11b; *HAHS* 21.327; Lin Hsiu-chung, *Chu Hsüan Tsa Chu*, 3.8a.
31. *SHY, shih-huo* 14.45a (1170), 65.95b (1167).
32. *SHY, shih-huo* 14.38a–39a.

by men from the top three grades—from upper (*shang*) and middle (*chung*) households.[33] After the reform of 1156, middle households also appear to have supplied most Large Guard Chiefs.[34]

Naturally, men wanted to avoid being enrolled in these higher grades. At times, rather than bear the burdens associated with high grade, families would sell their property and become itinerant workers or guest households or simply abandon their homes and flee.[35]

Information on grade was also included in other documents, which the yamen clerks compiled on the basis of wealth registers and records supplied by the village officers.[36] These other documents were necessary if miscellaneous levies were to be gathered,[37] if the militia was to function properly,[38] and most pertinently if the assignment of accountability for providing services was to be equitable.

Special registers seem to have been employed in determining service assignments. Village officers and yamen clerks cooperated in their compilation. On the lowest level, village officers drew up records of property and militia rolls. On the basis of the information in these records the clerks then made lists for the selection of servicemen.[39] One source indicates that three copies of the service selection registers were needed—one for the superior guard, one for the subprefecture, and one for the prefecture. Every seven years

33. *HAHS* 18.270. Lin Hsiu-chung asked in 1132 that Superior Guard Leaders always be from first-grade households. Lin Hsiu-chung, 3.8a; See also *SHY, shih-huo* 14.40a (1164), 14.38a–39a (1161), 65.95b (1167).

34. *SHY, shih-huo* 14.33b–34a (1156), 65.89b (1157); Shu Lin, 3.11b; *HAHS* 21.326; Lin Hsiu-chung, 3.8a.

35. Lin Hsiu-chung, 3.8a (1132); *SHY, shih-huo* 14.36b.

36. *SHY, shih-huo* 14.22b.

37. For a description of the records used in collecting under the *ho-mai* system, see *SHY, shih-huo* 66.25b–26a.

38. *SHY, shih-huo* 66.29a–b; *CHTK* 2.23.

39. *SHY, shih-huo* 14.22b, 66.29a–b.

the old copies seem to have been sent to the legal offices for storage.[40]

The nature of these service registers is not wholly clear. Contemporary witnesses call them by different names, which in some cases may be synonyms. In other cases the discrepancies may stem from varying local customs or from changes over time. In general these registers were of two types: one type, based on the subprefecture as the unit, divided the people into five grades, each of which had its own register; the other type, based on the smaller *pao-chia* units, did not divide the people into grades. Ch'en Fu-liang, criticizing the Southern Sung village officer system because it followed *pao-chia* precedents and not the older village service precedents, said:

> The service system (*i-fa*) used the Five-Grade Registers (*wu-teng pu*). The *pao-chia* system used the Fish Scale Registers (*yu-lin pu*). The Five-Grade Registers were based on the whole subprefecture as the unit. From the first [grade] down to [the fifth grade], using the wealth of the households [as the basis for arrangement] each [grade] made a register. The Fish Scale Registers were based on the neighborhood units. From the first guard to the last, one register was drawn up [for each guard] without consideration being given differences in wealth. [Under the Five-Grade System] each [grade] had its own register. Thus, among first-grade households, even if they differed in wealth, they still were all "upper households." In the second grade, although there were different degrees of opulence, [the households] were still all "middle households." Their strengths were generally comparable and therefore the assessments of services were equitable. [But, if you base the assessment of services on the Fish Scale Registers, this will be unjust, for, if all the families in a superior guard] are put together in one register, when there are many well-to-do families in the superior guard the length of time between their being called

40. *KCSMHC* 7.3b.

for services will be long, but if the superior guard has numerous poor households then [the few families rich enough to be called for services] will have only short terms of leisure from services. Or, if all the households in a [guard] are poor, some will unavoidably be placed in the first or second grades and treated as rich households and they will have no leisure. Because the wealth of households differs so greatly, the burdens of service is inequitable. When the *pao-chia* was initially practiced, it was charged with control of banditry and that was all. At first it had no connection with the hired service system. But, in 1074, for the first time they used *pao-chia* militia personnel to act as Heads of Tithing to gather taxes, and Elders, Household Chiefs, and Stalwart Men were abolished.[41]

Ch'en wanted the authorities to separate the *i-fa* from the *pao-chia* and hoped that service personnel would again be chosen from the Five-Grade rather than the Fish Scale type of register.[42] In practice both sorts of registers seem to have been used. A contemporary of Ch'en complained that men were being drawn not on the basis of residence (that is, from Fish Scale Registers) but on the basis of wealth (Five-Grade Registers). This resulted in hardships, since men might be forced to collect taxes in cantons other than their own, or villagers might be asked to gather city levies.[43] Still another contemporary, Huang Kan, complained that men were being called from the particular superior guard involved (that is, from Fish Scale Registers). This encouraged the practice of shifting legal residences from poor, underpopulated areas to richer, more populous regions. In poor areas the few liable households would frequently be drafted. Therefore they sought relief by changing their legal residence to richer areas, where they would be called

41. Ch'en Fu-liang, 21.2b–3a.
42. Ibid. See especially 21.2a and 21.3b.
43. Wang Yü-chih, "Chou Li Ting I," in Na-lan Ch'eng-te, *T'ung Chih T'ang Ching Chieh* (Yüeh Tung Shu Chü ed., 1873), 21.11b.

on less often. City men, forced to adopt a legal residence in rural areas, also sought registration in rich cantons. They might transfer registration from one superior guard to another (*hsi-tu*) or from one canton to another (*hsi-hsiang*).[44] Reformers proposed various plans to eliminate this practice. Some advocated selection from larger administrative units;[45] one local administrator divided the rich up among the cantons, irrespective of actual residences, and then adjusted the resulting burdens according to distances;[46] and Huang Kan asked that Household Chiefs be chosen from among the richest men in the canton rather than the richest men in the superior guard,[47] in effect advocating a compromise between the five-grade policy based on the subprefecture, and the Fish Scale policy based on the superior guard.

The argument between the supporters of the two different systems can be stated succinctly: those in favor of the fish scale system said that men who were chosen to work only in their home areas would know local conditions; those who advocated the five-grade system maintained that men chosen on the basis of wealth rather than residence would be better able to bear the financial burdens involved in the offices.

Although the term Fish Scale Register does not appear in other sources, it seems to be a synonym for the frequently mentioned Rat Tail Registers (*shu-wei pu* or *shu wei tu pu*). These Rat Tail Registers were based on the superior guard as the unit, and listed the wealth of the top three household grades, the length of time since previous service, and the number of adult males in the family.[48] Rat Tail

44. *SHY, shih-huo* 66.29a; Yüan Hsieh, *Chieh Chai Chi*, 13.4b.
45. Yüan Hsieh, 13.4b.
46. Li Ching-te, *Chu Tzu Yü Lei*, 111.4384.
47. Huang Kan, *Mien Chai Chi*, 25.8a.
48. *SHY, shih-huo* 66.30b (1212), 14.38a (1161); *HCP* 474.6a–b.

Registers were still used for conscripting servicemen during the Yüan dynasty.[49]

The service registers are also sometimes called Flowing Water Registers (*liu-shui pu*)—an allusion to the fact that men were listed on them, and in theory chosen from them, from top to bottom in rank order of wealth. The nature of these Flowing Water Registers is not wholly clear. During the Yüan they were property records used in determining taxes but apparently not in assigning village service obligations,[50] though during the Southern Sung they were so used. Ts'ao Yen-yüeh wrote:

> Nowadays the injury caused by the prefectural and subprefectural [authorities] who collect taxes using tax vouchers (*pan-pu*) that [are based on] taxes listed even though the patrimony involved no longer exists, and the injury caused by the prefectural and subprefectural [authorities] who requisition village officers from Flowing Water [Registers] that [are based on] taxes listed even though the patrimonies involved no longer exist, indeed may be called "disorderly."[51]

A *Sung Hui Yao Chi Kao* document dated 1161 also indicates the use of these records in assessing village service levies:

> Therefore in using the Rat Tail [Registers] and the Flowing Water [Registers] in conscripting servicemen, [the officials] necessarily want wholly to draft those who have not served previously,[52]

and in 1192 Hsü I said:

> As for drafting servicemen under the old system using Flowing Water [Registers], men were drafted in rotation from the beginning to the end.[53]

49. Wang Wei, *Wang Chung Wen Kung Chi* (Ts'ung-shu Chi Ch'eng ed.), 6.168–70.
50. Ibid.
51. Ts'ao Yen-yüeh, 10.2a.
52. *SHY*, shih-huo 14.38a.
53. *SHY*, shih-huo 66.27b (1192).

Although there are still some unanswered questions about the exact nature of these service registers, their general character is clear. Like the other critically important types of Sung population registers, they were records on the basis of which the government could assign responsibilities. As such, they contained those items of information most closely connected with making such assessments—the names and addresses of the household heads, the value and character of their landholdings and other properties, the number of adult males, and so on.

At bottom, the working of this registration system rested on the acts of the village officers, who during the Sung were the chief figures in the compilation of local records. They were in a position to judge the accuracy of reports submitted by individual households, and to draw up documents which they could then pass on to the clerks—the other vital group in the making of registers.

The central government was interested in collecting sufficient revenues and in having certain rural functions performed, while avoiding creating excessive discontent in the countryside. The first two of these objectives (and, judging from government performance, the more important ones) did not really demand the keeping of accurate records. However, if the state wished to avoid creating unrest, the information on these records had to portray fairly correctly the actual situation. Inaccurate registers might benefit a few corrupt clerks and a handful of rich and dishonest families, but only at the cost of provoking the wrath of the majority of taxpayers.

But if records had always been compiled according to the letter of the official regulations, the costs would have been enormous. Although it had created an elaborately detailed system for making records and collecting revenues the government did not insist that all its prescriptions be followed in practice. Instead, it merely demanded that local leaders submit gross aggregates of revenues, provide minimal services, and keep the local records current enough to preclude violent resistance by long-suffering taxpayers. In theory the state determined the burdens even of individual households, but in fact the higher authorities did not bother with the details of the apportionment of responsibilities. Of course, the flexibility inherent in this policy could not benefit all rural households equally. The flexibility meant, not that these costs could be avoided, but that their distribution was determined by the outcome of agreements and decisions made on the local level. The key figures in the making of these decisions were the clerks and village officers, and their power in this case was intimately connected with their control over the system of documents on which such determinations were supposedly based—documents which could be used to support their judgments and acts before the law.

Even so cursory an examination of Sung registration procedures and records as undertaken in this chapter reveals the *paperasserie* characteristic of the Sung—the trait in which it least resembled contemporary governments in other parts of the globe and most resembled our modern bureaucratized states—but it cannot fully reveal how these records were used, to what ends, and for whose benefit. Of the households on the service lists, which ones were actually requisitioned and how was the selection actually made?

]7[Further Criteria of Liability and Procedures of Conscription

In addition to household status and economic standing, the length of time since a family had last provided a village officer was also a factor in determining service burdens.[1] When a household had been drafted, a red notation (*p'i-chu*) was made after its name on the register. Since the spaces after the entries of those that had not yet been requisitioned were blank they were known as "white bases" (*pai-chiao*) to distinguish them from the "red bases" (*chu-chiao*) that were serving or had already served. The term "white base" might refer to a family that was liable but had not yet been called, or to one that was so poor that it was ineligible.[2]

At the beginning of the Southern Sung the ordinary practice was for clerks to select from among the liable in order of wealth. They avoided calling repeatedly on those whom, having previously served, had red marks after their names. In 1156 an official complained that this policy was not just. He pointed out that many of those listed as red bases were in fact richer, even after service, than the white bases currently being drafted. He suggested the modification of a system used during the late Northern Sung, under which families were to be freed for a fixed period following a

1. *HCP* 227.2a.
2. Lou Yüch, *Kung K'uei Chi* (Wu Ying Tien Chü Chen Pen Ch'üan Shu ed.), 26.5a; *HNYL* 173.2843; "SIFS" p. 261; *SHY shih-huo* 14.34a.

term of service and were then to become eligible again.[3] Such rulings on leisure periods continued to be part of the service code in the early Southern Sung.[4] The regulations suggested in 1156 provide the first detailed description of these rulings from the Southern Sung period. Under them, after the end of a leisure period of six years the wealth of a household would be compared with that of those families currently being called on to provide servicemen. If the red bases were more well-to-do than the white bases, they would again become liable and would be reclassified as white bases.[5] Within a few years a number of officials had attacked this new policy.[6] One critic cited a hypothetical example of an area in which the wealth of the top ten families ranged from 10,000 strings to 9,000 strings by units of 100. Under the six-year policy, men worth 9,000 strings, fabulously wealthy by common standards, might never have to serve.[7] The system was also attacked by men who declared it unworkable in very poor regions, where rich families were too few to permit them six years of respite from services. As a result of these criticisms the policy was abandoned in 1158, and although Hung Kua suggested a modified version of it in 1161 it does not seem to have been revived.[8]

The system of multiple service (*pei-i fa*), a more detailed scheme for making relief periods directly proportional to real wealth, seems to have been proposed in the early 1140s,[9] restated in the 1180s,[10] enforced experimentally in

3. *HCP* 407.14a; 464.9b.
4. *SHY, shih-huo* 14.29b. Under one system in use in 1091, if a household that had not been at leisure for four years was again called, it was to be paid for service. See *HCP* 464.9b.
5. *HNYL* 173.2843; *SHY, shih-huo* 14.32b–33a.
6. *CHTK* 2.24; *HNYL* 179.2970; Lou Yüeh, 26.5a.
7. *HNYL* 179.2970.
8. Hung Kua, *P'an Chou Wen-chi* (*Ssu Pu Ts'ung K'an* ed.), 41.1b; *HNYL* 189.3161.
9. *SHY, shih-huo* 14.29b (1145); Ma Tuan-lin *Wen Hsien T'ung Kao*, 13.138.
10. The original documents are no longer extant, but the descrip-

Liang-che after 1194,[11] and in theory extended to the whole empire in the early thirteenth century.[12] A document from 1194 describes the law of 1187.

> Ch'un-hsi fourteenth year, eleventh month, twenty-third day—the officials memorialized asking that a comparison be made of the wealth and taxes paid [by families]. [Those households] rated at a half-fold (*pan-pei*) should be permitted to be free from service for ten years. [At the end of the ten years] they should again be treated as white bases. Those worth one-fold should be free for eight years and then again be treated as white bases. Those worth two-fold should be free for six years and then again be white bases. Those worth three-fold should be free for four years and then should be treated as white bases.[13]

tions written in the last decade of the twelfth century and the early thirteenth century describe the practice in broad outline. These later reports seem to be discussing two systems, one set up in 1187 (*SHY, shih-huo* 66.27b), and a second in 1189 (*SHY, shih-huo* 66.30b), but the similarity between the two policies is so great that it seems almost certain that only one plan is being described, and that one of the two descriptions contains several errors including an erroneous date.

11. *SHY, shih-huo* 66.27b. The date of this document appears at first glance to be 1191 but it is given as the intercalary seventh month. A check of dates indicates that this almost certainly is a copyist's error for the intercalary tenth month, which would make the year 1194.

12. *SHY, shih-huo* 66.30b.

13. *SHY, shih-huo* 66.27b. The system of 1189 as described in a document dated 1212 changes the ratios of wealth used in determining the lengths of time during which a family would be at leisure but otherwise is identical with the system of 1187. Under the 1189 law a family worth one-fold would be free for ten years, one worth two-fold would be free for eight, one worth three-fold for six years and one worth four-fold for four years, and a family worth more than four-fold would also be free for four years. *SHY, shih-huo* 66.30b. There are other indications that the two systems are identical. The document dated 1194 is a request that the scheme of 1187 be put into effect (apparently up to that time it had only nominally been in use). This request was granted but only on an experimental basis and only in Liang-che circuit. *SHY, shih-huo* 66.27b. But, the document dated 1212, which purports to describe the system of 1189, is a request that the system in use in Liang-che be extended to the whole empire. *SHY, shih-huo* 66.30b. This interpretation is also supported by a laconic entry in the annals, which under the date of the third month of 1210 says, "It was

These reforms—aimed at increasing the weight given to real wealth in assigning burdens—were symptomatic of a general trend of policy. The Southern Sung increasingly emphasized wealth as the most important characteristic to be used in distinguishing families. This trend was also reflected in localized practices. Local officials did have considerable power to assess services as they saw fit,[14] but in general they were advised to adhere to local custom, which in some regions meant calling men on the basis of the amounts of money they paid in taxes. The author of the handbook for magistrates, *Chou Hsien T'i Kang,* advised local officials that if, in the past, Superior Guard Leaders were drawn from men who paid at least three hundred cash in taxes, future candidates for this position should also be men who paid this amount.[15]

The trend was also reflected in a host of reform proposals which had as their aim the more delicate adjustment of responsibility to richness. In 1158 it was suggested that if family A was worth twice as much as family B, then A should be liable for twice the service of B.[16] Three years later it was proposed that the households in a superior guard should be ranged on a ten-point scale on the basis of the amount of land that they owned. Those worth three points could be called as Guard Chiefs. Those worth seven points could be drafted as Superior Guard Leaders for a single term. Those rated at ten points could be used as Superior Guard Leaders for two terms.[17] In 1166 an offi-

---

ordered that the 'multiple service system' (*pei-i fa*) of Liang-che circuit be used in all circuits." T'o T'o et al., *Sung Shih,* 39.8b. The difference of two years between the date given in the annals and the date of the *Sung Hui Yao Chi Kao* request is presumably a scribal error.

14. Wei Ching, for instance, on taking office as a local administrator, promised that he would exact no unreasonable services. Wei Ching, *Hou Lo Chi,* (Ssu K'u Ch'üan Shu Chen Pen edition), 19.28b.

15. *CHTK* 2.23.

16. *SHY, shih-huo* 14.34a; ibid., *shih-huo* 65.90a.

17. *SHY, shih-huo* 14.37b.

cial advocated making the lower cutoff point for liability for call as a Superior Guard Leader an amount fixed for each superior guard according to its poverty or opulence.[18] Under a similar scheme devised by Lou Yüeh, a household worth 100 strings would be responsible for a month of services and a household worth 1,000 strings for ten months of services. The policy could be adapted to local conditions. In a rich area, households worth 300 or 500 strings might be accountable for the costs of only one month of services; in a poor region, those worth only 30–50 strings might have to provide funds to pay for a month's services.[19] Possibly as a result of this proposal, a system rather like that outlined by Lou Yüeh seems to have been used in Ming prefecture, households being required to provide funds to pay for a certain number of days of service.[20]

In 1172 it was again suggested that service be proportional to landholding. A household that owned 10–20 *ch'ing* (about 150–300 acres) would be liable for one period of service. Those owning 21–40 *ch'ing* would be accountable for two terms. A household that had 41–60 *ch'ing* would be liable for a triple term.[21]

In 1191, the Lesser Lord of Imperial Sacrifices, Chang Shu-ch'un said:

> [As for] the system of drafting servicemen, using the wealth of the household as the basis, Flowing Water [Registers] are made, [and the officials] wholly draft [from this list]. . . . I humbly say that in broad cantons and in narrow there is no policy as equitable as dividing the wealth of men into ten ranks. Those in the top five ranks will be liable for call as Superior Guard Leaders or their Assistants. Those in ranks six through nine will be liable for call as Guard Chiefs. Those poor

18. *SHY, shih-huo* 14.40a.
19. Lou Yüeh, 26.5a–b.
20. *KCSMHC* 7.2a. Poor households might only be responsible for the costs of a few days of services. This system obviously implies that substitutes were hired to do the actual work involved.
21. *SHY, shih-huo* 61.80a–b, 6.5b–6a.

people in rank ten will be exempt. I say that if their wealth is between 500 and 3,000 strings, they will be Superior Guard Leaders or their Assistants. If their wealth is between 400 and 200 strings, they will be Guard Chiefs. If their wealth exceeds these figures, they should be treated in accord with the rules covering the length of relief from services. In broad canton if [a household's] worth does not reach to 100 strings, or in a narrow cantons if it does not reach to 50 strings, then that household should be exempt.[22]

As with several other such proposals, there is no evidence of government action. Taken together, however, the proposals demonstrate that during this period there was continuing pressure to make the service system more equitable by distributing its costs progressively according to real wealth.

Selection of candidates appears generally to have occurred between eight and four weeks prior to the date on which the selected households were to become responsible for services. Yüan Shuo-yu suggested that the decision be made two months before the expiration of the terms of the incumbent officers,[23] and, since the warrants of conscription were dispatched into the rural areas one month before the beginning of the new service terms, the determination clearly had to be made before that date.[24]

The service lists were drawn up by the Canton Scribes, together with other clerical workers. The handbook for local officials, *Tso I Tzu Chen,* advises local administrators:

> Drafting of servicemen cannot be done casually. First, [on the basis of] the grade registers and the current canton notices, produce a red book (?) [saying,] "Such and such a year, [this household] formerly filled such

22. *SHY, shih-huo* 66.26b.
23. Yüan Shuo-yu, *Tung T'ang Chi,* 9.15a–16b.
24. *CHTK* 2.24. An official in 1134 had asked that the choosing of candidates be done one month before the beginning of their terms, to which the Ministry of Finance replied that rules already covered that sort of procedural detail. *SHY, shih-huo* 14.21b.

and such service posts, [it] has or has not undertaken affairs, [it] has left uncompleted business, or has had men come to substitute and help out, [it] has now been at leisure for so many years." Afterward carefully compare and examine the wealth and tax records. Then decide the assignment of responsibility either according to rules or according to your colleagues' [judgement] as to who can be drafted.[25]

Thus, the new personnel were to be selected under the direct supervision of the subprefectural administrator or his civil service subordinates.[26]

During the early years of the Southern Sung, selection seems to have followed a pattern of rotation, under which Large Guard Chiefs were selected from among those serving currently as Small Guard Chiefs, and Superior Guard Leaders and their Assistants were chosen from among Large Guard Chiefs. In 1133 an official reported that this practice had led the rich to bribe the clerks to list them, not in the same *pao-chia* units as their poorer neighbors, but in units comprised only of wealthy households. When this was done, the well-to-do were able to serve less often than their affluence would otherwise have required. The official asked that the system be altered to end such chicanery by modifying the wording of the current *i-fa* regulations. His suggestions were enacted in two parts, in 1135 and in 1139. Although the original rules are no longer extant, the various references to this reform make it possible to reconstruct their possible form. They appear to have read originally: "If there are vacancies among the Large Guard Chiefs, they should be filled by selecting and requisitioning from among the Small Guard Chiefs. If there are vacancies among the

25. *TITC* 4.19a. Both *tien-ya* and *shou-fen* are mentioned as assisting the Canton Scribes. For the former see *SHY, shih-huo* 66.30a. For the latter see Yüan Shuo-yu, *op. cit.*, 9.15a–16b.

26. Yüan Shuo-yu, 9.15a–16b advocates the use of the *ling-tso*, and the *SHY, shih-huo* 66.30a (1207), says that this was the responsibility of the assistant subprefect (*hsien-ch'eng*).

Superior Guard Leaders and their Assistants, they should be filled by selecting and requisitioning from among the Large Guard Chiefs." When the text had been changed by deletion and addition to fit with the suggestions of the official, it read: "If there are vacancies among the Large Guard Chiefs, they should be filled by selecting and requisitioning from among all [the men in] the large guard. If there are vacancies among the Superior Guard Leaders and their Assistants, they should be filled by selecting and requisitioning from among all [the men in] the superior guard."[27] Although one reference implies that the rotation policy may have been followed in some places as late as 1161, after the 1130s the candidates generally seem to have been chosen from among all the men in the unit under consideration.[28]

The clerks seized on this process of selection as a way for extracting bribes from the people. In filling one post they would approach several families in succession, being paid by each to go on to assign the duties to some other household. Under the Head of Tithing system the general name for such fraudulent charges was Head of Tithing money (*chia-t'ou ch'ien*), but to disguise their depredations the clerks sometimes said that the cash was "being used to aid the garrisons and stockades" (*ying fu chen chai*) or was "being forwarded to the prefecture" (*chieh fa pen chou*).[29]

Once a household had been chosen, the clerks drew up a draft warrant (*ch'ai-chang*), which included the name of the head of the household and the title of the service post.[30] One month before their service was due to begin, these

27. *SHY, shih-huo* 14.20a, 14.19b, 14.48a–b.
28. *SHY, shih-huo* 14.37b, records a memorial that asked that it no longer be required that men called as Superior Guard Leaders or their Assistants have seen previous service as Guard Chiefs.
29. *SHY, shih-huo* 14.45b–46a (1170); Wang Ying-ch'en, *Wen Ting Chi*, 5.44. Liu Ts'ai-shao, *Fan Ch'i Chü Shih Chi*, 8.23b.
30. *TITC* 2.9a. For the term *ch'ai-chang* see *CHTK* 2.24; *SHY, shih-huo* 66.30a.

warrants were sent to the parties chosen.[31] It appears that on arrival in the countryside they were publicly read and signed in the presence of the neighborhood group standing as witnesses, and copies were posted publicly at the subprefectural headquarters.[32]

Drafted households had the right to appeal the decision, and very frequently did so, refusing to begin their terms until some legal verdict had been reached.[33] In theory these cases were supposed to be ruled on within one month, but in fact, because of the welter of suits involved, judgments were often long delayed.[34] One contemporary official said that 30–40 percent of the assignments were felt to be unjust.[35] The people were granted the right to appeal conscription decisions outside the regular channels, bypassing the subprefectural and prefectural authorities and directly informing the circuit intendants or the censorate.[36] Frequently the men already serving as village officers were compelled by the authorities to go on serving until a final judgment had been reached.[37] Reformers occasionally suggested that a man newly called be forced to serve provisionally until his case had been settled, so that the incumbent could retire,[38] and in 1174 it was ruled that if a man lost a suit against service, the length of time between the date on which he was supposed to enter office and the date of the final judgment would be added to his term. If the officials ruled against a man who, when called for a two-year term, had instituted proceedings that delayed his assuming office for a season, he would be required to serve a term of two

31. *CHTK* 2.24.
32. *TITC* 2.9a, 7.36b.
33. *CHTK* 2.24.
34. *SHY, shih-huo* 66.28b.
35. Ch'eng Hsün, *K'o-an Hsien-sheng Tsun Te Hsing Chai Hsiao Chi* (Chih Pu Tsu Chai Ts'ung-shu ed.), 2.6a–7b.
36. *SHY, shih-huo* 66.28b.
37. *SHY, shih-huo* 14.31b (1149), 66.21a (1174); *CHTK* 2.24.
38. *CHTK* 2.24; Yüan Shuo-yu, 9.15a–16b. These suggestions apparently were not widely adopted. *SHY, shih-huo* 66.28b.

years plus one season. If he won his suit and the clerks were judged at fault, someone would be hired to fill out the time until a suitable candidate could be found.[39]

The prevalence of corruption among the clerks and the tendency of many local officials to leave the running of the system entirely in the hands of these underlings exacerbated the inequities of the system and the legal tangles that resulted.[40] The author of the mid-twelfth-century handbook *Chou Hsien T'i Kang* says:

> If the subprefectural administrators are not enlightened, the clerks will use the drafting of servicemen to seek bribes. If they call on family A and get a bribe, they will switch to family B. If they call on family B and get a bribe, they will suddenly change and draft family C. Originally they were supposed to draft one household, but the injury extends to several households. The attendant disorders will continue for a long time without affairs being settled. Therefore, the first thing that must be done in drafting for services is to admonish the clerks severely. If a man who has been conscripted has a complaint, you should order all the families that were accountable for [that particular post] to assemble. In the offices you should look into the draft warrant and examine the registers to determine the selection so that there will not be repeated problems. If the family first called on is not in fact serving, you must judge them guilty [of bribery].[41]

Families that did not succeed in bribing the clerks to bypass them entirely in the conscription process might still seek to have the beginning of their terms deferred. During the mid–twelfth-century the beginnings of the terms of Superior Guard Leaders and their Assistants were divided

---

39. *SHY, shih-huo* 66.21a.
40. *SHY, shih-huo* 14.22b (1134), 14.23a (1134), 14.30a (1146), 14.34a–35a (1156).
41. *CHTK* 2.24. The proliferation of lawsuits that resulted from this sort of corruption naturally also increased the opportunities for bribery. *SHY, shih-huo* 14.19a–b (1131).

into the first and second halves of the month. Men who learned that they were being called to serve at a time when duties were particularly onerous frequently paid the clerks to shift them to the next segment and call others in their stead.[42]

The clerks were the chief, but not the sole, cause of the problems in drafting. Lou Yüeh pointed out that the right of appeal against unfair drafting could be used by the rich to evade their responsibilities. He said,

> If family A is called on to serve, they will inevitably say "Family B is richer than we are." If family B is called on, they will say "The property of Family C is double ours."
>
> If the prefecture decides that family A is eligible, family A will ceaselessly complain to the Office of the Fiscal Intendent; then if family B is used, family B will complain to the Office of the Ever Normal Granary; and so it will reach to family C! If the records of the suits are examined, [it will be seen that they are] based on rules and cite precedents that cannot be broken. These three families will bring suit, and if they do not win [their cases] will not stop [appealing]. Eventually the powerful have their way, and the injuries are passed on to the lower households.[43]

After all the legal processes had been passed through, the day came when an individual household became responsible for the performance of certain village officer duties. The requisitioned family might have a member serve in person for the time specified or, in the cases of many families, might be able to procure a substitute. Households headed by men residing in other subprefectures or cantons, men living in the city, Buddhist and Taoist priests, some widows, single adult male family heads, officials, and some other groups were permitted to engage proxies. By the end of the twelfth

42. *CHTK* 2.18. The author suggests the abolition of this bi-weekly system.

43. Lou Yüeh, 26.4b.

century, rich families that were not legally allowed to avoid serving in person often used substitutes. The only effective restriction seems to have been that people were to be held legally accountable for the acts of the men they hired to take their places.[44]

Although relatively little information touches on the use of proxies, it appears to have been widespread.[45] But who were these substitutes? There are complaints about the use of men who had been mustered out of the armies (*fang t'ing chün jen*),[46] but apparently by far the most common candidates for these posts were clerks or ex-clerks from the local yamen.[47] The government tried to prohibit the use of clerical personnel and to define the qualifications of suitable candidates. In 1160 it was ordered that clerks who served as village officers should be beaten one hundred strokes.[48] A decade later the minister of finance Yang T'an asked that substitutes be chosen from men of fixed residence who were natives of the subprefecture. Households were not permitted to employ men mustered out of the army or clerks. Despite these injunctions, many village officers were clerical personnel who worked as servicemen for long periods of time. Huang Kan claimed that although those conscripted nominally served in person, in fact they engaged proxies who held the village posts for several tens of years. He called

44. *SHY, shih-huo* 66.26b (1191); ibid., *shih-huo* 14.44a. This system of private hiring seems to be a revival of a Northern Sung practice that was legal during at least part of Che-tsung's reign but apparently became illegal thereafter. *HCP* 389.6b.

45. Hiring was obviously used under most variations of the righteous service system described in chapter 8. It was also current in Ming prefecture. *KCSMHC* 7.2a ff. It also seems to be implied in many of the schemes used to tie liability more closely to actual wealth.

46. *SHY, shih-huo* 65.100a, 14.36a. For the meaning of this phrase see *HCP* 90.14a. Such men seem to have been released because they were too old, ill, or disabled for further military service.

47. Liu Ts'ai-shao, 8.23a–b; Ch'en Fu-liang, *Chih Chai Wen-chi*, 21.1b; *SHY, shih-huo* 14.36a.

48. *SHY, shih-huo* 14.36a.

them evil shiftless youths who were familiar with village affairs.[49]

According to a document dated 1160,

> Among the Superior Guard Leaders and their Assistants in the prefectures and subprefectures there are hired replacements, many of whom are clerks or clerical workers who were working in the yamen but who were not included in the legal quota of clerks (*ssuming*). . . . [People] just see that there is much business in the public offices and that it is not carried out with dispatch, [and yet] they do not know that this problem is rooted in [corruption among the clerks]. I beg that a clear system of punishments and rewards be set up, and that men be permitted to make accusations in accord with the system of heavy punishments (*chung-chih*). The employees should also be considered equally guilty. A decree ordered the Ministry of Justice to set up a system. The Ministry of Justice said, "From now on, as for all cases of men hired as substitutes, if they are men who have been mustered out of the army, or are incumbent or ex-servicemen or clerks, then they and their employers will be beaten one hundred strokes with the heavy rod. Their accusers shall be given a reward of fifty strings of cash." [This suggestion of the Ministry of Justice was] accepted.[50]

These recommendations are themselves proof of the widespread use of the practices against which they inveigh. Complaints about the system are legion, but it should be noted that one commentator praised the change, saying that professionals who knew procedures were able to restrict corruption.[51]

There is no way of knowing what proportion of those drafted as Superior Guard Leaders, or their Assistants, or as Guard Chiefs chose to act in person, and what proportion turned their tasks over to professional workers. Nor can we

49. Huang Kan, *Mien Chai Chi*, 25.8a.
50. *SHY, shih-huo* 14.35b–36a.
51. *HNYL* 160.2594.

assess accurately the relative costs of personal service versus paying for a substitute. But it is clear that the wealthy thought the hiring of replacements was to their advantage (they engaged proxies in the twelfth century even though during much of that period the practice was illegal), while the government recognized the benefits involved, for it continued to treat the right to employ substitutes as a privilege to be accorded men as a reward. As a result, despite the retreat after the 1070s from the system of hiring village officers using government funds, there was a continuing movement during the Southern Sung toward the use of professionals in the more important village service posts. Private hiring of substitutes had been permitted under the antireform policies of Ssu-ma Kuang[52] but does not seem to have been allowed under the policies enforced after A.D. 1093. Then, in the Southern Sung, the use of long-term paid workers crept in under the guise of the hiring privilege accorded privileged groups. In many areas the real question, eventually, was not whether the workers themselves would be professionals but how to distribute the cost of paying for their services and how to manage the system of hired agents.

52. *HCP* 389.6b; *CPCSPM* 108.5b.

Problems
and the Search
for a Solution

Distributing local service costs was the heart of the problem of *i-fa* in both the Northern and the Southern Sung. Someone had to bear the costs if local government was to continue to function, but any distribution that ruined the families bearing the cost weakened the state and could not be employed for any long period. From the 1020s on, statesmen and commoners sought solutions for this quandary. The solution eventually tried by the Northern Sung was the outcome of official planning and suggestion; the answer adopted by the Southern Sung seems to have been largely the creation of the people. But although the Southern Sung is in this regard noteworthy as a period of popular initiative, the history of the period also reveals the role of the state as supporter of and advocate for institutions created outside the formal halls of government.

The most radical Northern Sung plan for allocating costs had been championed by Wang An-shih, who pressed for a national system of salaried clerical officers reimbursed with income from a special impost. During the years 1071–74 a part of the revenue from this impost had been used to reimburse village officers, a practice which was revived under Che-tsung (1085–1100). The salaried officer system designed during the reign of Che-tsung seems to have worked adequately during his reign and that of his successor, Hui-tsung (1100–1126),[1] but after the Jurchen invasions of 1126 the

1. The policy of reimbursing officers was again attacked imme-

Sung government was forced to devote almost all available income to defense spending. Various officials requested that the labor service monies be diverted into the general treasury so that they could be used by the armed forces. With the life of the dynasty at stake, the Court was sympathetic to all suggestions that might increase the funds available for military uses. During the 1130s and 1140s the categories of levies that had been set aside for labor service salaries were one by one transferred into the general account. By mid-century the last vestiges of the practice of compensating village servicemen using the labor service funds had disappeared. The taxes themselves were still collected,[2] but they were now merely one component of the general fiscal system and had no apparent connection with village services. In effect, the cost of paying for services had been redistributed. No longer did most households have to contribute twice a year to a fund used in defraying village service costs. Now the whole burden of performing certain duties was rotated among limited groups of families. The state had stopped using tax revenues to reimburse village officers; the officials and the people responded by advocating and instituting practices that relieved those requisitioned, and they changed the character of the village officers by promoting the rise of privately hired professionals. With the decline of Wang An-shih's policies, as the burden on those drafted increased, there was considerable discussion of *i-fa* among officials, conditions conducive to the spread of the charitable service system arose, and, because great responsibilities were placed

---

diately after the death of Che-tsung, when the Hsiang-t'ai empress dominated the government, but as soon as Hui-tsung assumed control the Shao-sheng policies were reaffirmed. See *TSKSK* p. 583.

2. T'o T'o et al., *Sung Shih*, 26.15b. In fact, the rates were raised as time passed, at least in some areas. Chao Shan-kua, *Ying Chai Tsa Chu*, 1.6a–b; Ch'en Liang, *Yen Chou T'u Ching*, 1.35–36; Liao Hsing-chih, *Sheng Chai Chi*, 5.15b. In addition to the regular levies, officials even collected extralegal surcharges. *SHY, shih-huo* 68.26a (1221); Yüan Ts'ai, *Yüan Shih Shih Fan*, 2.28b.

on individual well-to-do households, the hiring of substitutes became attractive.

The functioning of Wang An-shih's system throws light on the practices of local taxgathering; its decline illuminates the fiscal problems of the central government and sets the stage for the transformation of village services in the second half of the Southern Sung. Descriptions of the working of the system are fragmentary. As originally established during the reign of Shen-tsung (1067–85), the top three grades in the countryside and the top five grades in the cities contributed a graduated tax twice a year to defray the costs of services.[3] During the Southern Sung this impost seems to have been assessed as a fixed percentage of the land tax. Chao Shan-kua remarks that before 1152 a man who paid taxes of thirty strings of cash (each string in theory containing one thousand coins) had to contribute nineteen coins per string as labor service money, but that by the 1180s those paying a mere ten strings a year in taxes had to contribute twenty-five coins per string in service money.[4] The regular village officers collected this impost when they were taking in the Twice-a-Year Tax.[5] During the same era in some prefectures special desks staffed by yamen clerks were responsible for keeping accounts of this income. These desks, which also dealt with the Ever Normal Granary revenues, were called *mien-i ch'ang-p'ing an*. This practice reflects the close connection between the labor service money system and the Ever Normal Granary system, which on the circuit intendant level were the responsibility of a single office.[6]

3. *HCP* 227.2a.
4. Chao Shan-kua, 1.6a–b.
5. T'o T'o et al., 66.31a–b, and *SHY, shih-huo* 14.18a, for the Southern Sung. *HCP* 2506.21b–22a for the Northern Sung.
6. For these "desks" see Li Ching-ho, *Chia-t'ai Wu Hsing Chih*, 7.5a. This gazetteer describes conditions in Hu prefecture in Liang-che at the turn of the thirteenth century. For the official responsible see Lo Chün, *Pao-ch'ing Ssu-ming Chih*, 6.13a, which indicates that in

In different regions civil servants of different ranks or positions handled the fund, and occasionally several departments in the same prefecture split the responsibility for control over this money. According to a Yüan gazetteer, in Ming prefecture after 1166 one category of labor service money was collected by the office of the prefectural vice-administrator;[7] a Sung gazetteer describing this same prefecture during the K'ai-ch'ing period (1259–60) indicates that in most subprefectures this fund was the responsibility of the assistant subprefect, but in one case it was handled by the subprefectural registrar;[8] and in 1251, in K'un-shan subprefecture of Su prefecture, the office of the assistant subprefect managed the labor service impost from three cantons while the office of the subprefect controlled the funds from the other two cantons in the subprefecture.[9] Such departments kept the records of the gathering of these levies and may also have managed part of the distribution of the income, but how such funds were disbursed to the village officers is not clear, nor is there any brief description of the accounting practices in the yamen offices.

But although the exact process by which the funds were gathered and expended cannot at present be adequately described, it is clear that during the first decade of the Southern Sung at least some of the revenue was used to reimburse village officers. In 1134 there was even an order increasing the rate of collection of labor service taxes to make possible the hiring of Elders and Household Chiefs.[10] However, most

---

Ming prefecture between 1225 and 1227 the labor service money collected from official households was managed by the official who ran the Ever Normal Granary system. During the Northern Sung the labor service money and the Ever Normal Granary money were collected at the same time by the same officers. *HCP* 2506.21b–22a.

7. Feng Fu-ching, *Ta-te Ch'ang Kuo Chou T'u Chih* (Sung Yüan Ssu-ming Liu Chih ed.), 6.25b.

8. *KCSMHC* 4.21b.

9. Ling Wan-ch'ing, *Yü Feng Chih*, 2.4b.

10. *SHY, shih-huo* 14.23a. This order says that either the dual sys-

of the money was diverted during the first and second decades of the period to meet more immediate problems. Once the money had been diverted, it was never again used to pay village officers. Ch'en Fu-liang writes:

> That which is called service exemption money was originally a means for showing mercy to the people, causing them to send out money to be used to hire service personnel, so that [the people] might have respite from labor. After [the state] stopped hiring Household Chiefs, the [Household Chief] money was still collected. It is now [placed] in general funds. After the state stopped hiring Stalwart Men, the money was still collected. It is now placed in general funds. After the state stopped hiring Elders, the money was still collected. It is now placed in general funds. Moreover, the state also took the "three-coin Bowmen hiring money"[11] and the one-coin surplus money,[12] and completely diverted them into general funds. . . . even the money collected when the rate of collection from official households was raised to parity . . . was ordered sent up.[13] Thus, the labor service money that was retained in the prefectures and subprefectures became

tcm was to be used after the pattern of Fukien or money was to be collected in larger amounts.

11. In 1128 the government raised the rate of the collection of labor service money by three coins. This surcharge was to be used to pay for the increased levies of Bowmen that had been established the previous year. *SHY, shih-huo* 14.23a; Ma Tuan-lin, *Wen Hsien T'ung K'ao*, 13.137; *HNYL* 15.325; *Huang Sung Chung-hsing Liang Ch'ao Sheng Cheng*, 3.18b.

12. This surcharge had been attached to the labor service tax from the founding of the system under Shen-tsung. At that time it was justified as a fund for contingencies such as famines, etc. Ma Tuan-lin 12.131. But Chao Ting, *Chung-cheng-te Wen-chi*, 50.9b, writing in the early Southern Sung, calls it a means for supporting the clerks.

13. In 1129, in order to raise extra revenue to pay for the recently increased number of Bowmen, the state raised the rate of collection of labor service money from official households so that it became equal to the rate used in collecting from ordinary households. *SHY, shih-huo* 14.17b, 14.17a; T'o T'o et al., 178.15b; Chao Ting, 50.9b; Chang Hsiao-hsiang, *Yü Chü-shih Wen-chi*, 17.9b; *CYTC* chia 15.205; Li Mi-hsün, *Yün Ch'i Chi* (Ssu K'u Ch'üan Shu Chen Pen ed.), 3.5a.

less and less, and the servicemen who were not salaried became numerous.[14]

When the emergency had eased, the labor service income was used for various purposes, including the hiring of yamen clerks, but not apparently for the compensating of village officers.[15]

After the collapse of the system of reimbursing village officers from labor service tax revenues, the burden on the families of men called to act was unbearable. Again and again contemporary observers report that people were ruined by the costs of these offices.[16] Sympathetic officials repeatedly suggested reforms, most of which called for some means of compensating servicemen for their work. In 1156 the acting governor of Fu prefecture, Chang Tao, asked that Household Chiefs in the underpopulated sections of Hu-pei and Ching-hsi circuits be paid. His request was apparently granted.[17] In the early 1180s Chu Hsi suggested a comparable policy. He commented that the root of the existing trouble in the service system was the stopping of salaries, and asked that Elders and Household Chiefs again be given

14. Ch'en Fu-liang, *Chih Chai Wen-chi*, 21.1a–b. See also *SHY, shih-huo* 14.23b; ibid., *shih-huo* 64.89b; ibid., *shih-huo* 64.92a; *HNYL* 84.1381; ibid., 86.1430; ibid., 88.1475; ibid. 105.1708; *Huang Sung Chung-hsing Liang Ch'ao Sheng Cheng*, 9.13b; T'o T'o et al., 29.14a, for other descriptions of this diversion of funds.

15. The local gazetteer of K'un-shan subprefecture in Su prefecture reported that, during the middle of the thirteenth century, "the salary money for the legal circuit clerks (*ti-hsing ssu li*) is 88 strings, 743 coins a month. . . . The salary money for the civil service clerks (*ti-chü ssu-li*) is 76 strings, 600 coins a month. The above items [are paid from] the labor service money collected from Hu-ch'uan canton and from miscellaneous monies (*tsa-se ch'ien*)." Ling Wan-ch'ing, 2.7b. See also Pien Shih, *Yü Feng Hsü Chih* (Peking National Library microfilm), 7b.

16. See for example *SHY, shih-huo* 14.18a (1131), 14.39a–40a (1164); 66.29a (1204); Ts'ai K'an, *Ting Chai Chi*, 5.1b.

17. *SHY, shih-huo* 14.32a–b. The text implies that Chang thought of the system of hiring Household Chiefs as a temporary expedient to be repealed when the population of these areas increased.

emoluments.[18] Yeh Shih advocated a similar plan, also in the second half of the twelfth century. The labor service funds would be kept in the prefectures and subprefectures where they would be used to reward the tax collectors. These tax collectors' superiors (the Superior Guard Leaders and their Assistants) would be compensated by having their Twice-a-Year tax quotas reduced by half.[19] Chen Te-hsiu had also asked for a return to the policy of paying village officers.[20]

Despite these proposals the closest the state came to making compensation of servicemen a general policy was the adoption in the early thirteenth century of the idea that those currently serving as village officers should not have to contribute labor service money while they were in office, a modest move that can be considered payment only in the broadest sense of the term.[21]

The state had subverted the policy of reimbursing servicemen from a special impost; it did not take decisive action to relieve the suffering caused by this change. Although many government leaders suggested reforms that might have aided the victims of the draft system, the most ingenious relief measure—the "charitable service" (*i-i*) system—was the creation of commoners. The state promoted the charitable service reform by creating an intolerable situa-

18. *HAHS* 21.326–28.
19. Yeh Shih, *Shui Hsin Wen-chi*, 3.20b–21a.
20. *HSWC* 29.4b–6b.
21. T'o T'o et al., 39.9a, implies that all servicemen were freed from the tax and gives the date as the fifth month of 1210. Ma Tuan-lin, 13.138, says that the *li-cheng* (i.e. *pao-cheng*) were freed from the tax, and gives the date as 1209. *SHY, shih-huo* 66.30b–31a, agrees with Ma that only *li-cheng* were exempted, but gives the date as the fifth month of 1212. It should be pointed out that the policy of exempting service workers from the labor service tax was first tried in 1071, when Stalwart Men were freed from paying labor service money. Ch'en Fu-liang, 21.2a. Occasionally other groups were freed from this levy. There are several instances of temporary exemption granted to men who lived in areas that had suffered because of recent military actions. T'o T'o et al., 26.8a; 38.15b.

tion, to which the people responded, and then supporting the charitable service system and encouraging its spread.

The charitable service system was first established by the rural people themselves, and only later taken up by the government as an answer to the problem of local services. The heart of the most noteworthy form of the system was an endowed estate, the revenue from which was used to recompense village officers. The first such estate seems to have been founded by the people of Chin-hua subprefecture, Wu prefecture, Liang-che circuit, in the middle of the twelfth century. From there it spread to certain areas of nearby Ch'u prefecture, where it was enthusiastically championed by local officials. Local variations occurred as the system, with the encouragement and sometimes the direct help of members of the government, spread to other areas. Foundations were endowed and managed in different ways, and sometimes the people involved actually determined the allocation of household grades and service duties.[22] During the last quarter of the twelfth century the functions of some of these charitable service estates seem to have become more complex. They were used not only to reimburse village officers, but also at times to support welfare services such as care for widows and orphans.[23] But, with the passage of time, the

22. There are two recent articles in Japanese on the *i-i* system, one by Osaki Fujio, "Sō-dai no Gi-Eki," *Shigaku kenkyū kinen ronso,* October 1950, pp. 261–85, and a more recent one by Sudō Yoshiyuki, "Nan-sō ni sukeru Gi-Eki no setsuritsu to sono unei," *Toyo Gakuho,* 48.4, pp. 425–63. There is also an even more recent and more detailed study in Chinese: Wang Te-i, "Nan Sung I-i K'ao," in *Sung Shih Yenchiu Lun-chi* (Taipei: Commercial Press, 1968).
23. Feng Fu-ching, 2.13a; Yüan Chüeh, *Yen-yu Ssu-ming Chih* (Sung Yüan Ssu-ming Liu Chih ed.), 14.41a; Lo Chün, 11.21a. It is possible that these charitable estates that were used to support welfare services were in no direct way related to the service estates, sharing only the name, but it seems more probable that they were related to the service foundations. We know, for instance, that when a foundation was established in Jun prefecture, the founders decided that excess profits would be used to establish a granary for charitable purposes. Liu Tsai, *Man-t'ang Wen-chi* (Chia Yeh T'ang Ts'ung-shu ed.), 23,13a–14a.

richer and more powerful local families began to abuse their power, either by diverting the revenues from some of the foundations into their own pockets or by donating estate lands to local officers in return for official favors. Critics of the system appeared, and, although charitable service was practiced in some regions until late in the dynasty, there was local option in most of the empire: if the residents of an area desired, they could follow the charitable service procedures, or they might choose to follow the old drafting policies. The charitable service system was finally destroyed under the Yüan dynasty when the government confiscated the estates.[24] The story of the rise of this institution, its spread, and its decline illuminates not only the practices of the village service system in the Southern Sung but also the whole problem of institutional innovation in Chinese society. It is an illustration of the intricate interplay between popular initiative and governmental action.

In 1169 the administrator of Ch'u prefecture in Liang-che circuit, Fan Ch'eng-ta, reported that the people in one or two of the superior guards of Sung-yang subprefecture had gathered to discuss the problem of village services. They had agreed that the burden could be distributed more equitably if they could set up some method for remunerating servicemen from common funds. They knew that a system of endowed estates had been in use in parts of neighboring Wu prefecture for several decades and decided to adopt this system. They then contributed land and grain to establish a perpetual "charitable foundation" (*i-ch'an*), which owned 3.300 *mou* (about five hundred acres) of fields, the income from which was to be utilized to pay village officers. Fan, who dubbed the system "charitable," commended it highly and asked that the government encourage its adoption elsewhere.[25] The Court ordered a general discussion of the in-

24. Feng Fu-ching, 2.14a.
25. *Huang Sung Chung-hsing Liang Ch'ao Sheng Cheng*, 60.12b. The system was also occasionally called the "aid system" (*chu-fa*). Ibid., 60.12a. On the system in Wu prefecture see Sudō Yoshiyuki,

novation and, finding that officials in other circuits were unenthusiastic, did not accept Fan's suggestion,[26] but in Ch'u prefecture the new system spread rapidly. In 1169 Fan reported that it existed in one or two superior guards of one subprefecture in Ch'u prefecture. Two years later he mentioned that "charitable service" was in use in six of the subprefectures of Ch'u prefecture. He asked that the Court order the new prefectural administrator to submit copies of the detailed agreements in accord with which the charitable service foundations were governed. He also said that the people were being permitted to adopt or reject the new system and asked that the authorities urge them to accept the innovation.[27]

The government aproved Fan's recommendations, and with official encouragement the system continued to spread. It seems to have been most widely used in Liang-che, Chiang-nan West, and Chiang-nan East circuits, but it also occurred in Fukien.[28]

---

pp. 425ff. On Ch'u prefecture see especially *SHY, shih-huo* 66.22a–b, and *Huang Sung Chung-hsing Liang Ch'ao Sheng Cheng* 60.12b. See also *SHY, shih-huo* 14.46a–b. The figure 3,300 *mou* appears both in *SHY, shih-huo* 66.22a–b, and in *CYTC chia* 7.92.

26. *Huang Sung Chung-hsing Liang Ch'ao Sheng Cheng* 60.12b.

27. *SHY, shih-huo* 66.22a–b.

28. The apparent prevalence of the system in these areas and the relative paucity of references to its use elsewhere may in part be illusory—a result of the fact that these areas are more fully described than are more peripheral circuits. However, it seems at least equally plausible that the system was more widespread in these more economically sophisticated regions of the empire. A brief survey of the sources indicates the presence of the system in Ch'ang prefecture in 1179 (*CYTC chia* 7.92); in Shan-yin subprefecture of Shao-hsing prefecture (about 1181; *HAHS* 18.270); in Hui prefecture (Cheng Hsün, *K'o-an Hsien-sheng Tsun Te Hsing Chai Hsiao Chi* (Chih Pu Tsu Chai Ts'ung-shu ed.), 2.6a–7b; in Te-hsing subprefecture of Jao prefecture about 1184 (*CYTC chia* 7.93); in Ch'in-t'an subprefecture of Jun prefecture about 1213 (Liu Tsai, 21.20a–b); in Ch'u prefecture (Yüan Fu, *Meng Chai Chi* [Ts'ung-shu Chi Ch'eng ed.], 3.35); in Chi-shui subprefecture of Chi prefecture in 1184 (Wen T'ien-hsiang, *Wen Shan Hsien-sheng Ch'üan Chi* [Ssu Pu Ts'ung K'an edition], 9.205); in Ming

prefecture (*KCSMHC* 7.1a); and in Hsien-yu subprefecture in Fukien in the early thirteenth century (*HSIVC* 46.10a). This list could be further extended, but adding more references would merely make more obvious the concentration of the institution in these circuits. From the beginning there was much local variation in the ways the charitable service system was organized and managed. Apparently the state gave its general endorsement to the key concept of the system—the right of the people to contribute in a regular way to a fund used to help village officers. There seem to have been cases in which these funds were not used to buy land, but in the system of charitable services most frequently described the contributions were invested in a revenue-producing estate, the income from which was to be used to compensate village officers. Occasionally the government also gave financial support to the estates, but it permitted the local officials and the people wide discretion in the adjustment of the general idea to local conditions.

The endowments were built up in various ways, sometimes by the people alone, sometimes by the people with official advice and guidance, and sometimes with government financial aid. It seems probable that the original pattern was one of popular action without much government help. This is clearly true of the system as it was adopted in Ch'u prefecture,[29] and there are other cases in which the initial funding was carried out without state help.[30]

Contributions might be assessed in various ways. In some cases men gave fields that formed a fixed proportion of their landed holdings, or they might contribute the grain from a fraction of their farms or money equal to a portion of their land taxes, or subscribe various amounts voluntarily.[31]

29. *SHY, shih-huo* 66.22a–b.
30. Yüan Fu, 3.35; *HAHS* 18.270; Feng Fu-ching, 3.5a. Yüan Fu received his *chin shih* in 1214, which suggests that his report concerns the second quarter of the thirteenth century.
31. Liu Tsai, 23.13a; ibid., 23.21a. See also Feng Fu-ching, 3.5a; Ch'eng Hsün, *K'o-an Hsien-sheng Tsun Te Hsing Chai Hsiao Chi*, 2.15a–16b.

Writing in 1213, the official Liu Tsai describes the founding of an estate by the natives of his home prefecture without official help or advice. His essay provides the following rare, vivid picture of community action among the people:

[As for] the beginning of this practice [of *i-i,* there was] in one superior guard a family [surnamed] Chiang [composed of] an elder brother named Kung and a younger brother named Hsiung-fei. Their nephews were named I-k'uei, Wen-hsien, Yao-min, and Sung-nien. In the same superior guard [there was] a family surnamed Teng, [with members] named Tsu-yu, Lin-kuang, and Fu-ch'i; a Wang family [with members] named Li-cheng, Li-min, and Li-ting; a Ch'en family [headed by a man named] Yung-k'ou; and a T'ang family [with members] named Ch'eng-yüan, Liang-kao, Ju-shan, Liang-jung, and [a man named] Yüan Kung-ming. [These men] planned [together], saying, "We are men in the same occupation. Although we are not very rich, yet no others in the superior guard are preeminent before us. Now the services daily cause difficulty, and affairs also are troubled. [As for] long-range plans [for dealing with the problem], none are as good as the charitable service system. Yet if it is not arranged in a public and just manner, it will not be adequate to succor men. Therefore, [with regard to] the given fields, in each case we must set forth their strength. This must be done. Also, if [the endowment] is not liberal, it will not be sufficient to be handed on for a long time, Therefore, in calculating costs we must make the profits public and just and constantly collect them plus a surplus. This must be done. If it is done in this fashion, even if there is much discussion men will not be able to say that [the foundation] is being used for private [profit]. Because the income plus the surplus is collected even if there is a bad harvest, we do not need to fear that the principal will be used up. Then [the system] will be completely excellent."[32]

Concerned lest their plan be executed without care, the founders went on to decide that a house should be pledged to serve as the headquarters of the foundation. The rele-

32. Liu Tsai, 23.13a–14a.

vant documents could be kept there in safety and the work-
ings of the project could be easily investigated. Any profits
would be used to purchase more land. If this secondarily
purchased land showed a profit, this would be distributed
to the original donors. Any surplus beyond this would be
used to found a community granary after the pattern popu-
larized by Chu Hsi.[33]

In many cases the estates were founded and endowed
through the combination of this kind of local popular initiative and official encouragement. In Ch'u prefecture the
first estate had been created by the people. But during the
1170s the *i-i* system there seems to have had financial problems. Around 1180 a commoner named Yang Chuan asked
that the government reform and revive the *i-i*. In response
to this request, the Court ordered the local administrator,
Chi Hsiang, to submit his recommendations for changes.
Chi suggested a plan under which official households, commoner households, and households headed by Buddhist or
Taoist priests would all have to give two *mou* out of every
hundred to the charitable estates.

His recommendation was sharply attacked on the grounds
that it unfairly burdened the privileged household types,
and that in any case it would be extremely difficult to force
official households to support the system. Chi rebutted these
objections and won the support of some high central government figures, but the Court finally decided that local
authorities could treat his policy as optional.[34] Despite the
critics, the system was retained in Ch'u prefecture, for in

33. Ibid. In what may be another reference to the headquarters of
a charitable estate, the *Ta-te Ch'ang Kuo Chou T'u Chih* first describes
the previous history of a postal station (*i*) and then says, "At present
it is the headquarters building of a 'charitable estate' (*chin wei i-'t'ien
chuang-wu*)." Feng Fu-ching, 3.23b. However, in the late Southern
Sung "charitable fields" (*i-t'ien*) or "charitable estates" (*i-chuang*) were
sometimes welfare institutions as well as service institutions. See Lo
Chün, 11.21a; Yüan Chüeh, 14.41a. We cannot tell which sort of
estate is being referred to by Feng Fu-ching.

34. *CYTC chia* 7.92–93; *HAHS* 18.270; *Huang Sung Chung-hsing
Liang Ch'ao Sheng Cheng* 60.12b; ibid. 61.1a.

1181, when Chu Hsi passed through the area while on an inspection tour, he submitted a report on the *i-i* which included his suggestions for its reform. On the building up of the charitable foundations, he said:

> This prefecture some time ago received an imperial order to follow the request of the commoner Yang Chuan in establishing a charitable service system. . . . But in this prefecture at present the practices are not wholly good. If you order upper households, official households, and households headed by Buddhist and Taoist clergy to contribute fields in order to fill out the charitable fields, this is truly good! But in this prefecture lower households who may own only one or two *mou* of land have also been ordered to give land, or money to buy property, which is then presented to the officials. And men from upper households who own many fields sometimes plan and reduce what they contribute to a trifle. These lower households nowadays have to give land, [and] by and by, [if] they are not willing to act as servicemen, the officials without grounds again demand rent for the fields. This is to oppress the poor in order to benefit the upper households.[35]

The difficulty of trying to get fields from official households is also reflected in an essay on charitable services by Ch'eng Hsün. He begins by distinguishing two forms of charitable service. In the first form, the service period was divided into units of time, and the local people themselves seem to have performed the tasks involved; in the second (which apparently corresponds to the more widespread pattern of *i-i*), the people gave either grain or land and, with the income, hired professionals to do the work. Hsün himself preferred the policy of land contribution. He suggested that the cantons should appraise the amount of agricultural land within their boundaries and the costs of hiring the requisite servicemen, and then levy assessments against the landowners according to the amount of land they owned

35. *HAHS* 18.270.

and the amount of money needed. But he specifically excludes from his list of eligible properties official fields (*kuan-t'ien*), imperial gift fields (*tz'u t'ien*), and fields owned by official households within their tax-free quotas (*kuan-hu hsien-t'ien*).[36]

Officials were occasionally able to supply more tangible aid to the estates. In 1179, in response to the plea of the administrator of Ch'ang prefecture, an order was issued that the recently confiscated property of a superior guard clerk should be sold. The proceeds were to be divided among the forty-five superior guards in the prefecture and used to purchase fields for the charitable estates. The order stated that this ruling was not to be treated as a precedent,[37] but there are other examples of official gifts of lands to the estates.[38]

An essay by Liu Tsai illustrates the complex interplay of governors and governed. Liu Tsai, acting not in his official capacity but as a leading native son of Chin-t'an subprefecture, suggested the establishing of a charitable service foundation. His proposal was accepted, and the estate was founded by voluntary subscriptions of money. Later, the foundation secured lands that had been confiscated by the government. Liu wrote:

> Because my ancestors were all buried in superior guard [number twenty-one of Chin-t'an subprefecture's Yu-hsien canton], I have always looked upon its elders as my fathers and elder brothers, and looked upon its younger people as my sons and younger brothers. I saw that those who owed services could not escape being beaten, and moaned by the streams and roads. In the period before they were called, those who had not acted as servicemen used a hundred devices to avoid serving. After this they shriveled in fear, to the point where they no longer dared to acknowledge the graves

36. Ch'eng Hsün, 2.15a–16b.
37. *SHY, shih-huo* 66.21b; *CYTC chia* 7.92.
38. *CYTC chia* 7.92; Liu Tsai, 21.21a.

of their ancestors. I humbly grieved over this. [Then]
in the autumn of 1212 I stopped at the ancestral grave
at Yün-pien. A member of a local landowning family
visited me. His surname was Chang. He was a man of
Wu-hsing and clearly a scholar. I asked why he had
come. He said: "My family owns more than three hundred *mou* of fields. [This is so much land] it cannot
all be cultivated. The mountainous sections are even
larger than the fields, and we cannot guard against
illegal grazing and the gathering of firewood. The authorities constantly tax it. In the autumn [the grain]
comes in [as harvest] and in winter it goes out [as
taxes]. What is picked up from high and low is only
adequate to pay the authorities. . . . Day and night I
constantly think about this and it always makes me
sick at heart." I asked, "Why don't you sell [the land]?"
He said, "Men dread the services. Even if I begged
to give it to them they would not be interested." When
I heard this I was deeply grieved. I thought that if the
servicemen needed for the summer and autumn [tax
periods] were hired, it would not cost more than one or
two hundred strings. The family of Chang is indeed
large and yet its strength is not sufficient [to farm all
of its land]. Thus, the potential profit of some of the
land has been lost. If the servicemen households got
[the benefits], gathering their strength in order to cul-
tivate [this land], and grazed and collected firewood,
except for the paying of regular taxes, the management
of [this land] would not be difficult. Thereupon I in-
vited Chang to discuss the buying of these fields and
pointed out the advantages of having the fields bought
and given to the servicemen. The multitude of households in the area were delighted and hopeful. The city
resident Lü Tsung-k'o led off by subscribing some sil-
ver. In this way he persuaded his nephew [Lü] Tsung-
ch'ia and others to agree with it. Within a ten-day
period we raised two hundred and sixty strings of cash
with which we paid Chang, and also eight hundred
strings extra in order to purchase adjoining properties.
A year later there was a drought, and the price of land
declined. There had already been some men who tried
to sell me low land in other superior guards. I advised
the estate to meet their price of 395-odd strings. The

contract had already been drawn up when the landowners became involved in litigation. At the time when this land was confiscated, the present Office Division Chief, Wang Chün-chi, who was passing through the subprefecture, praised the completeness of the charitable service system in the superior guards; and used the confiscated lands to aid [the estates].[39]

Management of the estates did not always follow the pattern described by Liu Tsai. Sometimes control was rotated annually among the subscribers.[40] In other areas special administrators called "service heads" (*i-shou*) oversaw the collection of the income from the fields. These men had to be chosen from among the upper households in the unit or they would not be capable of handling the job adequately, but they tended to abuse their powers, taking advantage of the poor and favoring the rich and the official households by lying about sales of property and divisions of families.[41]

Chu Hsi said that in 1181 in Ch'u prefecture these "service heads" not only collected the income from the foundation lands but also determined the terms of service. He remarked that in Shan-yin subprefecture of Shao-hsing prefecture the terms of service were fixed by the officials in the local yamen, and suggested that this Shan-yin practice was preferable to the usages current in Ch'u prefecture.[42]

In still other regions the estate lands were set aside for the use of Superior Guard Leaders and Household Chiefs. Each officer had a fixed quota of such land, which was recorded in the regular land registers. Presumably the management of the fields was in their hands.[43]

Under another interesting variant of the charitable service system the people themselves determined the household

39. Liu Tsai, 21.20a–22a.
40. Feng Fu-ching, 3.5a.
41. *KCSMHC* 7.2a ff.
42. *HAHS* 18.27o.
43. Ibid. This would also seem to have been the system followed in the area described by Liu Tsai, 21.20a–22a.

grades and the terms of service and then informed the officials. This version of charitable services was sometimes called "service by discussion" (*i-i*). According to a gazetteer of Chiang-ning prefecture from the Ching-ting period (1260–64):

> For a number of years now the people of Che-chung have practiced charitable service and the people of Chiang-hsi have practiced service by discussion. They find [these systems] convenient . . . Service by discussion is a system in which household ranks and terms of service are fixed in public discussion, and after this has been done the officials are informed.[44]

Most contemporary observers approved of the charitable service policies,[45] but it also had many critics. Some of the earliest opponents were concerned about the way that the system was run in Ch'u prefecture. In 1176 the retiring administrator of the prefecture submitted a memorial criticizing the charitable service system for breaking down in practice because of the differences in wealth between the families in superior guards. In poorer areas he considered the policy a hindrance rather than a help. The Ch'u prefecture pattern was again criticized after the prefectural administrator Chi Hsiang made contributions compulsory in 1180. The later critics also asked for local option.[46] In rebuttal, a supporter of the *i-i* contended that the charitable service system was bitterly hated by corrupt clerks who found it difficult to extort money in areas where it was in

44. Chou Ying-ho, *Ching-ting Chien-k'ang Chih*, 41.16b–17a. See an essay by Yüan Fu in which he describes policies followed in Ch'ü prefecture whereby the people determined household grades and terms of service and then informed the officials. Yüan Fu calls this "charitable service" (*i-i*). Yüan Fu, 3.35.

45. Ch'en Fu-liang, 40.8a–b; T'o T'o et al., 389.8b; ibid., 404.8a; ibid., 401.9b; Liu Tsai, 21.21b; Hu T'ai-ch'u, *Chou Lien Hsü Lun*, p. 16; Wen T'ien-hsiang, 9.205.

46. *SHY, shih-huo* 66.22b. Passages in the standard history seem to suggest that these recommendations were accepted. See T'o T'o et al., 178.17a–b, 35.14a–b.

use. These clerks had had men from several subprefectures submit arguments against *i-i,* but the true popular attitude was reflected in a stone tablet erected by the citizens of Te-hsing subprefecture to commemorate their gratitude for the founding of the system.[47] Chu Hsi, who investigated the situation in Ch'u prefecture shortly after the reforms of Chi Hsiang, also found fault with the *i-i* there, not because it injured the normally exempt groups but because the poor also had to contribute to the estates. Chu Hsi further complained that poorer households sometimes had to serve without pay. If they refused, they would be dunned for taxes by the officials. These injustices in apportioning the costs were compounded by the "service head" system, which resulted in an unfair assignment of service burdens.[48]

Unjust allocation of the costs of service might result from deliberate fraud. The more powerful families in an area might not subscribe their fair share to the original estates,[49] or they might buy permanent immunity from being called by making large initial gifts.[50] They might even eventually absorb the estates and use them as if they were private property.[51] Some officials disliked the system because the demands it placed on a household were proportional to that household's wealth. The wealth of the people was reassessed at best every three years, and during the interim there were often great changes in the relative affluence of the families in the superior guard, but the *i-i* system did not take these changes into account.[52]

Liu Tsai noted that the procedures for assessing contribu-

47. *Huang Sung Chung-hsing Liang Ch'ao Sheng Cheng* 61.1a.
48. *HAHS* 18.270; *KCSMC* 7.1a–b; *KCSMHC* 7.2a.
49. *HAHS* 18.270.
50. Hu T'ai-ch'u, p. 16.
51. This is the reason the founders of the charitable service estate described by Liu Tsai resolved to establish a foundation that could be investigated easily. See also similar complaints in Yüan Fu, 3.35; Hu T'ai-ch'u, p. 16; *KCSMC* 7.1a.
52. *HAHS* 18.270; Yüan Fu, 3.36.

tions were frequently changed. He said that in his native subprefecture men might be asked to give fields that formed a fraction of their property, or they might contribute grain from a portion of their fields or money equal to a part of their land taxes. Not only were different standards in use, but they were frequently changed, and the people were disturbed because they never knew what to expect next.[53] These criticisms provoked high-level discussion of the system[54] and led to the reintroduction of the option policy in 1193,[55] though not to the abolition of the charitable services. In the closing years of the dynasty there was even an apparent attempt to end local choice and enforce charitable services throughout the empire. In 1268 the annals note that "the charitable service system was practiced,"[56] and in 1274, only five years before the final triumph of the Mongols, "it was ordered that the prefectures and subprefectures practice the system of charitable fields and charitable service,"[57] but it is doubtful that in those last chaotic years of the dynasty's life these orders of the state were enforced. With the collapse of the last Sung strongholds in 1279, the history of the charitable service system as an effective local institution ended.

Reforms in Chinese institutions might originate on the local level, as a result of popular initiative, but the history of the charitable services also demonstrates the vital role of the state. Changes, once introduced, might be treated by the authorities as desirable, undesirable, or of no consequence.

53. Liu Tsai, 21.13a.
54. See, for instance, an order of 1222 that the Ministry of Finance discuss the charitable service system in detail. T'o T'o et al., 40.11b.
55. T'o T'o et al., 35.14b, 35.14a.
56. Ibid., 46.11b.
57. Ibid., 47.2b. A curiously similar system for aiding local service was established in 1324, under which large landholders in South China were requested to set aside a portion of each *ch'ing* of land and to devote the revenues from this parcel to helping pay the expenses of the *i* system. See Franz Schurmann, *Economic Structure of the Yüan Dynasty* (Cambridge: Harvard University Press, 1956) pp. 79–80.

If the state chose to encourage the spread of a new system, it could bring to bear the considerable legal and fiscal powers under its control. The government as a body of men also served as a chief means for the dissemination of ideas and information, even when these ideas were not embodied in state rulings. In premodern China the civil service was, in effect, the only national organization. Since it was a small group of men who were frequently shifted from area to area, to the capital and to the circuits, the communication of information was both easy and assured.

When any large body of men within this group became aware of a problem, they responded by proposing alterations in current policy. The nature of these proposals and the positions of the men who submitted them might vary widely; the path of proposals from submission through acceptance to execution followed certain defined routes. In their history can be read the character of the government that dealt with them—its problem, its aims, its methods, and its effectiveness.

In Southern Sung times most of the officials who labored to improve the system of village services were concerned with one fundamental question—How was the cost of performing these services to be distributed among the people? Seeking to distribute this burden in accord with their concepts of social justice and political practicality, these men inadvertently helped create a new system for the performing of local functions. Changing the answer to the question "Who must pay?" they also changed the answer to the question "Who will act?" The professionalization of local service personnel was a logical if undesired corollary of the attempt to make privileged groups within the populace share the cost of village services. In many cases it was impractical for members of privileged households to perform the requisite duties in person. The officials who demanded that such people bear the costs involved had perforce to tolerate the use of substitutes. The privilege of hiring replacements was progressively extended to larger groups of households, and many took advantage of that privilege. The hired seem in many cases to have been clerks from the local yamen. In this roundabout way the provision of local services in the late Southern Sung passed at least partly into the hands of professionals.

The character of the services themselves does not seem to have changed much during the dynasty. There are few disputes over what functions should be performed on the village level, only arguments over what officers should perform them. And even in these controversies about the distribution of duties the key issue seems to have been the costs involved for the officers.

Moreover, Southern Sung reformers did not concern themselves with how local functions were to be carried out. The late Northern Sung handbook for local officials, the *Tso I Tzu Chen,* describes procedures for dealing with some local officer duties, such as caring for stricken travelers or collecting certain taxes, but details like these did not enter the recorded debates of the higher officials.

Higher authorities did concern themselves with some broader aspects of the system of village services. There are numerous expressions of imperial interest[58] and repeated orders that the system of services be examined and made equitable.[59]

Many officials on all levels of the government discussed *i-fa.* Most frequently they were men serving in the Ministry of Finance,[60] but they also came from other ministries in-

58. T'o T'o et al., 178.17a (1128); *SHY, shih-huo* 14.36a (1160), 66.23b (1185).

59. *SHY, shih-huo* 14.36a (1160); T'o T'o et al., 178.17a (1128), 34.9a (1170), 35.7a (1180), 35.17a (1185), 38.9a (1205), 40.11b (1222).

60. Such as the Ministers of Finance, Chang I (*SHY, shih-huo* 14.24a [1135]), Yang T'an (ibid., *shih-huo* 65.100a–101a [1172]), and Yeh Chu (ibid., *shih-huo* 66.25a [1190]), and the Executive of the Ministry of Finance Li Jo-ch'uan (ibid. *shih-huo* 14.42a). For the other Ministry of Finance memorials see ibid., *shih-huo* 14.19b, 20b, 22b, 27a, 32a, and ibid., shih-huo 66.28b.

cluding Rites, Justice, and Personnel,[61] from the Secretariat
Chancellory, the Department of Ministries,[62] the censorial
organs,[63] and various other agencies.[64] Even the chief minister Ch'in Kuei discussed the problem of services,[65] and in
1196 the Minister of the Personnel, Hsü Chi-chih, began to
compile a book on the subject. He entitled it *The Essentials
of the Service System,* and when it was finished in 1199 the
Left Grand Councillor Ching T'ang presented it to the
emperor.[66]

Such agitation for reform involved the whole hierarchy
of fiscal officers in the Southern Sung. At the top, the general
direction of fiscal policy, including control and reform of
i-fa, was vested in the Department of Ministries.[67] Under
the Department of Ministries the Ministry of Finance controlled *i-fa* affairs;[68] below Finance these affairs were supervised by the circuit intendant offices of the Ever Normal

61. Such as the Custodial Judicial Investigator of the High Court
of Justice, Huan Chou (*SHY, shih-huo* 14.29b [1145]); the Provisional
Executive of the Ministry of Rites Hsin Ts'u-ying (ibid., *shih-huo*
14.33a [1158]), and the Executive of the Ministry of Justice Wang
Ta-yu (ibid., *shih-huo* 14.43b [1169]).
62. The Drafting Official of the Secretariat of Sun Chin (*SHY,
shih-huo* 14.21a [1135]); the Provisional Assistant Office Chief in the
Department of Ministries Wang Pao (ibid., *shih-huo* 14.30b [1149]).
63. Such as Li Yüan-yüeh (*SHY, shih-huo* 14.21b [1134]); Li Jo-ku
(ibid., *shih-huo* 14.29b [1145]); T'ang P'eng-chü (ibid., *shih-huo* 14.33a
[1156]); Hsieh E (ibid., *shih-huo* 66.22b [1184]); Hsü Hung (ibid.,
shih-huo 66.30b [1209]); and Chang K'uei (ibid., *shih-huo* 66.28a
[1199]).
64. *SHY, shih-huo* 14.18a, 14.43a, 66.24a, 66.26b, 66.30a.
65. T'o T'o et al., 30.12a (1147).
66. T'o T'o et al., 178.17b–18a. This book was called *I-fa T'i Yao.*
For a variant report on this work see *CYTC chia* 9.77. This was not the
only work on the service system of this era. A contemporary bibliog-
raphy also lists a book called the *Ch'ang-p'ing I-fa.* Yu Mao, *Sui Ch'u
T'ang Shu Mu* (Hsi Shan Yu Shih Ts'ung-shu K'an Chia Chi ed.), p.
12b. This probably was a copy of the compilation of the rules governing the Ever Normal Granary system and the labor service system
which was compiled (in 54 chapters) in 1144. *CYTC* 5.12a.
67. *HNYL* 6.164.
68. Ibid.

Granary system,[69] and below the intendants by the administrators of the prefectures and subprefectures.

A survey of the memorials preserved in the *Sung Hui Yao Chi Kao* sections on village services suggests that prefects and circuit intendants were the most active local officials in the debates over reforms in the system of village services. In this body of documents there are fourteen cases in which prefects are mentioned as participants in reform discussions, and eleven cases of circuit intendants.[70] Very few memorials are attributed to subprefectural officials—there is one from a subprefect and there are two others from assistant subprefects.[71]

The memorials preserved in the *Sung Hui Yao Chi Kao* are not a random sampling of those submitted to the throne

69. *SHY, shih-huo* 14.22b (1134). Although the Intendant of the Ever Normal Granaries was the most important official on the circuit level, the other intendants also sometimes participated in discussion of village service reform. For instance, in 1128 the Fiscal and Judicial Intendants memorialized the Ministry of Finance concerning some changes. Ibid., *shih-huo* 14.23b.

70. In this body of documents there are fourteen cases in which prefects are mentioned as participants in the reforms discussions, and eleven cases in which circuits intendants are mentioned. In only one case is the office concerned given simply as the Office of the Intendant of the Ever Normal Granary. In the other cases the memorials came from the offices of Fiscal Intendants, Intendants of Tea and Salt, or from people holding concurrent positions—i.e. concurrently Fiscal Intendant and Intendant of the Ever Normal Granary, or concurrently Judicial Intendant and Intendant of the Ever Normal Granary. For the documents see *SHY, shih-huo* 14.17b, 20a, 24b, 27b, 29a, 30a, 36b, 43a, 47a, and ibid., *shih-huo* 66.25b, 26b, 30b. Since there were far more prefects than there were circuits intendants, it is an interesting indication of the important role these intendants played that they should be so overrepresented in the sample. At the same time, the prefects played a much more important role than did the subprefects. For the documents see ibid., *shih-huo* 14.25a, 26a, 31a, 32a, 34a, 38a, 40a, 42b, 44b, 46a-b, and ibid., *shih-huo* 66.22a, 22b. It should be noted that there were two cases of prefects holding other positions concurrently, in one case a man was concurrently the circuit pacification officer, and in the other case the prefect was concurrently the circuit regulator.

71. *SHY, shih-huo* 14.24b, 26b, 34a.

in the Southern Sung. For the most part they are suggestions that were approved. Moreover, historical accident has destroyed a large part of the original collection, and so the coverage of time is spotty. But, even with these qualifications, the analysis of the origins of these documents is suggestive. There were several thousand subprefectural officials and hundreds of prefects, but only some dozens of intendants. The overrepresentation of intendants and the virtual absence of subprefectural officials may be explained in several ways, but all the explanations in the end merely indicate the key role of the intendants in determining policy.[72]

Intendants clearly played an important role in discussing reforms, but several documents show that the central authorities, when faced with local problems, solicited the opinions of the administrators on the spot. A representative document, dated 1167, saying:

> There has been much talk about village services, but no definitive discussion. . . . Now I ask that the intendants of the Ever Normal Granaries pass on to their subordinate prefectures and military prefectures [an order] to report on the good and the bad points of usages that could long be practiced, for submission to the Department of Ministries within one season.[73]

72. The disproportions revealed can be explained in a number of ways. Possibly the officials of the subprefectures and prefectures did not submit many proposals. Possibly the proposals they submitted were sent up through the circuit offices and not directly to the central authorities, and, when the documents were recorded, credit for the ideas was given the intendants involved, not the administrators. Possibly proposals coming from intendants were more likely to obtain approval (and thus qualify for inclusion in the *Hui-yao*). Possibly many of the documents we have that merely say "officials said" stemmed originally from local administrators. The documents in the *Sung Hui Yao Chi Kao* are abbreviated. Possibly when documents were abbreviated, the names and titles of lower officials were the first to be deleted. In any event, it does seem clear that intendants were very influential in discussions about these laws, for whatever reasons.

73. *SHY, shih-huo* 65.96a–b.

Solicited and unsolicited proposals might also be submitted directly to the throne. If the throne felt they deserved further study, it would ordinarily order the Ministry of Finance to investigate the suggested policies and to submit its recommendations to the Department of Ministries within a limited time, frequently five or ten days.[74] If accepted, the reforms were often tried provisionally in a limited region for a set period, at the end of which their success was evaluated.[75]

Many individual officials did submit their ideas on service reform to the throne. Sometimes their suggestions sound conservative (Chao Ting in 1129 suggested that all traces of the reforms of Wang An-shih should be eradicated),[76] sometimes they sound traditionalist (Wang Ying-ch'en criticized the critics in 1167 by saying that the problem of *i-fa* was men, not institutions),[77] but frequently these erstwhile advisors addressed themselves to very real problems in constructive ways.

Corruption among the clerks in the yamen, a problem that continued to plague later dynasties, was a major concern of a number of Southern Sung reformers,[78] as was the tendency for these clerks to form alliances with rich local families or with the men called as village officers.[79] During the Southern Sung, officials suggested two contradictory lines of policy for dealing with these problems. Some men wanted more strictly detailed regulations, including restrictions on the entrance into the group of hired workers,[80] while others insisted that the most important root of the problem of corruption was the proliferation of regulations

74. *SHY, shih-huo* 14.20b (1133), 14.26b (1137).
75. Lou Yüeh, *Kung K'uei Chi*, 26.6a; *SHY, shih-huo* 14.45b.
76. Chao Ting, 50.9b; *SHY, shih-huo* 14.23a–b.
77. *SHY, shih-huo* 14.42b.
78. Lou Yüeh, 26.5a; Ch'en Yüan-chin, *Yü Shu Lei Kao,* 1.1b–2a; Kao Ssu-te, *Ch'ih T'ang Ts'un Kao* (Ts'ung-shu Chi Ch'eng ed.), 2.37; *SHY, shih-huo* 14.24a–b, 65.96a–b, 66.21b.
79. Cheng Yao and Fan Jen-kung, *Ching-ting Yeu Chou Hsü Chih,* 2.22; *SHY, shih-huo* 14.47b, 14.28b.
80. *SHY, shih-huo* 65.100b–101a (1172).

to the point where the civil service officials did not know which directives to follow so that control over local affairs gravitated into the hands of the clerks.[81]

This plethora of rules, another problem that plagued later dynasties and led to the creation of the position of legal secretary under the Ming and Ch'ing, had become a serious hindrance to administrative efficiency by the middle of the Southern Sung. The size of the problem is indicated by the results of an investigation of village service regulations carried out in 1158 by the Minister of Personnel, Wang Shih-hsin. Wang reported at the time of this study there were a total of thirty-eight applicable general directives. Fifteen of these were rules stemming from the Ever Normal Granary System set up in the Shao-sheng period (1094–97) as reaffirmed in the Ever Normal Granary and Labor Service System of the Shao-hsing period (1131–62), and twenty-three were continuing directives that had been issued to clarify rules of the Ever Normal Granary and Labor Service System of the Shao-hsing period. In particular, Wang was distressed to discover four important but potentially conflicting rules on the assessment of *i-fa* burdens.[82]

Southern Sung reformers did not halt the proliferation of laws or end dishonesty among the clerks. At best they reduced the severity of the problems. In another sense they even contributed to the growth of corruption among clerical personnel. In their zeal to distribute the village service burdens in a just and workable way, these officials inadvertently fostered the partial professionalization of the village officers. The professionals were apparently mostly clerks and ex-clerks, and so, by promoting a system in which such men were employed, the officials created fresh opportunities for corrupt practices without creating any new means for policing the system.

81. *SHY, shih-huo* 14.33a–34a (1158); Chou Lin-chih, *Hai Ling Chi* (Ssu K'u Ch'üan Shu ed.), 4.2b.

82. *SHY, shih-huo* 14.32a–34a (1158).

]9[*Conclusions*

The system of local control established by the Chinese in the last centuries B.C. remained remarkably stable during the imperial period, in broad outline and down to the subprefectural level. But superficial structural stability disguised a continuing if slow evolution.

Below the subprefectural level, political institutions changed also. Dynasties maintained a considerable degree of functional continuity and some degree of structural continuity with their predecessors, but at times they used dissimilar means to approach their common goals. Under most dynasties vital functions in rural areas were divided among a variety of groups of functionaries. Village officers were an important category of such functionaries, but in most eras they were not the only figures of authority in the countryside. Particularly during the last dynasties local functions and powers seem to have been shared by numerous individuals and groups. Gentry, clerks, runners, and *pao-chia* officers all participated in the rural political system. The Sung, by contrast, is distinguished by the degree to which vital tasks and powers were concentrated in the hands of one group, the village officers.

This peculiarity presumably reflects some social reality characteristic of the Sung. Standing as they do between the rulers and the ruled, these boundary figures seem particularly sensitive to changes in the character of either group. The evolution of the institutions they staff may thus reflect with particular clarity the transformation of the social system. The village officer system's near monopoly of most rural political functions is a characteristic of the Sung dynasty as a whole, setting it off from other eras in Chinese imperial history. Within the Sung, too, there were variations in service systems. The changes that produced these variations reflect the continuing metamorphosis through which Chinese society was passing. This metamorphosis had little impact on rural political functions but was mirrored in changes in personnel policies and in structure.

Some of the structural changes in the Southern Sung village service system seem at first glance to have been of minor importance. The shift from the township to the superior guard as the chief unit of organization does not appear to have caused much alteration in other facets of the system. But perhaps this change should be viewed as a side effect of one of the key structural changes of the period—the increase in the size of the superior guard and its consequent evolution into a geographical unit. According to the original rulings, most Sung village officers oversaw fixed numbers of households. The largest major unit during the late Northern Sung, the superior guard, by law numbered 250 households. During the Southern Sung, in both concurrent and dual service regions, the number of people under the jurisdiction of the Superior Guard Leaders grew until in some areas they numbered between 1,000 and 2,000 households. This process led to the redefinition of the superior guard unit, on an areal rather than a demographic basis. As a result of the transformation, the village officers became areal administrators rather than group leaders, with both augmented powers and heavier responsibilities.

This increase in unit size occurred in both dual and concurrent service areas and so does not seem to have been intimately connected with the second major structural change of the Southern Sung, the rise of concurrent service as the normal pattern of rural organization. As originally conceived, the concurrent system was to have been the normal pattern, with the dual variant used under special conditions. But, in fact, the dual system predominated in the Northern Sung. Then, during the troubles attendant on the Chin invasions, the state found that the taxation officers under the dual system were unable to perform their jobs satisfactorily in disturbed regions. *Pao-chia* leaders were therefore coerced into concurrent service, probably in the hope that they would use their police and military powers to squeeze sufficient revenues from the people. The concurrent pattern was then found to be particularly useful in areas of heavy population and taxation, and was retained, in all except a few outlying regions, after the ending of the emergency. The spread and permanent adoption of concurrent service occurred in the richer, more densely populated sections of the empire, and it seems to have been closely interwoven with fundamental changes in the nature of the rural social system.

Before the late T'ang, while there was still a rural "aristocracy" of sorts, the men chosen by the government to exercise control in the countryside either were members or clients of families already influential, or else they shared their authority with such families; in the Ming and Ch'ing, rural influence and power were shared by a number of groups—clerks, runners, gentry families, and the leaders of the *li-chia* and *pao-chia* organizations. But in the Sung the earlier system was already moribund, and the later system was only in its infancy. Control of major functions in rural areas seems to have been almost entirely in the hands of the village officers. Taxes, communications, services, minor police functions, and even some military functions were largely under their control. The *pao-wu* militia might bear some of the burdens of self-defense, and clerical personnel might under some circumstances preempt certain functions, but the heaviest responsibilities and the widest powers were given to the village officers.

Such powers came at a price. We must not assume that the village officer households were pleased to receive control over important functions from the state. On the contrary, they sought in many ways to evade the responsibility for services. But while it is probable that the burdens of service were occasionally passed on to the truly poor, this surely cannot have been the rule. Poor families simply could not have borne the costs associated with service, which were great enough to ruin many relatively prosperous households. The continuing stability and strength of the Southern Sung seems clear evidence that the duties were adequately performed, and this in turn indicates that in most cases relatively well-to-do families provided members to act as village officers, or hired replacements (and oversaw the replacements' work). With the advent of charitable service, these households could accept their responsibilities without great cost to themselves. The households were then given vital duties as well as powers. The working of this system need not have meant that the chosen households enjoyed great prestige (although they might well do so), nor did it mean that other households in the area in question did not have some influence, but rather that the functions performed by other households were of limited importance.

With the spread of the concurrent service system, general oversight of the various duties of the village officers came to be centered in the hands of one key officer, the Superior Guard Leader, who thus became the pivotal figure in administration below the subprefectural level since he exercised discretionary control over questions vital to his neighbors. He might in part determine the tax burdens of individual families, might give evidence in disputes over land titles, and was the chief figure in the creation of the registers from which fiscal burdens were computed. He frequently controlled the local militia, had some other police powers, and had constant and privileged (if not always welcomed) access to the clerks. Whether he sought to or not, he can hardly have avoided wielding great influence over local affairs.

This near monopoly of rural political functions by the village officers contributed to another, perhaps even more distinctive trait of the Southern Sung rural social order: the critical importance of wealth per se in determining the distribution of responsibilities and influence in rural areas.[1]

This trait of Sung society seems to be tied in with the general movement within Chinese society and economy in the Sung period, toward a more mobile and open system. Without denying the continued existence of groups that had definite limits placed on their personal liberty, it still seems clear that the society of Sung times was more fluid and open than had been the case in earlier times. On the highest level of the elite, in the graded civil service, this was achieved through large-scale use of the system of competitive examinations—a practice that prefigured the creation of the gentry group. On the level below the graded civil service this fluidity resulted from the use of wealth as a key determinant of social position—a phenomenon connected with the "capitalistic" tendencies of the Sung era. The rise in the relative role of wealth in fixing status was thus in turn partly the product of another economic development of the time, the spread of a money economy, which made both feasible and just the redistribution of rural responsibilities primarily on the basis of wealth and resulted in the steady attrition of the privileges of a variety of households.

When it became feasible to hire replacements, the draft-

1. This is not to say that wealth was not an important source of influence during other eras of Chinese history. Nor does it mean that Sung rural society did not include families that derived their influence from noneconomic roots—from being "old" families with traditional prestige. It does mean that, during the Sung, wealth in and of itself seems to have been more important in determining the distribution of discretionary control over rural responsibilities (and thereby of influence) than it had been in the previous period or than it was to be in the gentry-dominated society of the future.

ing of rich but previously privileged households became both politic and just. To force a household headed by a woman, an elderly person, or a youth to contribute the services of a family member to the state would have been cruel. To force such a household, if it was rich, to hire someone to be a serviceman was both fair and possible— given a widespread money economy.

In addition, the rise of a money economy may have helped indirectly to encourage the spread of a system of professional servicemen employed by these rural rich or by endowed estates established to defray service costs. Commutation of various duties and the hiring of replacements had a long history before Sung times. The Sung is remarkable, not for the birth of commutation as a practice, but for the rapid growth of a system of commutation that involved a huge number of individuals and reached down into the smallest hamlets of the empire.

Those drafted as Sung village officers controlled, personally or by proxy, most rural political functions. But who were these men? From scattered information it is possible to patch together a portrait that may be helpful.

Perhaps most important, they were largely well-to-do landowners. Most village officers were chosen from households registered in the top four grades of rural families which taken together seem to have comprised only a small fraction of the total rural population. Although, no doubt, some rich families successfully sought to evade service by bribing the local clerks, this can hardly have been a universal practice. And in any case it seems clear that in almost all cases the eventual victims were also relatively well-to-do, even if they were not so wealthy as those able to bribe their way out of serving.

In seeking to evade service, potential village officers reveal themselves to have been well informed about the law and not fearful of litigation. Suits against service, brought by commoners who based their arguments on the details of the legal codes, seem to have been even more frequent than attempts at bribery. Indeed, it sometimes appears that a majority of the men called went to court before they were willing to accept the local officials demands that they act as servicemen. The profound fear of involvement with the law often said to have been characteristic of the people in Ming and Ch'ing times does not seem to have afflicted the Sung rural elite. Contentious and litigious, these families were willing and able to go to law to achieve their aims, citing rulings and precedents to confound the will of the authorities, and appealing their cases to higher levels if unsatisfied.

Their litigious character, combined with the nature of the jobs they were supposed to perform as servicemen, indicate that such people were ordinarily presumed to be literate. Such limited pictures as do appear in the sources show them using their literacy and other skills primarily in managing estates, even while they sought connections with the official elite through their children, marrying their daughters to *chin shih* or encouraging their sons to study for the examinations. In this light they seem much like the later gentry, though in the Sung they had not yet espoused so enthusiastically the values of the literati.

Occasionally such men came together to organize as groups for joint activities. Such organizations, which cut across kin lines, occurred in pre-Sung times also but then they frequently clustered around Buddhist monasteries, and had religious or charitable functions. By the Sung, many were wholly lay in orientation. As illustrated by the charitable service estates, such rural associations were formally organized, with their own bylaws, records, and offices.

From all the limited evidence there emerges a dim picture of an assertive rural class, a country counterpart of the emergent bourgeoisie of the Sung cities. The developments that had given rise to these two groups—the bourgeoisie of the cities and the rural, market-oriented estate owners in the countryside—had been born in the late T'ang, and reached a temporary apogee in the Sung. In later times the values they embodied would give way before the values of the literati-dominated gentry society, but in the Sung these two potentially conflicting styles of life, both born in the T'ang, hung in temporary balance, giving the Sung its own distinctive character. This exquisite balance is displayed in miniature in the figures of the village officers. Representatives of the owners of the commercialized estates, co-opted into the service of the mandarins who were at this time the prime carriers of the competing ideal of the gentry, they brought to the performance of their duties both the legalistic and commercial skills of their class and the often mouthed if not always observed ideals of the literati.

Bibliography

WORKS IN WESTERN LANGUAGES

Balazs, Etienne. *Le traité économique du "Souei-chou."* Leiden: E. J. Brill, 1953.

Buriks, Peter. "Fan Chung-yen's Versuch einer Reform des chinesischen Beamstenstaates in den Jahren 1043–44." *Oriens Extremus* 3 (July–December, 1956): 57–80, 153–84.

Chang Chung-li. *The Chinese Gentry: Studies on their Role in Nineteenth Century Chinese Society.* Seattle: University of Washington Press, 1955.

Ch'en, Kenneth. "The Sale of Monk Certificates," *Harvard Theological Review* 49, no. 4 (October, 1956): 307–27.

Ch'ü T'ung-tsu. *Local Government in China under the Ch'ing.* Cambridge: Harvard University Press, 1962.

Eichhorn, Werner. "Gesamtbevölkerungsziffern des Sung-Reiches." *Oriens Extremus* 4: 52–69.

Franke, H. "Die Agrarreformen des Chia Ssu-tao," *Saeculum* 9 (1958).

Friese, Heinz. *Das Dienstleistungssystem der Ming-Zeit (1388–1644).* Hamburg: Gesellschaft für Natur- und Völkerkunde Ostasiens, 1959.

Hartwell, Robert. "Classical Chinese analysis and economic Policy in T'ang and Sung China," *International Congress of Orientalists in Japan, Transactions* no.13 (1968), 70–81.

———. "A Cycle of Economic Change in Imperial China: Coal and Iron in Northeast China, 750–1350," *Journal of the Economic and Social History of the Orient,* 10 (July 1967), 102–59.

————. *A Guide to Sources of Chinese Economic History, A.D. 618–1368.* Chicago: Committee on Far Eastern Civilizations, University of Chicago, 1964.

————. "Markets, Technology, and the Structure of Enterprise in the Development of the Eleventh-century Chinese Iron and Steel Industry." *Journal of Economic History* 26 (March 1966): 29–58.

————. "A Revolution in the Chinese Iron and Coal Industries During the Northern Sung, 960–1126 A.D." *Journal of Asian Studies* 21 (Feb. 1962): 153–62.

Ho Ping-ti. *The Ladder of Success in Imperial China.* New York: Columbia University Press, 1962.

Hsiao Kung-ch'üan. *Rural China: Imperial Control in the Nineteenth Century.* Seattle: University of Washington Press, 1960.

Hsüeh Chung-san and Ou-yang I. *A Sino-Western Calendar for Two Thousand Years.* Peking: Hsin Chih San Lien Shu Tien, 1957.

Kracke, E. A., Jr. *Civil Service in Early Sung China.* Cambridge: Harvard University Press, 1953.

————. "Family versus Merit in the Chinese Civil Service." *Harvard Journal of Asiatic Studies* 10, no. 2 (1947): 103–23.

————. "Sung Society: Change within Tradition." *Far Eastern Quarterly* 14 (1954–55): 478–88.

Liu, James T. C. *Reform in Sung China.* Cambridge: Harvard University Press, 1959.

————. "The Sung Views on the Control of Government Clerks." *Journal of the Economic and Social History of the Orient* 10, nos. 2–3 (Dec., 1967): 317–44.

Liu, James T. C., and Golas, Peter, eds. *Change in Sung China.* Lexington: D. C. Heath and Co., 1969.

McKnight, Brian E. "Administrators of Hangchow under the Northern Sung." *Harvard Journal of Asiatic Studies* 30 (1970): 185–211.

Schurmann, Franz. *Economic Structure of the Yüan Dynasty.* Cambridge: Harvard University Press, 1956.

Twitchett, Denis. "Chinese Social History from the Seventh to the Tenth Centuries." *Past and Present* no. 35 (Dec. 1966): 28–53.

———. "Documents on Clan Administration: I. The Rules of Administration of the Charitable Estate of the Fan clan. Annotated Translation of the *I-chuang kuei-chü*." *Asia Major* 8 (1960): 1–35.

———. *Financial Administration under the T'ang Dynasty.* Cambridge, Eng.: Cambridge University Press, 1963.

———. "Lands under State Cultivation under the T'ang." *Journal of the Economic and Social History of the Orient,* 2 (1959): 162–203.

———. "The Monasteries and China's Economy in Medieval Times." *Bulletin of the School of Oriental and African Studies* 19, no. 3, 526–49.

———. "Monastic Estates in T'ang China." *Asia Major* n.s. 5, pt. 2 (1956): 123–46.

———. "Recent Work on Medieval Chinese Social History by Sudo Yoshiyuki." *Journal of the Economic and Social History of the Orient* 1, pt. 1 (Aug. 1957): 145–48.

———. "The T'ang Market System." *Asia Major* 12 (1966): 202–48.

Yang Lien-sheng. "Ming Local Administration." In *Chinese Government in Ming Times: Seven Studies.* edited by Charles O. Hucker. New York: Colombia University Press, 1969.

Yu Ping-kuan. "The Reform of the Public Services of the Northern Sung Dynasty and Its Related Measures." Unpublished Master's thesis, Far Eastern and Russian Institute, University of Washington, Seattle, 1959.

Works in Chinese and Japanese

Chai Ju-wen [翟汝文]. *Chung Hui Chi* [忠惠集]. Ssu K'u Ch'üan Shu Chen Pen edition. The collected short writings of Chai Ju-wen (1076–1141).

Chang Fang-p'ing [張方平]. *Lo Ch'üan Chi* [樂全集]. The

collected short writings of Chang Fang-p'ing (1007–91). Yüan manuscript edition. National Library of Peking microfilms.

Chang Hsiao-hsiang [張孝祥]. *Yü-hu Chü-shih Wen-chi* [于湖居士文集]. Ssu Pu Ts'ung K'an edition. The collected short writings of Chang Hsiao-hsiang (1139–1169).

Chang Pang-chi [張邦基]. *Mo Chuang Man Lu* [墨莊漫錄]. Ts'ung-shu Chi Ch'eng edition. A collection of occasional notes by a twelfth-century writer.

Chang Shou [張守]. *P'i Ling Chi* [毘陵集]. Ts'ung-shu Chi Ch'eng edition. The collected short writings of Chang Shou.

Chao Pu-chih [晁補之]. *Chi Chu Chi* [雞肋集]. Ssu Pu Ts'ung K'an edition. The collected short writings of Chao Pu-chih (1053–1110).

Chao Shan-kua [趙善括]. *Ying Chai Tsa Chu* [應齋雜著]. Yü Chang Ts'ung-shu edition. The collected short writings of Chao Shan-kua (fl. twelfth century).

Chao Ting [趙鼎]. *Chung-cheng-te Wen-chi* [忠正德文集]. Ch'ien-k'un Cheng Ch'i Chi edition. The collected short writings of Chao Ting (1085–1147).

Chao Yen-wei [趙彥衛]. *Yün Lu Man Ch'ao* [雲麓漫鈔]. Ts'ung-shu Chi Ch'eng edition. A collection of occasional notes by a twelfth-century writer.

Chen Te-hsiu [眞德秀]. *Hsi Shan Cheng Hsün* [西山政訓]. Ts'ung-shu Chi'eng edition. A collection of comments of government practices by Chen Te-hsiu (1178–1235).

———. [眞德秀]. *Hsi Shan Wen-chi* [西山文集]. Ssu Pu Ts'ung K'an edition. The collected short writings of Chen Te-hsiu (1178–1235).

Ch'en Ch'i-ch'ing [陳耆卿]. *Chia-ting Ch'ih Ch'eng Chih* [嘉定赤城志]. T'ai Chou Ts'ung-shu edition. A gazetteer describing T'ai prefecture in Liang-che circuit, dated 1223. Ch'en Ch'i-ch'ing was a native of Lin-hai in T'ai prefecture. He received his chin-shih in the fifth year of Chia-ting (1212).

———. *Kuei Ch'uang Chi* [篔窗集]. Ssu K'u Ch'üan Shu Chen Pen edition. The collected short writings of Ch'en Ch'i-ch'ing (chin-shih 1212).

Ch'en Fu-liang [陳傅良]. *Chih Chai Wen-chi* [止齋文集]. Ssu Pu Ts'ung K'an edition. The collected short writings of Ch'en Fu-liang (1137–1203).

Ch'en Liang [陳亮]. *Yen Chou T'u Ching* [嚴州圖經]. Ts'ung-shu Chi Ch'eng edition. Ch'en Liang was an Administrator of Yen prefecture. The preface to this local gazetteer is dated 1139–40.

Ch'en Yüan-chin [陳元晉]. *Yü Shu Lei Kao* [漁墅類稿]. Ssu K'u Ch'üan Shu Chen Pen edition. The collected short writings of Ch'en Yüan-chin (b. 1184).

Ch'eng Hsün [程洵]. *K'o-an Hsien-sheng Tsun Te Hsing Chai Hsiao Chi* [克庵先生尊德性齋小集]. Chih Pu Tsu Chai Ts'ung-shu edition. The collected short writings of Ch'eng Hsun.

Cheng Yao [鄭瑤] and Fang Jen-jung [方仁榮]. *Ching-ting Yen Chou Hsü Chih* [景定嚴州續志]. Ts'ung-shu Chi Ch'eng edition. These two men were officials in Yen prefecture during the Ching-ting period (1260–64). They compiled this local gazetteer as a continuation of the Yen Chou T'u Ching, beginning their account with the Ch'un-hsi period (1174–89) and continuing their record to the Hsien-ch'un period (1265–74).

Ch'ien Shuo-yu [潛說友]. *Hsien-ch'un Lin-an Chih* [咸淳臨安志]. Ch'ien-t'ang Wang Shih Chen-ch'i T'ang blockprint edition, 1830. A gazetteer of Lin-an prefecture, dated 1268.

Ch'in Hsiang-yeh [秦湘業]. *Hsü Tzu-chih T'ung-chien Ch'ang-pien Shih Pu* [續資治通鑑長編拾補]. Chekiang: Shu Chu blockprint edition, 1883. The reconstructed final portion of Li Tao's Hsü Tzu-chih T'ung-chien Ch'ang-pien.

Chou Ch'u-fei [周去非]. *Ling Wai Tai Ta* [嶺外代答].

Chih Pu Tsu Chai Ts'ung-shu edition. A series of notes on southern China, Hainan, and foreign trade.

Chou Hsien T'i Kang [州 縣 提 綱]. Ts'ung-chu Chi Ch'eng edition. A handbook for local magistrates, compiled in the mid–twelfth century. The author is unknown.

Chou Li [周 禮]. Ssu Pu Pei Yao edition. The "Rites of Chou," a book purporting to describe the political system in use under the Chou founders.

Chou Lin-chih [周 麟 之]. *Hai Ling Chi* [海 陵 集]. Ssu K'u Ch'üan Shu edition. The collected short writings of Chou Lin-chih (died after 1201).

Chou Ying-ho [周 應 合]. *Ching-ting Chien-k'ang Chih* [景 定 建 康 志]. Ssu K'u Ch'üan Shu edition. Gazetteer of Chien-k'ang prefecture from the Ching-ting period (1260–64).

Chu Hsi [朱 熹]. *Chu Wen-kung Cheng Hsün* [朱 文 公 政 訓]. Ts'ung-shu Chi Ch'eng edition. A collection of brief comments on the conduct of government affairs by Chu Hsi (1130–1200).

———. *Hui-an Hsien-sheng Chu Wen-kung Wen-chi* [晦 菴 先 生 朱 文 公 文 集]. Ssu Pu Ts'ung K'an edition. The collected short papers and writings of Chu Hsi (1130–1200).

Chu Yü [朱 彧]. *P'ing Chou K'o T'an* [萍 洲 可 談]. Ts'ung-shu Chi Ch'eng edition. A collection of miscellany including reports of local customs, second-hand reports on the Liao, and other material on government compiled by an author who lived during the second half of the eleventh century.

Ch'üan Han-sheng [全 漢 昇], "Nan-Sung Tao-mi te Sheng-ch'an yü Yün-hsiao," [南 宋 稻 米 的 生 產 與 運 銷], *Chung-yang Yen-chiu Yüan, Li-shih Yü-yen Yen-chiu So Chi-k'an* X (1942), 403–31.

———. "Pei-sung Pien-liang te Shu Ch'u-ju Huo-i," [北 宋 汴 梁 的 輸 出 入 貿 易], *loc. cit.*, VIII (1939), 189–301.

Chung Hua Shu Chü [中 華 書 局], compiler. *Sung Ta Chao Ling Chi* [宋 大 朝 令 集]. Peking: Chung Hua Shu Chü, 1962. A collection of Sung documents.

Fan Ch'eng-ta [范 成 大]. *Wu Chün Chih* [吳 郡 志]. Tse Shih Chü Ts'ung-shu edition. A local gazetteer for Su prefecture in Liang-che circuit, written shortly after 1218.

Feng Fu-ching [馮 復 京]. *Ta-te Ch'ang Kuo Chou T'u Chih* [大 德 昌 國 州 圖 志]. Sung Yüan Ssu Ming Liu Chih edition. A Yüan dynasty local gazetteer describing Ch'ang-kuo sub-prefecture in Ming prefecture.

Feng Shih-hsing [馮 時 行]. *Chin Yün Wen-chi* [縉 雲 文 集]. Ssu K'u Ch'üan Shu Chen Pen edition. The collected short writings and papers of Feng Shih-hsing (d. 1163).

Han Yüan-chi [韓 元 吉]. *Nan Chien Chia I Kao* [南 澗 甲 乙 稿]. Wu Ying Tien Chü Chen Pan Ch'üan Shu edition. The collected short writings and papers of Han Yüan-chi (b. 1118, d. after 1178).

Hsieh Shen-fu [謝 深 甫]. Ch'ing-yüan T'iao Fa Shih-lei [慶 元 條 法 事 類]. Peiping: Yen-ching Ta-hsüeh T'u-shu Kuan, 1948. Laws and regulations from the Ch'ing-yüan period (1194–1200).

Hsü Sung [徐 松], editor. *Sung Hui Yao Chi Kao* [宋 會 要 輯 稿]. Taipei: Shih Chieh Shu Chü, 1965. This work, the remaining part of the huge collections of selected documents made under imperial auspices during the Sung, is one of the primary sources for the study of Sung institutions. Most of the material in the Sung Hui Yao Chi Kao consists of proclamations or approved memorials, with occasional insertions of commentary.

Hsüeh Chi-hsüan [薛 季 宣]. Ken Chai Hsien-sheng Hsüeh Ch'ang Chou Lang Yü Chi [艮 齋 先 生 薛 常 州 浪 語 集]. Yung Chia Ts'ung-shu edition. The collected short writings of Hsüeh Chi-hsüan (1125–73).

Hu T'ai-ch'u [胡 太 初]. *Chou Lien Hsü Lun* [晝 簾 緒 論]. Ts'ung-shu Chi Ch'eng edition. A one-chapter work giving advice on the conduct of government affairs by Hu T'ai-ch'u (fl. 1234).

Huang Kan [黃 榦]. *Mien Chai Chi* [勉 齋 集]. Ssu K'u Ch'üan

Shu edition. The collected short writings of Huang Kan (1152–1221).

Huang Sung Chung-hsing Liang Ch'ao Sheng Cheng [皇宋中興兩朝聖政]. Taipei: Wen Hai Publishing Company, 1967. An annalistic history of two Southern Sung reigns.

Hung Kua [洪适]. *P'an Chou Wen-chi* [盤洲文集]. Ssu Pu Ts'ung K'an edition. The collected short writings of Hung Kua (1117–84).

Kao Ssu-te [高斯得]. *Ch'ih T'ang Ts'un Kao* [耻堂存稿]. Ts'ung-shu Chi Ch'eng edition. The collected short papers and writings of Kao Ssu-te (chin-shih 1229, d. after 1241).

Kato Shigeru [加藤繁]. *Shina keizai-shi kosho* [支那經濟史考證]. Tokyo: Toyo Bunko, 1952–53. A collection of some of the articles of the noted sinologist Kato Shigeru (1880–1946).

Koiwai Hiromitsu [小岩井弘光]. "Sōdai kokosu mondai ni kansuru shiken" [宋代戶口數問題に關する私見]. *Bunka* 22 : 641–57.

Lao Kan [勞榦]. *Ch'in Han Shih* [秦漢史]. Taipei: Chung Hua Wen Hua Ch'u Pan Shih Yeh She, 1964. A brief history of the Ch'in and Han dynasties by one of the world's foremost contemporary students of Chinese history.

Li Chao-ch'i [李昭玘]. *Yüeh Ching Chi* [樂靜集]. Ssu K'u Ch'üan Shu Chen Pen edition. The collected short papers and writings of Li Chao-ch'i, who was in office during the late eleventh century.

Li Ching-ho [李景和]. *Chia-t'ai Wu Hsing Chih* [嘉泰吳興志]. Wu Hsing Ts'ung-shu edition. A local gazetteer for Hu prefecture in Liang-che Circuit. Written during the opening years of the thirteenth century.

Li Ching-te [黎靖德], compiler. *Chu Tzu Yü Lei* [朱子語類]. Ying Yüan Shu Yüan blockprint edition, 1872. A collection of the sayings and discussions of Chu Hsi (1130–1200).

Li Hsin-ch'uan [李心傳]. *Chien-yen I-lai Chao-yeh Tsa Chi* [建炎以來朝野雜記]. Ts'ung-shu Chi Ch'eng edition.

Li Hsin-ch'uan (1166–1234) was a noted historian of the Southern Sung. This book contains brief discussions of a number of events that occurred during the reign of Kaotsung (1127–63).

———. *Chien-yen I-lai Hsi Nien Yao Lu* [建炎以來繫年要錄]. Peking: Chung Hua Shu Chü, 1956. An annalistic history covering the reign of Kao-tsung (1127–63) in two hundred chapters. This work is one of the most important sources of information on the events of the reign of Kao-tsung.

Li Mi-hsün [李彌遜] *Yün Ch'i Chi* [筠谿集]. Ssu K'u Ch'üan Shu Chen Pen edition. The collected short writings of Li Mi-hsün (1089–1153).

Li Tao [李燾]. *Hsü Tzu-chih T'ung-chien Ch'ang-pien* [續資治通鑑長編]. Taipei: Shih Chieh Shu Chü, 1954. Along with the Sung Hui Yao Chi Kao, this is the most important source for the study of the history of the Northern Sung. Completed in 1174, it is an annalistic history of the years 960–1127.

Li Yüan-pi [李元弼]. *Tso I Tzu Chen* [作邑自箴]. Shanghai: Commercial Press, 1934. A handbook for officials serving in local government posts. This is the most detailed official handbook on Sung local government. The author died in 1117.

Liang K'o-chia [梁克家]. *Ch'un-hsi San Shan Chih* [淳熙三山志]. Ming woodblock edition. A gazetteer of Fukien, from the Ch'un-hsi period (1174–89).

Liao Hsing-chih [廖行之]. *Sheng Chai Chi* [省齋集]. Ssu K'u Ch'üan Shu Chen Pen edition. The collected short writings and papers of Liao Hsing-chih (1139–78).

Lin Hsiu-chung [林秀仲]. *Chu Hsüan Tsa Chu* [竹軒雜著]. Ssu K'u Ch'üan Shu Chen Pen edition. The collected short papers and writings of Lin Hsiu-chung, who received his chin-shih during the Hsüan-ho period (1119–25) and was active in official life during the reign of Kao-tsung (1127–63).

Lin Shui-han [林瑞翰]. "Sung Tai Pao-chia" [宋代保甲]. *Ta Lu Tsa Chih* 20.7.4. An article on the Sung *pao-chia* system.

Ling Wan-ch'ing [凌萬頃]. "Yü Feng Chih" [玉峯志]. Yüan manuscript edition. Peking National Library Rare Books microfilm. The local gazetteer from K'un-shan sub-prefecture of Su prefecture in Liang-che circuit, dated 1251.

Liu Pan [劉攽]. *P'eng Ch'eng Chi* [彭城集]. Ssu K'u Ch'üan Shu edition. The collected short papers of Liu Pan (1023–89).

Liu Tao-yüan [劉道元]. *Liang Sung T'ien-fu Chih-tu* [兩宋田賦制度]. Shanghai: Hsin Sheng Ming Shu Chü, 1937. A study of the tax systems of the Sung dynasty by a contemporary Chinese scholar.

Liu Tsai [劉宰]. *Man-t'ang Wen-chi* [漫塘文集]. Chia Yeh T'ang Ts'ung-shu edition. The collected short writings of Liu Tsai (1166–1239).

Liu Ts'ai-shao [劉才邵]. *Fan Ch'i Chü Shih Chi* [檆溪居士集]. Ssu K'u Ch'üan Shu Chen Pen edition. The collected short papers and writings of Liu Ts'ai-shao (1086–1157).

Lo Chün [羅濬]. *Pao-ch'ing Ssu-ming Chih* [寶慶四明志]. Sung Yüan Ssu-ming Liu Chih edition. The local gazetteer of Ming prefecture in Liang-che circuit, dated 1227.

Lo Yüan [羅願]. *Hsin-an Chih* [新安志]. Blockprint edition, 1888. The local gazetteer of Hsin-an military prefecture in Liang-che circuit, dated 1175.

Lou Yüeh [樓鑰]. *Kung K'uei Chi* [攻媿集]. Wu Ying Tien Chü Chen Pan Ch'üan Shu edition. The collected short writings and papers of Lou Yüeh (1137–1213).

Lü Tsu-ch'ien [呂祖謙]. *Li Tai Chih-tu Hsiang Shuo* [歷代制度詳說]. Hsu Chin Hua Ts'ung-shu ed. Brief but detailed essays on government institutions by Lü Tsu-ch'ien (1137–81).

———. *Tung Lai Chi* [東萊集]. Hsü Chin Hua Ts'ung-shu edition. The collected short writings and papers of Lü Tsu-ch'ien (1137–81).

Ma Tuan-lin [馬端臨]. *Wen Hsien T'ung K'ao* [文獻通考]. Kuo Hsüeh Chi Pen Ts'ung-shu edition. An encyclopedia devoted to the history of Chinese intitutions, completed before 1319.

Maritani Katsumi [森谷克已]. *Chung-kuo She-hui Ching-chi Shih* [中國社會經濟史]. A Japanese study of Chinese social and economic history, in Chinese translation.

Matsumoto Yoshiyumi [松本善海]. "Rimpo-soshiki wo chushin toshitaru Tōdai no sonsei" [鄰保組織を中心とした る唐代の村政]. *Shigaku Zasshi* 53, no. 3 (1942): 323-71. A study of T'ang canton administration.

Mei Ying-fa [梅應發]. *K'ai-ch'ing Ssu-ming Chih* [開慶四明志]. Sung Yüan Ssu-ming Liu Chih edition. The local gazetteer from Ming prefecture in Liang-che circuit, dated 1259.

———. *K'ai-ch'ing Ssu-ming Hsü Chih* [開慶四明續志]. Sung Yüan Ssu-ming Liu Chih edition. A continuation of the K'ai-ch'ing Ssu-ming Chih. The continuation is also dated 1259.

Miyazaki Ichisada [宮崎市定]. "Kyo-ri no-baibi o chūsin to shite" [胥吏の陪備を中心として]. *Shirin* 30 no. 1 (May, 1945): 10-36. An article on Sung clerks.

———. "Sō-dai shu ken scido no yurai to sono tokushoku" [宋代州縣制度の由來とその特色]. *Shirin* 36 no. 2 (July, 1953): 1-27. An article on Sung local administration.

Nakamura Jihee [中村治兵衞]. "Sō-dai no chihō kukaku-kan ni tsuite" [宋代の地方區劃一管について]. *Shien*, no. 89 (December, 1962), pp. 85-115. A discussion of the *kuan* as a unit of local administration under the Sung dynasty, by a modern Japanese scholar.

Naba Toshisada [那波利貞]. "Tōdai rimpo-seido shakugi" [唐代鄰保制度釋疑]. In *Haneda Kakushi shōju kinen tōyō-shi ronsō* (Kyoto: 1950) 711-78. A study of T'ang cantonal and township administration.

Nieh Ch'ung-ch'i [聶崇岐]. "Sung I-fa Shu" [宋役法述].

Yenching Hsüeh Pao, no. 33 (December, 1947). 195–270. A discussion of the system of local services of the Sung dynasty by a modern Chinese scholar.

——. "Lun Sung T'ai-tsu Shou Ping Ch'üan" [論宋太祖收兵權]. *Yenching Hsüeh-pao* 34 (1948): 85–106. An article on the resumption of military control by the early Sung emperors.

Osaki Fujio [大崎富士夫]. "Sō–dai no Gi-Eki". [宋代の義役]. *Shigaku kenkyū kinen ronso,* October 1950, 261–85. An article on charitable service.

Ou-yang Hsiu [歐陽修]. *Ou-yang Wen Chung Kung Chi* [歐陽文忠公集]. Ssu Pu Ts'ung K'an edition. The collected short writings and papers of Ou-yang Hsiu (1007–72).

Ou-yang Shou-tao [歐陽守道]. *Hsüan Chai Wen Chi* [選齋文集]. Ssu K'u Ch'üan Shu. The collected short writings of Ou-yang Shou-tao (died after 1267).

Pien Shih [邊實]. "Yü Feng Hsü Chih" [玉峯續志]. Manuscript. Peking National Library microfilms. The continuation of the gazetteer of K'un-shan subprefecture in Su prefecture of Liang-che circuit, dated 1272.

Shih Hsiu [施宿]. *Chia-t'ai Kuei Chi Chih* [嘉泰會稽志]. Photolithographic reproductions. Chia-ch'ing recarved woodblock edition. A local gazetteer, dated 1202. from Shao-hsing prefecture in Liang-che circuit.

Shih Yao-pi [史堯弼]. *Lien Feng Chi* [蓮峯集]. Ssu K'u Ch'üan Shu Chen Pen edition. The collected short writings of Shih Yao-pi (1108–57).

Shu Lin [舒璘]. *Shu Wen Ching Kung Chi* [舒文靖公集]. Ssu-ming Ts'ung-shu edition. The collected short writings and papers of Shu Lin (chin-shih during the Ch'ien-tao period, 1165–74).

Sogabe, Shizuo [曾我部靜雄]. *Sō-dai zaisei-shi* [宋代財政史]. Tokyo: Dai Nippon Insatsu Kabushiki Kaisha, 1941. A study of the fiscal institutions of the Sung dynasty by a noted Japanese student of Chinese history.

Su Shih [蘇軾]. *Su Tung-p'o Liu Chi* [蘇東坡六集]. Ssu Pu Pei Yao edition. The collected short writings of Su Shih (1036–1101).

Sudō Yoshiyuki [周藤吉之]. "Nan-sō ni sukeru Gi-Eki no setsuritsu to sono unei," [南宋における義役の設立とその運宮]. *Toyo Gakuho* 48.4, 425–463. An article on charitable services.

———. *Sō-dai keizai-shi kenkyū* [宋代經濟史研究]. Tokyo: Tokyo Daigaku Shuppan Kai, 1962. A collection of studies of the fiscal and economic institutions of the Sung dynasty by a leading Japanese scholar.

———. *Tōsō shakai keizai-shi kenkyu* [唐宋社會經濟史研究], Tokyo: Tokyo Daigaku Shuppan Kai, 1965. Another collection of studies on the history of fiscal institutions of the T'ang and Sung periods.

Sun Yü-t'ang [孫毓棠]. "Kuan-yü Pei Sung Fu-i Chih-tu Te Fan Ke Wen-t'i" [關於北宋賦役制度的儿個問題], *Li-shih Yen-chiu*, no. 2 (1964), 135–67. An article on local service and corvee labor during the Sung dynasty by a mainland scholar. Not very useful.

T'o T'o [脫脫] et al. *Sung Shih* [宋史]. Taipei: Yee Wen Publishing Company, Ltd., 1965. The standard history of the Sung dynasty, completed in 1345.

Tou I [竇儀]. *Chung Hsiang Ting Hsing T'ung* [重詳定刑統]. Taipei: Wen Hai Publishing Co, 1954. A work on law by Tou I (914–66)

Ts'ai K'an [蔡戡]. *Ting Chai Chi* [定齋集]. Ch'ang Chou Hsien Chc I Shu edition. The collected short writings and papers of Ts'ai K'an (chin-shih 1166, d. after 1195).

Ts'ao Yen-yüeh [曹彥約]. *Ch'ang Ku Chi* [昌谷集]. Ssu K'u Ch'üan Shu Chen Pen Ts'ung-shu edition. The collected short writings and papers of Ts'ao Yen-yüeh (1157–1228).

Tseng Tzu-sheng [曾資生]. "Sung Chin Yü Yüan Te Hsiang-li Chih-tu Kai-huang" [宋金與元的鄉里制度概況], in Sung Shih Yen Chiu Chi. Volume 2. Taipei: 1965. An article on local administrative divisions during the Sung, Chin, and Yüan dynasties, by a modern Chinese scholar.

Wada Sei [和 田 清], editor. *Sō-shi shi-ka shi yakuchū* [宋 史 食 貨 志 譯 註]. Tokyo: Toyo Bunko, 1960. An annotated translation of the *shih-huo* section of the Sung Shih.

Wang Chih-wang [王 之 望]. *Han P'in Chi* [漢 濱 集]. Hu-pei Hsien Cheng I Shu edition. The collected short writings of Wang Chih-wang (d. 1170).

Wang Te-i [王 德 毅]. "Nan Sung I-i K'ao" [南 宋 義 役 考]. In *Sung Shih Yen-chiu Lun-chi*. Taipei: Commercial Press, 1968. An essay on charitable services.

Wang Wei [王 禕]. *Wang Chung Wen Kung Chi* [王 忠 文 公 集]. Ts'ung-shu Chi Ch'eng edition. The collected short writings and papers of Wang Wei (1322-73).

Wang Yang [王 洋]. *Tung Mou Chi* [東 牟 集]. Ssu K'u Ch'üan Shu Chen Pen edition. The collected short writings and papers of Wang Yang (1084-1153).

Wang Ying-ch'en [汪 應 辰]. *Wen Ting Chi* [文 定 集]. Ts'ung-shu Chi Ch'eng edition. The collected short writings of Wang Ying-ch'en (1118-76).

Wang Ying-lin [王 應 麟]. *Yü Hai* [玉 海]. Ch'eng Wang Shih edition. A famous encylopedia compiled in the Southern Sung by Wang Ying-lin (1223-96).

Wang Yü-chih [王 與 之]. *Chou Li Ting I* [周 禮 訂 義]. In Na-lan Ch'eng-te [納 蘭 成 德], T'ung Chih T'ang Ching Chieh [通 志 堂 經 解]. Yüeh Tung Shu Chü edition, 1873. A collection of writings on the Chou Li. Most of the comments included were by Sung authors, although a few are quotations of authors from the T'ang or earlier. Wang Yü-chih lived during the thirteenth century.

Wang Yüan [王 阮]. *I Feng Chi* [義 豐 集]. Yu Chang Ts'ung Shu edition. The collected short writings of Wang Yüan (d. 1208).

Wei Ching [衛 涇]. *Hou Lo Chi* [後 樂 集]. Ssu K'u Ch'üan Shu Chen Pen edition. The collected short writings and papers of Wei Ching (1159-1226).

Wen T'ien-hsiang [文天祥]. *Wen Shan Hsien-sheng Ch'üan Chi* [文山先生全集]. Ssu Pu Ts'ung K'an ed. The collected short writings of Wen T'ien-hsiang (1236–82).

Yao Kuang-hsiao [姚廣孝] *et al.* Yung-lo Ta-tien [永樂大典]. Peking: Chung Hua Shu Chü, 1959. A great encyclopedic compilation of Chinese writings done under the auspices of the Yung-lo emperor (r. 1403–25). Only a part of the original manuscript has survived.

Yanagida Setsuko [柳田節子], "Sō-dai gyō-sei-ko no kōsei," [宋代形勢戶の構成]. *Toyoshi Kenkyū* 27 no.3 (68.12) 100–17.

———. "Sō-dai no kakko ni tsuite" [宋代の客戶について]. *Shigaku Zasshi* 68, no. 4 (April, 1959): 1–38. An article on "guest" households during the Sung by a Japanese scholar.

Yang Chung-liang [楊仲良]. *Tzu-chih T'ung-chien Ch'ang-pien Chi-shih Pen-mo* [資治通鑑長編紀事本末]. Taipei: Wen Hai Publishing Co., 1967. Arrangement of the *Ch'ang-pien* in Chi-shih pen-mo format.

Yeh Shih [葉適]. *Shui Hsin Wen-chi* [水心文集]. Ssu Pu Ts'ung K'an edition. The collected short writings and papers of Yeh Shih (1150–1223).

Yu Mao [尤袤]. *Sui Ch'u T'ang Shu Mu* [遂初堂書目]. Hsi Shan Yu Shih Ts'ung-shu K'an Chia Chi ed. A catalog of items in the library called Sui Ch'u T'ang, by Yu Mao (1127–1194).

Yüan Chen [袁震]. "Liang Sung Tu-tieh K'ao" [兩宋度牒考] *Chung-kuo She-hui Ching-chi Shih Chi K'an* 7, no. 1 (June, 1944): 41–70. An article on monk certificates during the Sung dynasty by a modern Chinese scholar.

———. "Sung-tai hu-k'ou" [宋代戶口], *Li-shih Yen-chiu* 3 (1957): 9–46. An article on Sung population statistics.

Yüan Chüeh [袁桷]. *Yen-yu Ssu-ming Chih* [延祐四明志]. Sung Yüan Ssu-ming Liu Chih edition. A gazetteer describing Ming prefecture in Liang-che circuit. From the Yen-yu period (1314–20).

Yüan Fu [袁甫]. *Meng Chai Chi* [蒙齋集]. Ts'ung-shu Chi Ch'eng edition. The collected short writings and papers of Yüan Fu (*chin shih* 1214).

Yüan Hsieh [袁燮]. *Chieh Chai Chi* [絜齋集]. Ssu K'u Ch'üan Shu edition. The collected short writings of Yüan Hsieh (1144–1224).

Yüan Shuo-yu [袁說友]. *Tung T'ang Chi* [東塘集]. Ssu K'u Ch'üan Shu Chen Pen edition. The collected short writings of Yüan Shuo-yu.

Yüan Ts'ai [袁采]. Yüan Shih Shih Fan [袁氏世範]. Chih Pu Tsu Chai Ts'ung-shu edition. The family instructions of Yüan Ts'ai (*c.*1140–*c.*1190).

Glossary – Index

li-hou (distance markers)
[里堠], 69
li jen ya-ch'ien [吏人衙前], 26n
Li Jo-ch'uan [李若川], 172n
Li Jo-ku [李若谷], 173n
Li Te-lin [李德鄰], 100
Li Yüan-pi [李元弼], 54
Li Yüan-yüeh [李元瀹], 173n
Liang-che, 61, 71, 87, 88n,
  114; charitable service
  system in, 158, 160;
  concurrent service in, 80;
  system of multiple service in,
  139; system of unlimited
  landholding in, 115
liang-ch'u (two offices)
[兩處], 71n
Liao Hsing-chih [廖行之], 44
Lin-an [臨安], 76n
lin-pao (neighborhood group)
[鄰保], 44n. See also
  pao-lin
ling (subprefect) [令], 63
ling-tso [令佐], 143n
liu-nei (within the stream)
[流內], 1, 7, 8n
liu-shui pu (Flowing Water
  Registers) [流水簿], 134
Liu Tsai [劉宰], 162, 165, 167,
  169
Lou Yüeh [樓鑰], 141
Lu-ch'uan subprefecture
[瀘川縣], 78n, 93n
lu-hsia (salary boxes) [祿匣],
  64

Lü Hsi-ch'ang [呂希常],
  88–89
Lü Tsu-ch'ien [呂祖謙], 129

Ma-yang subprefecture
[麻陽縣], 74n
Male head tax (shen ting ch'ien),
  50
Messengers (ch'eng-t'ieh jen): as
  accusers, 114–15; as
  document carriers in the
  Southern Sung, 61; in the
  Northern Sung, 33n, 35, 37
mien-i ch'ang-p'ing an [免役常
  平案], 153
mien-i ch'ien (exemption
  money) [免役錢], 33. See
  also Labor service money
mien-i fa (hired service system)
[免役法], 32
Militia, in tax collection, 56.
  See also pao-wu; pao-chia
Military Service Supply Master
  (chiang li ya-ch'ien), 26n
min-hu (ordinary household)
[民戶], 98
Ming prefecture [明州], 76n,
  103n, 160n; hiring of service
  men in, 141; labor service
  money in, 154
Ministry of Finance, in service
  reforms, 99, 102, 106, 115,
  142n, 172, 173
mou [畝], 50, 163, 164, 166

Subprefect (*ling*), 8, 8n, 63, 154, 174

Subprefectures (*hsien*), 8–9, 11

Substitutes: groups permitted to hire, 147–48; hiring of, 147–50

Sun Chin [孫近], 173n

Sung-yang subprefecture [松陽縣], 159

Superior guard (*tu-pao*), organization of, 34, 76–78

Superior Guard Leader (*tu-pao cheng*), 34–37; key role of, 38–39, 66–67, 181–82; and law enforcement, 39–49; sometimes called *li-cheng*, 42n

Supply Masters (*ya-ch'ien*), 29–32; origins and evolution of, 25–26

Surplus money (*k'uan-sheng ch'ien*), 32

Surrender money (*chiao-yin ch'ien*), 46

Szechuan, 42, 80, 81

ta-pao (large guard) [大保], 34, 92n

ta-pao chang (Large Guard Chief) [大保長], 34

ta pi ch'iang tao [大辟強盜], 64

tai-fu [大夫], 119n

t'ai hsüeh sheng (Imperial Academy student) [太學生], 106

T'ai prefecture [泰州], 107

T'ai prefecture [台州], 88n, 103n

T'ai-tsu [太祖], 13, 127n

T'ai-tsung [太宗], 13

tan-ting hu (household with only a single adult male) [單丁戶], 96; loss of privileges, 101–03

T'ang, 3n; household grades in, 127n; privileges in, 101n, 109; rural organization of, 12–13, 23, 75

T'ang P'eng-chü [湯鵬舉], 173n

t'ao-hu [逃戶], 60

Tax brokers, 55, 55n

Tax collection: brokers and methods of delivery, 55–57; dunning, 57–58, 60; legal disputes, 58; records and maps used in assessment, 24, 51–53; as responsibility of village officers, 23–24, 35, 49–60, 83, 86–91; surcharges, 57; types of levies, 50; Twice-a-Year Tax, 50

Tax vouchers, in drawing up five-grade registers, 70, 128n. See *p'ing-yu*

te chieh (certified after examination) [得解], 106

te chieh chü jen (certified provincial graduates)

t'ui-p'ai [推排], 123, 123n
T'ung Kuan [童貫], 118
Twice-a-Year tax: collection
 of, 50, 80, 82; and collection
 of labor service money, 153;
 falls on resident households,
 126; process of collecting,
 52–57; regional variation,
 50; registers, 127; remission
 of, as payment for village
 officers, 157
tz'u-i ch'ien [辭役錢], 70n
tz'u t'ien (imperial gift fields)
 [賜田], 165
tz'u-yü (shrines) [祠宇], 69

Upper households. See *shang-hu*
Urban residents: legal rural
 residence system, 124–25;
 in the Northern Sung, 31n,
 32, 104; in the Southern
 Sung, 97, 104
Urgent communications
 (*hsin-p'ai*), 46

Village officers, 3, 10, 20; from
 the Ch'in through the Five
 Dynasties, 11–13; chain of
 official responsibility,
 173–74; and civil servants
 and subbureaucracy, 3, 22;
 combating locusts, 71; costs
 of service, 21, 156;
 distinctiveness of the Sung
 system, 178–79; fees paid

for document transmission,
 63; fire fighting, 27, 69;
 functions of, 5; and gentry
 6; gifts to clerks, 69–70;
 hiring of substitutes,
 147–50, 183, and lawsuits,
 47, 58; leisure periods,
 137–39; local welfare
 systems and, 67–68; in
 maintaining local order,
 39–49; making of maps and
 registers, 70–71, 130; in the
 Northern Sung, 23–25;
 process of selection, 142–47;
 providing construction
 workers and construction,
 military and official
 supplies, 66; punishment of,
 45; responsible for articles
 in subprefectural offices,
 65–66; responsible for
 roads, bridges, and other
 public facilities, 67–69;
 responsible for public
 notice boards, 63;
 responsible for tax quotas,
 59–60; responsible for
 traveling official needs, 65;
 rotation to clerical posts,
 25–26, 29, 71; social origins
 and character of, 182–85;
 terms of service, 23, 85–86;
 visits to the yamen, 58–59;
 wealth as criterion for
 choosing, 137–42, 182–83